NEW DIRECTIONS FOR COMMUNITY COLLEGES

Arthur M. Cohen
EDITOR-IN-CHIEF

Florence B. Brawer
ASSOCIATE EDITOR

Paula Zeszotarski
PUBLICATION COORDINATOR

Systems for Offering Concurrent Enrollment at High Schools and Community Colleges

Piedad F. Robertson
Santa Monica College

Brian G. Chapman
Columbus State Community College

Fred Gaskin
Maricopa Community College District

EDITORS

Number 113, Spring 2001

JOSSEY-BASS
San Francisco

ERIC®
Clearinghouse for Community Colleges

SYSTEMS FOR OFFERING CONCURRENT ENROLLMENT AT HIGH SCHOOLS AND COMMUNITY COLLEGES
Piedad F. Robertson, Brian G. Chapman, Fred Gaskin (eds.)
New Directions for Community Colleges, no. 113
Volume XXIX, number 1
Arthur M. Cohen, Editor-in-Chief
Florence B. Brawer, Associate Editor

New Directions for Community Colleges is indexed in Current Index to Journals in Education (ERIC).

Microfilm copies of issues and articles are available in 16mm and 35mm, as well as microfiche in 105mm, through University Microfilms Inc., 300 North Zeeb Road, Ann Arbor, Michigan 48106-1346.

ISSN 0194-3081   ISBN 0-7879-5758-5

NEW DIRECTIONS FOR COMMUNITY COLLEGES is part of The Jossey-Bass Higher and Adult Education Series and is published quarterly by Jossey-Bass Inc., 350 Sansome Street, San Francisco, California 94104-1342, in association with the ERIC Clearinghouse for Community Colleges. Periodicals postage paid at San Francisco, California, and at additional mailing offices. POSTMASTER: Send address changes to New Directions for Community Colleges, Jossey-Bass Inc., 350 Sansome Street, San Francisco, California 94104-1342.

SUBSCRIPTIONS cost $63.00 for individuals and $115.00 for institutions, agencies, and libraries. Prices subject to change.

THE MATERIAL in this publication is based on work sponsored wholly or in part by the Office of Educational Research and Improvement, U.S. Department of Education, under contract number ED-99-CO-0010. Its contents do not necessarily reflect the views of the Department or any other agency of the U.S. Government.

EDITORIAL CORRESPONDENCE should be sent to the Editor-in-Chief, Arthur M. Cohen, at the ERIC Clearinghouse for Community Colleges, University of California, 3051 Moore Hall, Box 951521, Los Angeles, California 90095-1521. All manuscripts receive anonymous reviews by external referees.

Cover photograph © Rene Sheret, After Image, Los Angeles, California, 1990.

Printed in the United States of America on acid-free recycled paper containing 100 percent recovered waste paper, of which at least 20 percent is postconsumer waste

CONTENTS

Principals Council—which creates a venue for principals and the college to discuss areas of mutual interest, and a variety of services provided by the college to local high schools.

EDITORS' NOTES

The terms *concurrent enrollment, dual credit, dual enrollment, postsecondary enrollment,* and *coenrollment* are used interchangeably to describe a rising trend in academic programming at community colleges that supports seamless education. Although some institutions make minor distinctions between these terms, there are no universally consistent definitions. The concurrent enrollment programs discussed in this volume are community college–level course offerings provided to high school students on either the high school or college campus. Students enrolled in these courses usually receive academic credit that is reflected on both their high school and college transcripts. The chapters collected in this volume outline several models of concurrent enrollment programming and focus on the challenges and issues associated with developing and maintaining such programs. Funding formulas, staffing issues, marketing, curriculum, faculty development, transferability of credit, student recruitment, and quality and effectiveness issues are discussed. These topics are addressed within the framework of different regions of the United States.

The reader will see throughout these chapters how closely the profiled community colleges and high schools have worked together to integrate the learning experience of their students. Santa Monica College, Cerritos College, Salt Lake Community College, Columbus State Community College, and community colleges in Maricopa County, along with Florida's New World School of the Arts and community colleges in Virginia and elsewhere, serve as examples of powerful collaboration. These concurrent or dual enrollment programs have been devised to ensure the development of critical thinking and technical and content skills through a wide spectrum of course offerings and in a variety of high school and community college settings. These outcomes have not occurred accidentally but rather through deliberate planning and the establishment of instructional standards. Although each collaborative venture has been developed and executed differently, clear evidence exists that these programs add significant value, in the form of positive personal and educational benefits, to the high school students who participate. In Chapter Three, for example, Margaret K. Peterson, John Anjewierden, and Cris Corser provide strong statistical data to support many of these outcomes. Additionally, the partnering institutions often create unique, and perhaps unexpected, learning environments and professional development opportunities for faculty members.

The opportunities for collaboration between higher education and the K–12 system have increased over the last decade. Instead of the finger-pointing of the past, in which different segments of our educational systems lay blame on one another, higher education leaders, with the cooperation of K–12 system leaders, have begun to explore how best to participate in programs of early intervention. There is no single approach to this type of collaboration; examples of innovation and creativity abound. Nancy Wolcott's description of The New World School of the Arts is a prime example of innovative collaboration at its best. Schools and colleges can adopt proposals to meet specific needs within their local communities. The chapters of this volume provide the reader with examples of many successful models being used throughout the country.

Certain tenets form the basis for the collaborations featured in this publication. The first tenet is that education is a continuum. Students accrue knowledge and continue to apply it at subsequent levels. If basic mathematics are not learned, students will have difficulty proceeding to algebra and calculus. If the ability to read, interpret, and understand the subtleties of the written word and to internalize information are not mastered, it is then impossible to appreciate poetry or to interpret the impact of historical events on the future. Envisioning the pattern of curricular and educational transition as a continuum addresses some of these important concerns.

The second tenet is that program course offerings complement the high school curriculum rather than supplant it. Beset by funding problems, many high schools have been forced to cut critical course offerings. For example, some large urban and small rural school districts have been forced to eliminate performing arts classes. Additionally, some school districts are now able to establish course offerings through dual enrollment that were never a part of their original offerings. As these districts work closely with college personnel, these courses can be at least partially restored to the curriculum. Examples abound of new courses that have become available because of these partnerships. A third-year foreign language class without the enrollment required by state board regulations; an advanced calculus class; an administration-of-justice class for a police magnet high school; art, music, and theater classes; and science classes—all are in high demand through dual enrollment programs. Technical courses that are not customarily available at the secondary level can be offered to enhance the curriculum of the urban, suburban, or rural high school. Salt Lake Community College, for example, has made strides in this area. The first-year experience or freshman seminar genre of courses can be offered to high school students, to instill confidence and foster goal setting among students who might not otherwise have seriously considered attending college.

The third tenet is concerned with accessibility. The setting for these programs may be the college or high school campus, or it may be a site linked through distance education technology. The precise location of the classes may have an impact on how accessible these programs are to the students. All the chapters of this volume provide a perspective on how colleges have attempted to bring the college campus to high schools students, in spite of barriers. In Chapter Eight, for example, Esther B. Hugo provides a compelling argument for access for all students, especially the underserved in California. Many program administrators have designed their programs for classes to be taught exclusively at the high school sites to save time and the costs of transportation. Some programs are offered during regular school hours; others take advantage of the empty classrooms after school or have weekend offerings, intensive summer programs, or both. Some programs effectively integrate high school students into the college campus through dedicated classes of high school cohorts or a mix of high school and traditional community college students. Access to academic resources is of paramount importance to the success of the high school student who is enrolled in a community college course; therefore, special consideration must be given to students who may not be familiar with community college resources and the expectations of college instructors.

The fourth tenet is concerned with providing financial support where necessary. In addition to considering place and time flexibility, as well as access to learning resources, program providers should carefully address financial need, because lack of financial support can be a significant barrier to higher education. Many programs do not charge students for tuition or fees, whereas others attempt to minimize the burden. In addition, the purchase of textbooks may be subsidized or other methods may be found to lower or eliminate textbook costs. High school students may not have been required to purchase textbooks in the past and therefore may not be prepared to deal with this increasingly expensive element of higher education.

The fifth tenet addresses the need for adequate academic support services for dual enrollees. Academic advising, precollege counseling, financial aid planning, study skills workshops, and assessment testing can and should be woven into these vital partnerships. Cooperation between college and high school counselors is a key element in the success of concurrent enrollment programs and the students they serve. The opportunity to attend college is transformed from an unattainable dream to a real possibility for many of the participating students. As one inner-city Los Angeles high school student stated in a Santa Monica College concurrent enrollment evaluation, "I never knew that I could go to college. I thought that I would just be lucky and get a job somewhere and not get shot before I was through."

Quality instruction is crucial to the success and credibility of concurrent enrollment programs. As witnessed by the authors of this volume, faculty qualifications and appropriate curriculum planning must be provided in order to maintain the integrity of and respect for high school–community college collaborations. Full- and part-time college instructors and credentialed high school instructors teach classes in these programs. Many programs have applied the same hiring standards to high school teachers that are applied in the selection of community college adjunct or full-time faculty members. Professional development, in-service training, orientation sessions, faculty recognition programs, ongoing instructor evaluations, and a formal faculty selection process are some of the elements that ensure quality instruction. The use of faculty liaisons from appropriate disciplines—along with the active involvement of community college department chairpersons, academic deans, and chief instructional officers—often provides the framework for an ever-improving concurrent enrollment program. High school principals, chairpersons, and faculty coordinators are also essential to the equation for success. Relationships among these individuals need to be deliberately cultivated and deepened. Faculty members from both organizations can contribute valuable ideas and significant assessment and evaluation of the student populations being served.

The fact that dual enrollment is an excellent model of accelerated placement is appealing to state legislators. Creating a cache of students who have completed anywhere from twelve to thirty credits of college while in high school is an additional guarantee of those students' persistence in college. That they arrive better prepared academically, with more self-confidence and a positive attitude toward college work, increases the probability of their success. The legislative actions regarding dual or concurrent enrollment programs have been mixed, but in many cases they have been positive. Informed legislators have often sponsored or cosponsored legislation that has created a framework for offering college-level courses to high school students. The Virginia Plan for Dual Enrollment and the actions in California and Utah are excellent examples. In Chapter One, Katherine Boswell provides a detailed account of many of these positive legislative activities. Although criticisms and accusations have surfaced in some states, such as Arizona, colleges and high schools can easily promote and defend their programs by maintaining high-quality instructional programs, hiring the finest instructors, holding themselves accountable to a set of specified goals and objectives, and clearly conveying their goals and cost-effective successes to elected officials, government agencies, governing bodies, and taxpayers. Boswell provides a comprehensive overview of concurrent enrollment programs throughout the United States. Setting the stage for the chapters that follow, she discusses state policies from the perspective of the current educational needs of students, legislative interest and concern, approaches to quality assessment, funding formulas, and the responsibilities of participating educational organizations.

In Chapter Two, Brian G. Chapman provides a step-by-step approach to creating a concurrent enrollment program. He discusses needs assessment, goals and objectives, policy and procedural issues, planning issues, staffing requirements, program pilots, marketing, customization, feedback and evaluation, and potential outcomes.

In Chapter Three, Margaret K. Peterson, John Anjewierden, and Cris Corser describe one of the largest concurrent enrollment programs in the United States. The success of Salt Lake Community College's program is attributed to a unique course approval process, faculty liaisons, and a strong emphasis on quality through curriculum review, problem solving, instructor evaluation, and ongoing professional development. This chapter includes statistical data from institutional research and comprehensive satisfaction surveys.

Chapter Four, by Donald E. Puyear, Linda M. Thor, and Karen L. Mills, provides an overview of the varied approaches to concurrent enrollment, in addition to a valuable sampling of supportive literature. The research presented in this chapter addresses standards, evaluation, uniformity, and academic success, followed by a detailed account of concurrent enrollment challenges at the state and local levels, along with related legislative and administrative actions.

In Chapter Five, Steven R. Helfgot emphasizes the importance of establishing programs that are high school centered. The need to carefully cultivate partnerships between community colleges and secondary schools is reinforced through efforts that are balanced, equitable, and consistent. Helfgot describes programming and planning that is deliberate and that can be cultivated over many years.

Rhonda K. Catron provides a concise overview of the seminal document, the *Virginia Plan for Dual Enrollment,* in Chapter Six. After tracing the roots of concurrent enrollment in the state of Virginia from early efforts toward articulation between educational enterprises, Catron addresses student eligibility, faculty selection, and funding. She also discusses outreach to rural areas, delivery issues, and faculty workload.

In Chapter Seven, Nancy M. Wolcott describes one of the most innovative concurrent enrollment programs in the country. A triorganizational venture, New World School of the Arts has achieved national acclaim, impressive student diversity, and outstanding alumni. Wolcott traces the success of this cooperative program over the past twenty years.

Esther B. Hugo examines issues of access and outreach in Chapter Eight, using a model program that has been highly successful in both inner-city and suburban Los Angeles. She casts a positive light on efforts to provide college access and exposure to a wide range of students who might not otherwise have the opportunity to experience the broad range of curriculum provided by Santa Monica College.

In Chapter Nine, Tammi C. Jordan examines the legislative actions in Ohio that led to the creation of the Postsecondary Enrollment Options program. She highlights how this legislation was used as the basis for creating a program at Columbus State Community College. This program provides a clear example of how student eligibility, quality standards, and proper placement testing can be used to develop a sophisticated set of program guidelines and procedures.

The rewards of these collaborative relationships between K–12 systems and community colleges can be best measured by the students' success within the program, their continued advancement in higher education, and the satisfaction of school district and community college administrators and faculty members at having collectively fostered the improvement of educational opportunities for students in their local community. The secret of success is to keep in mind the ultimate purpose: to provide educational opportunities for college coursework to students in high school and afford them a high-quality, efficient way to become productive citizens.

Piedad F. Robertson
Brian G. Chapman
Fred Gaskin
Editors

PIEDAD F. ROBERTSON is president of Santa Monica College, Santa Monica, California.

BRIAN G. CHAPMAN is a doctoral student in the Community College Leadership Program at the University of Texas at Austin and is employed in the enrollment services department at Columbus State Community College, Columbus, Ohio.

FRED GASKIN is chancellor of the Maricopa Community College District, Phoenix, Arizona.

1

Hundreds of thousands of secondary students across the nation—as many as 10 percent of high school students in some states—are participating in various forms of postsecondary enrollment options. State policymakers are considering a range of new policy options to accelerate student educational progress in light of projected demands for access to public colleges and universities by the "baby boom echo."

State Policy and Postsecondary Enrollment Options: Creating Seamless Systems

Katherine Boswell

There is a growing perception of a mismatch between what America needs and what it is getting from its educational systems. Policymakers, the media, and parents are calling for high schools, colleges, and universities to work together to provide access to a reasonably priced and relevant education in order to help students develop the critical thinking, technical, and content skills they will need in a changing economy. America's centuries-old model of higher education is being challenged as never before to work with the public schools to help transform practices to meet the educational needs of the children of the baby boom generation.

Parents are alarmed by reports of the rising cost of college, and policymakers worry about the need for a highly educated and trained workforce to compete in an increasingly global marketplace. These concerns result in an increasing interest among parents and politicians in providing a range of postsecondary enrollment options to high school students that accelerate student progress toward completing the baccalaureate degree. Across the country, an increasing number of community colleges are being called upon to cooperate with K–12 school districts in order to provide a variety of postsecondary options to high school juniors and seniors.

In response to these concerns, thirty-eight states have currently adopted state-level policies that encourage the provision of postsecondary enrollment options—usually in the form of concurrent enrollment of high school students in college-level classes. Concurrent enrollment agreements in ten additional states exist at the institutional level, although no state policies have been established to govern their use. Only two states report no policy or known practice of concurrent enrollment.

A Range of Postsecondary Enrollment Options

Over the past decade, policymakers have increasingly turned to concurrent enrollment options to provide access to college-level courses for credit in the high school. Although the terminology varies from state to state, there are typically two different approaches to concurrent enrollment courses.

College High programs represent agreements between high schools and colleges to offer college-level courses at the high school, typically for both secondary and postsecondary credit. The curriculum content and standards are determined by the appropriate college academic department, and the courses are usually taught by high school faculty members who hold the same academic credentials required of those teaching at the college (Zanville, 1999).

In contrast, concurrent enrollment programs typically enable high school students to register for college courses taught by college faculty members on the college campus, where they receive both high school and college credit for their coursework. Sometimes these college courses are delivered to the high school or home via distance education technologies such as the Internet. High schools often partner with local colleges to offer their students advanced-level math, science, or foreign language courses whenever there are not enough students to offer a similar course at the high school (Zanville, 1999).

The primary focus of this chapter is on dual and concurrent enrollment policies, but there are other enrollment programs used by state leaders to encourage educational acceleration.

AP/CLEP. The first early college admissions programs were created by the College Board in the 1950s. Advanced placement (AP) courses permit secondary students to take college-level courses while still in high school. Upon achieving a passing score on a national exam, students receive advanced standing when accepted at a college or university. The College Level Examination Program (CLEP) allows students to test out of beginning-level college courses at colleges and universities (Zanville, 1999).

International Baccalaureate. Another development that emerged twenty years ago is the International Baccalaureate (IB) program, designed for highly motivated high school students. The IB is a rigorous high school curriculum that includes foreign language study, literature, science, math, and social studies (Zanville, 1999). Upon successfully passing a national exam, students earn an IB diploma and then receive advanced standing when admitted to a college or university.

Tech Prep or 2+2. The most recent addition to the universe of postsecondary enrollment options are tech prep or 2+2 programs. Often funded by federal grants, these programs offer an articulated high school/community college curriculum, typically in professional or technical fields. The courses are designed to reduce duplication between high school and college so that students move seamlessly between systems. Courses may be taught by either high school or community college instructors at an approved location (Zanville, 1999).

Factors Driving Interest in Postsecondary Enrollment Options

Some of the benefits policymakers name for their increasing interest in creating postsecondary enrollment options include

- Reducing college tuition costs for students and their families
- Accelerating student progress toward a degree in order to free up additional space on campus to meet the projected demands for college access by the "baby boom echo"—children of the baby boomers, who are approaching college age
- Providing greater academic challenges to high school students who have "senioritis"
- Encouraging greater collaboration between high school and college faculty members
- Increasing student aspirations to go to college
- Providing greater academic opportunities for students at small rural schools
- Building closer ties between colleges and their communities

State Policies That Support Postsecondary Enrollment Options

Most states have adopted a range of policies governing the various postsecondary enrollment options. As previously mentioned, thirty-eight states currently have some form of state policy that governs these arrangements, although these policies vary widely from state to state. Some of the questions policymakers are asking include:

- Should there be a statewide policy ensuring access to postsecondary options, or is it best to allow communities and institutions to adopt those relationships that meet local needs?
- Is statewide funding required in order to ensure equity across the state?
- What financial incentives should be provided to encourage participation among secondary schools and colleges and universities? Or does providing per diem support to both colleges and universities represent "double-dipping" at the expense of the taxpayers?
- Should financial assistance or incentives be provided to students to pay for AP or IB tests, or to reduce or eliminate the tuition burden for high school students successfully completing college-level courses?

- How do we ensure that enrollment option programs are indeed providing high-quality college-level education to high school students?

Student Financial Incentives. Fifteen states—California, Colorado, Florida, Georgia, Iowa, Maine, Massachusetts, Michigan, Minnesota, New Jersey, New Mexico, Ohio, Utah, Washington, and Wisconsin—have statutes that require either the state or the local school district to pay all or most of the tuition costs for students enrolled in concurrent enrollment programs. However, in most states, school district subsidies only cover courses that are taken for dual college and high school credit. A class that is taken for college credit only is generally not subsidized. States typically require the student to cover costs for books and transportation, although some districts may choose to cover these expenses as well. Colorado House Bill 1162, a 1998 amendment to the Colorado statute, requires a student to pay for any tuition up front. Upon successful completion of the course, the student can apply for reimbursement from the local district. In California, tuition is waived but a small enrollment fee is required.

In an additional nine states—Alabama, Idaho, Illinois, Oregon, Pennsylvania, South Dakota, Tennessee, Virginia, and Wyoming—local districts determine whether or not to subsidize student tuition costs for dual and concurrent enrollment programs. Virginia's statute encourages but does not mandate that local school districts cover the cost of tuition.

In three states—Missouri, West Virginia, and North Dakota—students pay a discounted tuition rate. Although it varies by district, concurrently enrolled high school students in Missouri typically pay a deeply discounted tuition rate—about a third of the normal rate.

In eighteen states—Arizona, Arkansas, Connecticut, Delaware, Hawaii, Indiana, Kansas, Kentucky, Louisiana, Maryland, Mississippi, Nebraska, New York, Nevada, North Carolina, Rhode Island, South Carolina, and Texas—students are generally responsible for all tuition and fees, although they may receive some support from individual districts. Community college systems in a number of states, including Connecticut, Kentucky, and Texas, offer extensive tuition waivers to high school students who are enrolled in concurrent programs.

Institutional Incentives. A majority of states (twenty-seven) allow both the K–12 school district and the community college to count the dually enrolled high school student as an FTE (full time equivalent) or ADA (average daily attendance) student for purposes of generating state support. Eight states—Colorado, Georgia, Idaho, Kentucky, Ohio, Texas, Washington, and Wisconsin—adjust the K–12 funding formula to reflect a reduction in daily funds to the high school for the dually enrolled student. Thirteen states— Alabama, Alaska, Connecticut, Delaware, Iowa, Indiana, Massachusetts, Maine, Missouri, Montana, New Jersey, Rhode Island, and Vermont—do not allow community colleges to include high school students as part of their regular FTE when generating state enrollment support.

Student Eligibility. In many states, students must meet minimum academic performance eligibility requirements before they may enroll in a concurrent education program. Other states make such programs available to any junior or senior who is accepted by a college. Georgia and Oklahoma have very specific entrance requirements, including a formula based on a student's SAT/ACT score, grade point average, and class rank, as well as a written recommendation from the principal and the student's parents. Michigan requires students to show proficiency on the MEAP (Michigan Educational Advanced Placement) test to demonstrate their ability to benefit from college-level work. A few states make special provisions for students as young as those in the ninth grade, who are identified as gifted and talented, to participate in concurrent enrollment programs.

Other Special Requirements. Recognizing that participation in postsecondary enrollment options requires planning and preparation, many states require that school districts notify all eligible students by March 1 of any postsecondary enrollment options available for the following fall term. Other states mandate counseling for students and/or a signed permission slip from parents acknowledging that they understand the consequences that accompany a high school student enrolling in a college-level course.

Model State Programs

Growing interest in postsecondary enrollment options for students is generating interest on the part of many states to document the results of these programs and to expand their efforts to reach still more students.

Minnesota. The state of Minnesota takes credit for being the first state to institute concurrent enrollment policies for high school students. Many years of practice were finally codified in 1985 with the enactment of the Postsecondary Enrollment Options program. According to Minnesota statute Sec. 123.3514, the program is intended to "promote rigorous academic pursuits and provide a variety of options" for juniors and seniors in high school by providing them with the opportunity to take college courses at state expense. A report by the Minnesota Office of the Legislative Auditor (Mar. 1996) stated, "Policymakers hoped that the competition from colleges and universities might force secondary schools to become more responsive to the needs of students and parents" (p. ix).

The Minnesota legislative auditors (Mar. 1996) studied the experience of students who left their secondary schools for at least part of the day to take one or more college courses on a postsecondary campus during the 1994–95 school year. They found that the vast majority of students, parents, and college administrators were satisfied with the program, although some high school administrators expressed a range of concerns about the program's educational, financial, and administrative burden. They found that "6 percent of Minnesota public school juniors and seniors took courses at postsecondary schools . . . [although] student participation rates varied considerably across the state" (p. xi). This variability in student participation was related to the accessibility to college campuses in different parts of the state. The study also reported that program participants generally received higher grades than regularly admitted postsecondary students.

"School administrators, students and parents said that the most important reasons why students participated in the program were to get a head start on college credits and to save on postsecondary costs" (Minnesota Office of the Legislative Auditor, Mar. 1996, p. xiv). The auditors estimated that students who participated in the Postsecondary Enrollment Options program—as opposed to enrolling in the same postsecondary courses without the program—saved approximately $10.9 million in costs for tuition, fees, and books.

Washington. The Running Start program was created by the Washington state legislature in 1990 to expand educational opportunities for public school students. It began as a pilot program and then went statewide in 1992–93. By 1998–99, the number of students had increased to 12,355—or 6 percent of eligible Washington public high school students (Crossland, 1999).

Running Start permits eleventh- and twelfth-graders who pass a test demonstrating that they have the skills needed to succeed at college to take college-level courses, tuition-free, at Washington's thirty-two community and technical colleges. Because K–12 basic education funds are used, students who participated in 1998–99 are estimated to have saved $12.5 million in college tuition costs. Taxpayers also benefit significantly by paying only once to support Running Start students in both high school and college. It was estimated that this "two-for-one" aspect of Running Start saved taxpayers about $24.6 million in 1998–99 (Crossland, 1999).

The Running Start progress report also describes the results of a University of Washington (UW) graduation follow-up study on the original Running Start transfer students who had entered the university in 1993. Running Start students graduated with an average GPA of 3.42—significantly higher than the average GPA (3.14) of students who began their college admission at UW. The Running Start students also earned bachelor's degrees within four years at a rate of 41 percent, which was higher than the rate for students who had started their postsecondary education at UW, which was 31 percent within four years (Crossland, 1999).

Utah. The state of Utah has encouraged high school participation in dual and concurrent enrollment for many years, partly as a means to accelerate students' educational progress to cope with a burgeoning demand for access at the state's colleges and universities. In 1999, Governor Michael Leavitt announced an initiative to award a New Century Scholarship to any Utah high school graduate who had accelerated his or her education process and completed the requirements for an associate's degree prior to September 1 of his or her high school graduation year. The New Century Scholarship awards the student 75 percent of actual tuition costs for two years at any of Utah's state-operated baccalaureate-granting institutions (Utah State Board of Regents, 2000). The associate's degree may be earned by a combination of credits earned through concurrent enrollment, AP, and/or summer school attendance.

Concerns of Policymakers

Although interest and support for postsecondary enrollment options among state policymakers remain high across the country, certain concerns are being raised, including the following:

- Policymakers in some states have become concerned about the "double-dipping" impact on taxpayers when both K–12 districts and community colleges receive state support for secondary students concurrently enrolled in postsecondary classes.
- In 1997, the Oregon Joint Boards of Education (the Board of Education and the Board of Higher Education) approved a statewide study of current practices and policies to determine the need for a more uniform early options program (Zanville, 1999). Concerns have been expressed about inequitable access to college courses across the state. Increasingly, as students attend multiple institutions as they proceed through their college careers, different transcript systems at different state colleges and universities create problems for the students.
- Although the articulation and transfer of dual enrollment credits is generally not an issue at public colleges and universities, some students who seek to transfer to elite private institutions find that concurrent enrollment credits earned while they were in high school will not transfer.
- There is concern about the quality of programs, such as the College High classes that are being offered at high schools. Liabilities include the excessive workload for the high school teachers selected to teach the college-level courses, as well as the perception that the college curriculum needs to be "dumbed down" in order to be accessible to high school students.

Conclusion

Despite these and other concerns, there is no evidence that there is less interest among state policymakers in promoting postsecondary enrollment options as a means to ensure more seamless education systems. The goals of most state early option programs will continue to focus on

- Providing challenging educational opportunities for high school students
- Improving the college preparation of all students, thus reducing the need for remediation at the postsecondary level
- Increasing the number of citizens who participate in some form of postsecondary education in order to ensure a trained, competitive workforce

- Accelerating the educational progress of students through postsecondary education, saving both students and taxpayers significant dollars
- Fostering collaboration between high schools and colleges, resulting in reduced redundancy and ensuring a more seamless K–16 public education system

References

Colorado House Bill 1162, 61st General Assembly, 2nd Reg. Session, Colo., 1998.

Crossland, R. *Running Start: 1998–1999 Annual Progress Report.* Washington State Board for Community and Technical Colleges, Dec. 1999.

Minnesota Office of the Legislative Auditor. *Postsecondary Enrollment Options Program Executive Summary.* Minnesota Office of the Legislative Auditor, Mar. 1996.

Utah State Board of Regents. Rule 604. "New Century Scholarship." [http://www.utahsbr.edu/*.*/policy/r604.htm]. June 27, 2000.

Zanville, H. "Oregon Early Options Study." Oregon University System [http://www..ous.edu/aca/earlyoptions.htm]. Jan. 20, 1999.

Additional Resources

Blair, J. "More Teens Blending High School, College." *Education Week.* [http://www.edweek.org/ew/vol-18/31dual.h18]. Apr. 14, 1999.

Colorado House Bill 1217, 58th General Assembly, 1st Reg. Session, Colo., 1991.

Education Commission of the States. *Advanced Placement Courses and Examinations State Level Policies.* Denver: Education Commission of the States Clearinghouse Notes, 2000.

Education Commission of the States. *Choice: Postsecondary Options/Dual Enrollment.* Denver: Education Commission of the States Clearinghouse Notes, 1997.

Education Commission of the States. *1996–1997 State Issues Report.* Denver: Education Commission of the States, 1997.

Education Commission of the States. *1998–1999 State Issues Report.* Denver: Education Commission of the States, 1999.

Education Commission of the States. *Survey on Community College Finance.* Denver: Education Commission of the States, 2000.

Education Commission of the States. *Survey on Transfer & Articulation.* Denver: Education Commission of the States, 2000.

Minnesota Postsecondary Enrollment Options Act, Minnesota statute Sec. 124D.09, 1999.

Utah State Board of Regents. Rule 355. "Planning, Funding, and Delivery of Courses and Programs via Statewide Telecommunications Networks." [http://www.utahsbr.edu/*.*/policy/r355.htm]. June 27, 2000.

Utah State Board of Regents. Rule 471. "Transfer of Credit." [http://www.utahsbr.edu/policy/r471.htm]. June 5, 2000.

Utah State Board of Regents. Rule 165. "Concurrent Enrollment." [http://www.utahsbr.edu/*.*/policy/r165.htm]. June 27, 2000.

KATHERINE BOSWELL serves as director of the Center for Community College Policy at the Education Commission of the States, Denver, Colorado.

2

*This chapter provides guidelines for establishing a part-
nership between a community college and a single high
school or school district. In addition to outlining the steps
necessary for developing the program, discussions of how
to maintain quality and meet the needs of the individual
institutions are included.*

A Model for Implementing a Concurrent Enrollment Program

Brian G. Chapman

Concurrent enrollment programs enable students to earn college-level credit
while enrolled in high school. These collaborations have served to make college less financially burdensome for the student participants and their parents. Students who otherwise might not have even begun a college
education because of financial concerns or a variety of other factors have
achieved this heretofore unreachable goal.

Concurrent enrollment also brings substantial benefits to the participating educational institutions. Although the model described here is based
on a large urban community college district, it can also be successfully
established in a suburban or rural setting. This chapter presents just one of
the possible models for implementing a concurrent enrollment program.
Using this model, one urban college was able to complete the process in just
one year and increased its enrollment from six hundred to approximately
two thousand students in eighteen months.

Determining the Need for a Concurrent Enrollment Program

The first step is to determine if there is sufficient interest among the potential participants. A concurrent enrollment committee or task force should
be instituted at the originating college. A representative committee makeup
should include at least the chief academic officer, the dean of students, a
curriculum committee member, an admissions administrator, counselors,
advisors, and department chairpersons, as well as faculty members repre-
senting a cross-section of technical and liberal arts programs. All of these

individuals are key players in this process, and it is imperative to have their commitment to the program, as well as that of the board of trustees and the college president.

The committee—or selected members—should arrange to meet with the administrators, counselors, and faculty members of the school districts. It is unlikely that a single meeting would be sufficient; a series of meetings will probably be required. The first meeting will serve as an opportunity to present a complete outline of the proposed program. The high school contingent should be given time to review the proposal and seek input from supervisors, peers, and reporting staff. Should there be general interest in moving forward, subsequent meetings can serve to identify student needs, curricular needs, available resources, and potential roadblocks.

Identifying Program Goals and Objectives

Candid, open communication between community college and high school administrators is necessary to define the program's goals and objectives. To develop the student-related goals, the committee or task force should address the following questions: In what areas is the high school curriculum lacking? Are the arts and science offerings sufficient? Is college attendance emphasized as an option for all students? Are students being adequately prepared for the transition to college? and Is enough attention being paid to encouraging all students to attend college, and not just the high achievers? One important goal should be to minimize the expense of the program for the student participants.

Next in line are the goals of the individual educational institutions. What result does each institution want from the program? How would each entity define success? Are the expected outcomes realistic?

Clearly defined goals and objectives will aid in gaining support for the program from parents, teachers, faculty members, administrators, elected officials, and both high school and college students. They will also provide a framework with which to evaluate the success of the program.

Under the umbrella of the larger goal of fostering improved relationships between community colleges and K–12 systems, more specific goals should be established. Some examples of other goals and objectives are to (1) provide a wide variety of college-level courses for students, (2) provide student development-oriented, first-year experience courses to high school students, (3) enhance the performing and visual arts curricula in high schools, (4) enhance science and language offerings in high schools, (5) expose as many students as possible to a college-level experience, (6) provide a college-level experience for the most academically talented students, (7) allow students to "get a jump" on their college education, (8) provide a seamless transition from high school to college, and (9) encourage students who do not aspire to attending college to explore the possibility of continuing their education.

Once the decision has been made that a concurrent education program is right for the community, special care should be taken to design a program that will successfully meet the needs, goals, and objectives identified in the preliminary meetings. This is not the time to move forward blindly; indeed, this is the most crucial stage of implementation.

Before developing the plan for the program, policy and procedural issues that could create barriers to program implementation should be addressed. Some items to consider are:

- How well do the community college and high school schedules integrate?
- Will transportation be an issue?
- Will the students be covered under community college or high school insurance in the event of an injury?
- How will registration be handled?
- How will grade reporting take place?
- How will attendance reporting be handled?
- How will concurrent enrollment courses be noted on the college and high school transcripts?
- Will there be any textbook subsidies in place through either the high school or the college?
- Will the perception of "double-dipping" for state funds be an issue in the community?
- Where will courses be held?

Next, establish a financial framework. The community college should provide funding for the required personnel. What fees and charges, if any, will apply? Will there be registration fees? Will there be any compensation for providing the facility for the classes? Will there be any tuition charge for the courses and, if so, will the high school pay the tuition or will students be individually responsible for their tuition payments? If there is a tuition charged, will there be a reduction from the regular cost?

Once procedural issues have been addressed, the committee can move on to designing the course offerings. Naturally, these courses must meet the needs of the high school and its students. Using the information obtained in the preliminary meetings, the community college should prepare a preliminary selection of courses to be presented to the participating high school(s).

Staffing Requirements

Although a program such as this will likely require coordination and management by at least one full-time college employee, initially the project can be guided and molded by a team of campus professionals who are dedicated to the concept.

The start-up process for a concurrent enrollment program can be managed by a small group of campus administrators and faculty members whose agenda includes establishing concurrent education as an enduring college offering. As with any college instructional program, at least one full-time administrator will ultimately be required to manage and coordinate the program. Ideally, once firmly rooted, the program will include the following personnel:

1. *An on-site liaison from each high school.* This position would require at least part-time effort. A participating high school guidance counselor willing to accept the additional duties above and beyond his or her high school responsibilities often fills this role; the college should provide compensation for the additional duties. The liaison's role would include coordinating academic calendars, attending to facility requirements, managing instructional needs, and overseeing organizational procedures.

2. *A community college admissions/registration liaison to each high school.* This position also would generally be part-time, although there could be instances in which a full-time employee would fulfill some of these duties. These individuals should be considered regular employees of the college and should be trained in all aspects of the college admissions and registration process. Their duties would include assisting students in submitting and completing applications to the college and providing information to instructors regarding class rosters, add/drop deadlines, final grades, and all other admissions and registration procedures.

3. *An outreach liaison from the community college.* This position may be full- or part-time, but it is indispensable in facilitating direct communication between the community college and participating high schools. Responsibilities would include scheduling classes, working with high school faculty members and administrators, organizing and facilitating orientation sessions, answering questions as they arise, and addressing student services and faculty issues.

4. *Faculty.* Instructors can be drawn from the high school, the community college, or outside sources. High school teachers should possess the appropriate academic credentials required to teach at the community college level in their subject area. Faculty members who elect to teach in the program may already be affiliated with the college as full-time or adjunct faculty members. The program must maintain quality while extending the college's instructional services.

Selection of Faculty

A program, no matter how well designed, cannot exceed the talents of the instructors. Choosing instructors for the concurrent education courses may be difficult. Ideally, there will be a large number of applicants from which to choose. However, it is better to eliminate a course offering than to keep it on the roster with a less than stellar instructor. Faculty members for this program must be aware of the unique nature of the courses they will be teaching and should be willing to make an effort to be responsive to their new students' concerns. Even just one mismatch between a faculty member and a course in the program could spell disaster for the success of the program.

Beginning with a Pilot Program

Regardless of the potential size of the concurrent education program, it is prudent to start with a minimum of one semester of limited course offerings. This will allow transition time for all the personnel involved. Where possible, plan carefully for future growth. This will help avoid the pitfalls frequently associated with popular programs that grow at an unmanageable rate—such as the inability to evaluate the program properly, procure faculty and staff members, and provide adequate support services. In addition, carefully managed expansion will allow for a quicker and more effective response to the inevitable but unforeseen challenges. A high-quality program will continue to grow steadily and gracefully, and the college's reputation will benefit.

Feedback and Evaluation

Especially in the beginning, a vehicle for formal feedback between community college and high school officials is imperative. These feedback sessions should involve liaisons from each administration as well as from participating department chairs and instructors. It is critical to know right away what is working and what is not. Regularly scheduled feedback sessions— perhaps once a month for the first semester or two—can ensure that problems are identified quickly and resolved expediently. There should be a formal input and response process to prevent problems and concerns from "slipping through the cracks."

Marketing the Program

Once the program has been organized, a marketing plan should be developed. Follow-up promotional meetings with faculty members and administrators at high schools can be used to present what a college has to offer students. A list of courses the program has offered or is willing to offer should be included, and it should be noted whether the courses are intended to be offered on-site at the high school or the community college or at an off-campus site. In developing the package, the transportability of the course, the availability of instructors in specific disciplines, and the geographic constraints of the instructors should be considered. The broadest set of options, when presented to the high school decision makers, will afford an opportunity to match their needs with the instructional services the college has available.

In addition, marketing should be aimed directly at the students and their parents and guardians. Such marketing can include such methods as planning for a presence at high school parents' nights, mailing fliers to parents and guardians, distributing fliers to students at the high schools, and featuring articles in alumni publications and local newspapers. It is also a good idea for colleges to include a section on their concurrent enrollment program in the college catalog. Both students and parents should be made aware of the financial benefits associated with the courses. If textbook subsidies are available, they should also be featured.

Because student interest in the program is a key factor in its success, colleges should consider putting additional effort into highlighting the benefits of the program to the students. One effective method for attracting students is to hold a concurrent enrollment fair on the community college campus. This type of event is easily tailored to showcase the hosting institution's particular strengths. The event should include an orientation session for the students—where they would be given an overview of the program and informed of application and selection procedures as well as course offerings. The day could also include a tour of the community college campus, the opportunity to sit in on an actual or staged classroom session, a showing of the art work of current students and faculty members, a display of completed or in-progress science projects, a reading by student and faculty authors of their works of poetry, fiction, or nonfiction, and a display or presentation by each department that will be offering courses to the high school students. The agenda for the day is limited only by the imagination of the organizers.

Customizing to the Unique Needs of Each High School

Once the pilot program is completed and a college has begun expanding to additional schools or course offerings, it will probably need to customize its selection of offerings for each individual high school. The concurrent enrollment program is intended to complement rather than supplant the high school curriculum, and the unique needs of each participant high school should be considered. This is the only way to ensure that the course offerings are relevant to the students. For example, a high school that has limited offerings in the art department or has no physics teacher will be especially interested in offerings in those areas. And a high school with a strong life sciences curriculum and advanced placement courses in that discipline may not need college-level biology classes.

Maintaining Program Support and Success: A Focus on Quality

The success of this type of program depends on the experience of the participating students and the perception of the quality of the program by high school administrators, parents, legislators, and taxpayers. The concurrent enrollment program must provide college-level instruction of the same quality and academic rigor that is afforded to students enrolled in classes on the college campus. The students must be held to the same standards of excellence that incoming first-year college students are.

The college should consider providing midterm evaluations to the students and their counselors. After each semester, a team set up to monitor participant progress should review students' progress. Assessment of each student's progress should be used as a counseling tool to identify any individual challenges that he or she may face at the earliest possible stage and to provide the student with strategies for tackling these challenges. Every attempt should be made to work directly with students to increase the likelihood of their success.

In addition to the formal feedback sessions mentioned earlier, students should be given the opportunity to evaluate their instructors at the end of each semester. The academic departments of the college should provide evaluation of the participating faculty members, consistent with the campus guidelines.

A follow-up study should be performed at the end of the first semester to measure previously designated success indicators. Among these indicators may be course completion rates, course success rates, and grade point averages.

Institutional Benefits of Concurrent Enrollment

How students benefit from a concurrent enrollment program is clear, but what are the possible benefits to the community college and the high school?

For the college, a program of this type is an excellent recruitment tool. The college attracts better-prepared students who will experience fewer transition difficulties than do incoming freshmen who did not go through the program. In addition, concurrent enrollment programs generate a positive image in the community, faculty members gain from the experience of teaching a college course in a high school setting, the administrators and instructors of the community college gain in-depth knowledge of new student populations, and colleges build a solid base for future collaborations with the K–12 institutions.

The high school benefits from an enhanced curriculum that may better capture the imagination and interest of juniors and seniors, as it helps build the image of the high school as a place where students can take college courses, and the curriculum boosts student performance as well as graduation and high school-to-college transfer rates. In addition, high school teachers with appropriate credentials have the opportunity to teach courses that are more content intensive, and they can work with the community college, enhance their professional development, and become even better teachers. These opportunities will attract top-notch teachers to the high school. Although the outcomes will likely differ among programs and institutions, these are potential outcomes for any concurrent enrollment program.

Conclusion

A thoughtfully planned and executed concurrent enrollment program can be an asset to any community college, bringing benefits above and beyond any related program costs. Through the program, the college can assist in meeting the educational needs of the high school students in the community, and it can develop effective partnerships with K–12 institutions. At the same time, the college can reap the benefits of increased visibility in the community, of having better-prepared incoming first-year students, and of having in place an effective recruitment tool.

BRIAN G. CHAPMAN is a doctoral student in the Community College Leadership Program at the University of Texas at Austin and is employed in the enrollment services department at Columbus State Community College, Columbus, Ohio.

3

*At Salt Lake Community College the concurrent enroll-
ment department has structured a program that provides
quality instruction for students by focusing on faculty
development, and it creates a healthy partnership between
public and higher education institutions.*

Designing an Effective Concurrent Enrollment Program: A Focus on Quality of Instruction and Student Outcomes

Margaret K. Peterson, John Anjewierden, and Cris Corser

Each year, educators, administrators, and concerned parents grapple with the question of how to keep high school seniors engaged in learning and prevent an apathetic attitude popularly labeled "senioritis." Two questions arise from this goal: How can educators make the senior year of high school meaningful and significant for students? and How can educators make this year a solid transition into either the workforce or higher education?

Concurrent enrollment programs have been created to address these questions; they offer qualified high school students the opportunity to take college courses for college credit prior to high school graduation and have been implemented in school districts nationwide with a variety of structures and methods of operation. Salt Lake Community College (SLCC) in Salt Lake City, Utah, has created a successful program that focuses on quality instruction. The primary features of this program include a course approval process, liaisons, in-service training, and the Instructional Assessment System (IAS) evaluation instrument (created by the University of Washington), which have helped the program become a statewide model.

Background

Concurrent enrollment began a number of years ago at SLCC in response to state legislative action. The Utah state legislature passed a bill allocating $200,000 to fund the program. Their purpose was to establish a program that would give high school seniors—and some juniors—an opportunity to begin earning college credit, thus making the third and fourth year of high school a more meaningful, challenging transition into either higher education or the workforce. At the same time, legislators hoped to save money by using secondary school facilities for higher education courses.

In conjunction with the Utah State Board of Education and the Utah State Board of Regents, the legislature also provided guidelines for constructing this program, which included

- Establishing a program that creates a partnership between secondary and higher education institutions
- Establishing a program that gives control over college courses to the sponsoring college
- Allowing only high school seniors with a "B" average in high school coursework, with the addition of some juniors and sophomores with outstanding qualifications, to participate in the program
- Specifying that the textbooks, instructional materials, and tests for the program should be the same as those used for the courses taught on the college campus
- Requiring concurrent enrollment instructors to meet the same qualifications as regular adjunct faculty members

These guidelines were intended to establish a standard of instruction for concurrent enrollment equivalent to that of courses taught on the college campus, seeking to ensure that college credit was given for college-level coursework.

Initially, the concurrent enrollment program at SLCC grew out of what was known as "early enrollment." High school students were invited to come onto the college campus, take courses, and apply the credit they earned toward a high school diploma. Officially, the concurrent enrollment program came into being during the 1989–90 academic year. In 1993, the chair of the community education division inherited a program loosely structured and growing in popularity. As a result, he faced a major problem: how to provide quality instruction, given the looseness of the structure and the potential for rapid growth. In collaboration with several deans, he began to structure what has now become a model program. The features of this program are structured to maintain quality in the face of rapid growth.

Course Proposal Approval Process

One of the most important features of the program structure is the course proposal approval process. The program requires concurrent enrollment high school instructors to submit a course proposal form for each class they wish to teach. This form asks them to identify the course, list their academic qualifications for teaching the course, and outline the syllabus, specifying the textbook and any placement tests or prerequisites students must meet in order to enroll in the class. The completed form identifies the liaison or college contact person who will be working with the instructor, and it requires signatures from two school district administrators and three SLCC administrators—namely, the department coordinator, the division chair, and the dean associated with the course offering. First-time instructors must attach transcripts of all postsecondary work, as well as résumés and cover letters.

All course proposals and attachments are sent directly to the concurrent enrollment department, where they are logged in a spreadsheet to track the approval process. Before submitting the course proposal materials to the departments, division chairs, and deans for signature, the concurrent enrollment director and liaisons analyze the proposals, transcripts, and résumés to determine the academic preparation and qualifications of each instructor for teaching the course. Based on this analysis, particularly of the potential instructor's coursework, the concurrent enrollment department makes its recommendations.

After the course proposals have gone through the approval process, the concurrent enrollment department keeps copies of the proposal, transcripts, and résumés of each instructor on file. At that point, the director prepares college-approved contracts to be signed by each SLCC dean, the SLCC academic vice president, and the contract administrators for the five school districts served by the SLCC concurrent enrollment program. Copies of each course proposal become part of the concurrent enrollment contract.

In essence, each course proposal becomes an agreement between the instructor, the school district administrators, and SLCC. As such it becomes part of the foundation for monitoring and maintaining quality instruction.

Faculty Liaisons

Another feature that assists in maintaining program quality is the use of full-time concurrent enrollment liaisons, as well as college faculty members, who serve as part-time liaisons. Currently, the SLCC program employs five full-time liaisons and contracts directly with over fifty faculty liaisons, drawn primarily from the ranks of the full-time community college faculty. The role of the liaison is to monitor and maintain the quality of instruction. Therefore, his or her primary responsibility is classroom visitation. Full-time concurrent enrollment liaisons monitor classes in subject areas that have the largest enrollment: English, math, humanities, graphic communication, and art. College faculty liaisons monitor classes in which enrollment does not justify the hiring of a full-time liaison.

The liaison job title and description were chosen with the intent of establishing communication links between the department in which the class is offered, the concurrent enrollment department, and the high school instructor. Each college department chair assigns his or her faculty members to serve as liaisons and visit classes within their discipline two or three times a semester. Faculty liaisons will make more visits if instructors require additional assistance. During these visits, the liaisons observe instruction and interact with the students, and may participate in classroom activities. They may also give teaching demonstrations or substitute for the instructor on occasion to maintain college-level work when the instructor must be absent. The full-time visual arts liaisons often give teaching demonstrations in concurrent classrooms to demonstrate college-level art theory and skills development. The English and humanities liaisons regularly team-teach, conduct workshops on the principles of writing, and participate in peer-response groups by giving students feedback on their rough drafts as a part of the writing process. Mathematics liaisons also team-teach and work with individual students in the classrooms. In addition to these tasks, the liaisons answer questions students have about concurrent enrollment and making the transition to SLCC as a regular student.

Another primary responsibility of concurrent enrollment liaisons is to act as links between the college departments they represent and the concurrent enrollment high school instructors. For example, full-time liaisons regularly attend college faculty meetings, present any concurrent enrollment issues or concerns, and report back to concurrent enrollment high school instructors, keeping them abreast of departmental agendas. They also act as links between SLCC administrators and concurrent enrollment departments. Liaisons maintain contact with department coordinators and division chairs—answering questions, delivering messages, and carrying out department and division procedures.

In fulfilling their responsibilities, liaisons wear many hats and answer to a number of administrators. They must possess excellent written and oral communication skills and refined problem-solving ability, and they must meet the same academic qualifications as their campus counterparts in their specific disciplines. The liaisons overseeing academic disciplines must possess a master's degree and requisite teaching experience. Those overseeing vocational areas must also have the appropriate degree or experience equivalent to regular faculty members in their area. Each academic term, the full-time liaisons must teach one section on campus of the courses they visit in the concurrent enrollment program. Therefore, liaisons are departmental faculty as well as full-time concurrent enrollment liaisons. They are encouraged to stay current in their field, and money is allocated for attending and participating in conferences. The math liaisons attended two conferences during the 1998–99 academic year with colleagues from the math department; the English and humanities liaison gave a presentation addressing concurrent enrollment issues at the 1999 Two-Year College English Association–West Conference; the visual arts liaisons also participate in workshops to upgrade their art abilities as well as act as judges in the Sterling Scholar Program, a statewide college scholarship program for outstanding high school seniors.

The concurrent enrollment department has recently hired an academic advisor liaison. This liaison serves as a communication link between the academic advising department, the concurrent enrollment department, high school counselors, and concurrent enrollment students. The advisor liaison is responsible for assisting students in selecting courses appropriate for their anticipated majors and careers, as well as providing a resource for students as they make the transition from high school to college.

In-Service Training

The liaisons conduct annual in-service training for high school instructors to keep them current in the field and in harmony with the direction of on-campus instruction. Generally, the liaisons work in conjunction with department coordinators in planning and conducting these training sessions. The subject matter is discipline-specific and in-service varies according to the needs of the program. For instance, the director and personnel from the registrar's office implemented on-line registration and grade reporting to replace a cumbersome paper system, and they organized training for two hundred concurrent high school instructors to learn the new procedures. Participating school districts can now log onto the College Web site and register students, thus avoiding the need for paperwork. Although the on-line system experienced initial glitches and adjustments had to be made, it represents a much more efficient process for managing large numbers of students from multiple sites. The department also maintains a concurrent enrollment Web page that is updated regularly with new information, instructions, and deadlines. As a result, the use of on-line procedures has created room for further growth, basically turning what could be logistical problems into opportunities.

Another in-service project involved several liaisons, the director, and personnel from the assessment office in teaching the concurrent enrollment faculty and school district administrators how to use an on-line student placement testing procedure for math and English classes. All SLCC students are placed into English and math classes with CPT or ACT scores.

Each fall, the concurrent enrollment director, with the assistance of the full-time liaisons and office staff, conduct an in-service orientation for this same population. During this orientation, the concurrent enrollment staff distributes supplies, reviews policies and procedures, and updates participants on refinements within the enrollment, registration, and grading procedures. Among the materials the staff distributes to district administrators and teachers are updated editions of the program handbook and student handbooks (which contain registration instructions, disclosure statement forms, add/drop forms, and a calendar). Brochures are also provided that answer commonly asked questions and explain the features, benefits, and purpose of the program to students and parents. The program director revises and edits these materials each year in an effort to maintain the quality and integrity of the program.

In-service training for high school concurrent enrollment instructors during Summer 2001 includes an extensive off-campus session that addresses discipline-specific matters and instructional guidelines.

Throughout the year, the director holds additional quarterly meetings with district administrators, thereby strengthening the partnership between the college and the school districts. One of the problems the concurrent enrollment department faces is maintaining internal and external partnerships. Internally, problems have arisen between student services and concurrent enrollment because of the unique nature of registration, grade reporting, and maintaining student records for classes taught on a different academic calendar at multiple sites. These problems have been resolved through improved communication and coordination—although, externally, problems have arisen because of these internal improvements. The concurrent enrollment director has used in-service meetings as a means for creating dialogue and improving communications—key factors in building a healthy, viable partnership.

Another method for improving communications is the year-end awards program, at which outstanding teachers and liaisons are acknowledged for their hard work and efforts with students. This annual awards program enhances college administrators' and school district administrators' awareness of program quality and development. High school administrators nominate the teachers, each district selects its final recipient, and students from individual classes present the awards. In addition, concurrent enrollment instructors nominate liaisons from various disciplines and present awards at the program. And various students discuss the impact that concurrent enrollment classes have had on their academic success. For example, an architectural drafting student described how the concurrent enrollment class he attended influenced his decision to pursue an architectural career.

Teacher Evaluations

Beginning in Fall 1999, the program began pilot-testing a teacher evaluation instrument as an additional means of maintaining the quality of classroom instruction and as a tool for faculty development. Striving to achieve standardization with on-campus procedures, the program adopted the Instructional Assessment System (IAS) evaluation instrument, which SLCC uses to evaluate classroom performance of its full- and part-time faculty. This policy met with some resistance from the school districts because of high school faculty contract agreements. However, negotiations have resolved most of the resistance, and boundaries have been set and confidentiality maintained.

The IAS system supplies on-campus administrators with information from four questions, whereas other information from an additional series of questions goes directly and exclusively to the teacher receiving the evaluation. The first four questions provide information about students' assessment of the overall effectiveness of the course, the teacher's contribution to the course, the organization of the course, and the textbook. Analysis of these items has provided valuable information that the department plans to use for ongoing faculty development.

Currently, the department is creating strategies for the director and liaisons to use in doing intervention work with instructors who need improvement. One major component of the strategies is to establish specific, written goals for improvement, helping the teachers create a plan to meet these goals, measuring progress through observation, and providing supportive feedback.

In addition to maintaining the quality of instruction, the structure also seeks to manage logistical problems that have arisen as the program has grown from year to year—in some instances at a rate above 50 percent. One of the most effective strategies for managing growth and the size of the program (which has grown from 758 students in 110 sections to over 9,000 students in 610 sections over a ten-year period) has been the use of information technology, including the Internet and extensive use of database systems.

Outcomes Achieved

As a result of implementing this structure, the program has achieved several student outcomes. In April 1999, the department surveyed a stratified random sample of 604 students (approximately 12.5 percent) of the 4,817 students registered for concurrent enrollment courses in Spring 1999. The survey asked a set of questions designed to determine students' perception of concurrent enrollment courses, their plans for six months and then one year after high school graduation, and how the program affected their decision to attend college (Salt Lake Community College [SLCC], 1999).

In relation to students' perception of the courses, the research found that 26 percent of the students were completely satisfied, 41 percent were very satisfied, and 29.4 percent were satisfied (SLCC, 1999). Therefore, two-thirds of the students were at least very satisfied—and fewer than 3 percent were unsatisfied. In comparing these results with students' perception of regular high school classes, researchers found that 8 percent of those students were completely satisfied, compared with 26 percent for concurrent enrollment (SLCC, 1999). Research findings also show that 26 percent were very satisfied with high school classes, compared with 41 percent for concurrent enrollment. Overall, a greater proportion of students were at least very satisfied with concurrent enrollment classes, compared with regular high school classes, which suggests that the quality of instruction was better in concurrent enrollment classes than in regular high school classes.

In regard to student plans six months and then one year after high school graduation, the findings reveal that 45 percent of the students planned to attend college six months after graduation. That figure dropped to 38 percent one year after graduation. Analysis reveals that this drop might be attributed to graduates going to work, getting married, or serving religious missions (SLCC, 1999).

With respect to the effect that concurrent enrollment classes have had on students' decisions to attend college, 56 percent of the respondents reported that it encouraged them and 42 percent reported that it had no effect, and the courses discouraged fewer than 1 percent. During the summer of 1999, the concurrent enrollment department developed a research project using a stratified random sample to generate 1,097 student records. It systematically chose four years containing pertinent information from the ten years of the program's existence. It found that 55 percent of the concurrent enrollment students attended SLCC during the four-year period (SLCC, 1999).

These results indicate that the majority of participating students have been very satisfied with concurrent enrollment courses and that the program has been a positive influence on their decision to attend college, especially SLCC.

This study also indicates that during the four-year period prior to Spring 1999, 37 percent of concurrent enrollment students earned two-year degrees (SLCC, 1999). Analysis of the student records further indicates that students during this period took an average of three to four concurrent enrollment classes before high school graduation, which equates to an average total of 13.5 quarter credit hours per student. In general, the grade point averages of students in concurrent enrollment are comparable to those they have while attending SLCC, which are generally within the range of 0.3 grade points (SLCC, 1999).

The University of Utah's Department of Educational Leadership and Policy is currently conducting extensive research for the SLCC concurrent enrollment department, using data obtained for all students and concurrent enrollment students who enrolled at the college during the past seven years. Results and conclusions will be available in Spring 2001.

Other favorable outcomes of the program include the development of a state organization of concurrent enrollment programs—the Utah Alliance of Concurrent Enrollment Partnerships (UACEP). This organization acts as a sounding board for directors and assists in providing management guidelines. The concurrent enrollment program is also involved as a founding institution of the National Alliance of Concurrent Enrollment Partnerships (NACEP), which supports and promotes its constituent partners through quality initiatives, program development, national standards, research, and communication.

In addition, the program has achieved favorable outcomes with internal and external partnerships. Since its inception, concurrent enrollment has met with various forms of resistance. However, because of the strict requirements for teacher qualifications and consistent liaison monitoring since the current structure has been in place, that cloud is lifting. As a result, the concurrent enrollment program has gained more credibility and more respect from departments campuswide as a worthwhile, viable academic opportunity for students. In conjunction with this outcome, the offerings within school districts are expanding and additional highly qualified instructors are applying.

Through these outcomes, the concurrent enrollment program has become a foundation and has paved the way for further programs, such as the legislature-sponsored New Century Scholarship, which is awarded to students who have completed the equivalent of a two-year degree by the end of the summer of their senior year, thereby funding 75 percent of their remaining coursework toward a bachelor's degree. Finally, with an emphasis on maintaining the high quality of instruction and student outcomes, the structure of concurrent enrollment has created a bright, promising future for the program at Salt Lake Community College.

Reference

Salt Lake Community College (SLCC). *Salt Lake Community College Concurrent Enrollment Program Reports 1999*. Salt Lake Community College, Department of Concurrent Enrollment, Salt Lake City, Utah, 1999.

MARGARET K. PETERSON *is the director of concurrent enrollment at Salt Lake Community College.*

JOHN ANJEWIERDEN *is dean of the School of Business and Industry at Salt Lake Community College.*

CRIS CORSER *is the concurrent enrollment English and humanities faculty liaison at Salt Lake Community College.*

4

*This chapter presents a brief history of concurrent enroll-
ment initiatives and then gives an overview of activity in
Arizona, including research on student achievement, as
well as tracking studies. In spite of growth in the number
of programs and successes in student achievement, not
everyone in the state understands and appreciates the
benefits of the program; the final section of this chapter
describes some of the realities of politics and necessary
compromises.*

Concurrent Enrollment in Arizona: Encouraging Success in High School

Donald E. Puyear, Linda M. Thor, and Karen L. Mills

Studies of concurrent enrollment programs show that not only do they accelerate the attainment of a baccalaureate degree but they also create a comfortable transition to college. In addition, concurrent enrollment students perform as well as, if not better than, students who enter college at the traditional age. The literature substantiates that participation in concurrent enrollment need not be restricted to academically high-achieving students.

Overview

The patterns of concurrent enrollment programs are diverse. For instance:

- A concurrent enrollment course can be taught as an enhancement to or augmentation of a regular high school course. Unlike the regular high school students in the course, the concurrent students must do extra work to earn college credit.
- A high school teacher—generally recognized as an adjunct to the participating postsecondary institution—teaches a course, using the college curriculum or syllabus at the high school during the regular high school day, and the class is entirely composed of concurrent enrollment students or has a combination of concurrent and regular high school students. It is not unusual for this type of concurrent enrollment course to be linked via interactive television to other high schools, allowing those other students the opportunity to participate in college classes.
- A college course is taught at the high school during the school day, but the teacher is a postsecondary teacher who is not also a high school teacher.

NEW DIRECTIONS FOR COMMUNITY COLLEGES, no. 113, Spring 2001 © Jossey-Bass, A Publishing Unit of John Wiley & Sons, Inc.

- A college course is taught at a location other than the high school (often the college campus) but is limited to high school concurrent enrollment students.
- A college course is taught at a location other than the high school (often the college campus), and concurrent enrollment high school students are mixed with other college students.

Whatever the name and delivery model, today's concurrent enrollment programs are increasingly used to enrich a high school student's curriculum, accelerate his or her academic program, and provide that student with a smooth transition for entry into college.

The exact beginnings of concurrent enrollment are vague, but some attribute the original concept of eliminating the repetitive curriculum by awarding joint high school and college credit for a single course to J. W. Osborn. Osborn (1928) wrote about the repetition in curriculum between some high school courses and introductory college courses. About thirty years later, in 1956, his concerns were finally addressed with the development of the advanced placement (AP) examination—a single standardized test used to determine students' proficiency in certain subject areas (Greenberg, 1992).

Collins (1980) credits Jamestown Community College in New York with being the first institution to launch the practice of having high school students enroll in college courses for the purpose of receiving dual college and high school credit. In 1978, the community college invited the top eleventh-grade students to enroll in two college courses during the summer prior to their senior year. However, slightly preceding the Jamestown initiative was Project Advance, which came out of Syracuse University. According to an impact study for the university (Edmonds, Mercurio, and Bonesteel, 1998), Project Advance originated in 1973, when seven local high school principals and superintendents met with university staff members to develop a program that would "challenge high school seniors, many of whom had completed all of the requirements for high school graduation by the end of the eleventh grade" (p. 1). Although not documented in the literature, it is interesting to note that educators in the state of Connecticut boast of a concurrent enrollment program that existed as early as 1955. And Saint Louis University indicates that in 1959 they responded to pleas from the Saint Louis University High School to address the redundancy in curriculum between the last year of high school and the freshman year of college.

The literature is as rich with information about the history of how and when concurrent enrollment programs began as it is with dialogue about whether or not the programs should be provided, and whether or not students are performing at the collegiate level. This chapter, however, sets aside opposing arguments and opinions and focuses only on the research that supports the provision of concurrent enrollment.

The *Virginia Plan for Dual Enrollment* (1988) provides the best description of the relevance of concurrent enrollment programs nationwide by stating that these programs promote rigorous educational pursuits and encourage learning as a lifelong process while recognizing that high school students who accrue college credit are more likely to continue their education beyond high school than those who do not.

Although growth in the number of concurrent enrollment partnerships reflects a vibrant and far-reaching movement, presenting the demographics of this collaborative initiative is not unlike giving it a name or explaining how it works. It is dynamic in nature. Wilbur and Lambert (1995) provide perhaps the best attempt at presenting a national perspective. Their database includes information on more than 2,300 collaborative programs (not limited to concurrent enrollment), coordinated by the 861 institutions responding to the survey. The partnerships involve every kind of postsecondary institution and represent every region of the country. For concurrent enrollment specifically, the directory lists seventy programs in twenty-nine states. The postsecondary partners in these programs are both community colleges and four-year universities—public and private, large and small, well known and lesser known. A small number of the programs focus on very specific topics—for example, the International Academy at the University of Louisville's College of Arts and Sciences offers students the opportunity to explore world cultures and international affairs. Some of the institutions have programs that are offered only during specific times of the year, such as the Summer Youth College at Foothill College in California and the five-week residential summer college program at the University of Delaware. And some of the institutions work with a single high school partner, whereas others, like Syracuse University, work with a multitude.

In addition to history, research, and directories, an overview of concurrent enrollment programs would be incomplete without at least brief mention of the National Alliance of Concurrent Enrollment Partnerships (NACEP). This alliance is an association of higher education professionals who administer cooperative programs that link their institutions to secondary schools. It was created to establish and promote quality initiatives and national standards for concurrent enrollment programs, to research and disseminate information about such programs, to encourage strong relations between partner institutions (high school to college and college to college), and to support its membership through professional development and communication on issues of common concern. More information about this organization can be found by visiting their Web site (http://supa.syr.edu/nacep).

Concurrent Enrollment Activity in Arizona

Statewide reports show that all ten of the community college districts in Arizona are now participating in some model of concurrent enrollment partnership—a situation that has developed fairly recently.

Rio Salado College, in the Maricopa Community College District (MCCD), is the largest provider of concurrent enrollment programs in the state, and one of the largest in the country. Prior to 1992, their concurrent enrollment activities were limited to a single private school. But then, in the early 1990s, public high schools began to express strong interest in concurrent enrollment arrangements for their students. Therefore, Rio Salado College, along with community colleges throughout the state, found themselves addressing not only the logistics but, more important, the legalities of working with public high schools in concurrent initiatives.

Legal enablement of concurrent enrollment endeavors were substantiated within legislative statutes, which stated that high school governing boards could award Carnegie units and apply college courses toward high school graduation requirements as long as certain course stipulations were met. Additionally, a ruling by the then attorney general Bob Corbin stated that concurrent enrollment courses taught on the high school campus could be counted by the high school toward their average daily membership (ADM) calculations. ADM is the high school equivalent of FTSE (full-time student equivalent) and serves the same purpose of establishing base budget allocations. Therefore, not only did high schools aggressively pursue concurrent enrollment arrangements with postsecondary institutions, but they also became increasingly interested in having the programs be provided on the high school campus. Arizona's community colleges were committed to responding to the increasing number of requests for concurrent enrollment partnerships. However, they wanted to do so with some assurance of built-in quality. And so, the Arizona Council of Academic Administrators developed minimal standards that allow individual colleges to exceed these guidelines whenever appropriate. These standards state that (1) credit will be granted by the community college, (2) courses offered will have been evaluated and will have met the official college curriculum approval process—to include outline, competencies, grading policy, and attendance requirements, (3) students admitted to a college course will follow established admissions assessment and placement policies, (4) faculty members must have community college certification and must be selected and evaluated by the college, using approved college procedures, and (5) any text used must be college-approved.

During 1993, Rio Salado College began exhaustive efforts to track, study, and analyze every aspect of concurrent enrollment. The following summarizes what was learned from that research. Approximately one-third of the seniors who opted to enroll in a math class would not have taken the class had it not been offered for concurrent credit. Without this course, they would have chosen the "early out" option, which would have sent them home from school at 11:30 A.M. Most of the seniors taking dual enrollment classes did not need the high school part of the credit; they had met the minimum graduation requirements and wanted the college credit. Concurrent enrollment was increasing the motivation of freshmen and sophomore students—they were looking forward to working through a curriculum that would allow them to meet placement and prerequisite requirements for college-level classes. High school faculty members reported that classroom management became easier as students no longer complained about stringent class expectations and approached their college classes with a mindset that involved more study and attention.

One of the most compelling studies regarding the achievement of concurrent enrollment students comes from the MCCD Chemistry Instructional Council. Twenty questions are included in every final exam to see if selected chemistry classes are being taught uniformly across the district, including concurrent enrollment sections, and to see if letter grades are being assigned appropriately. The study is conducted annually and continues to document that all courses, including concurrent enrollment courses, are taught uniformly at a collegiate level and that assigned grades are appropriate.

Also within the Maricopa District are colleges that provide ACE (Achieving a College Education) and ACE+ programs. These programs are college campus-based programs, and ACE students are placed in classrooms with other high school–aged, concurrently enrolled students. It is important to note that ACE/ACE+ students are recruited from all quartiles of achievement during their sophomore year in high school. A 1997 report prepared for the Phoenix Think Tank (Finch, 1997) states that more than 90 percent of the high school participants in ACE/ACE+ programs graduate from high school, compared with a rate of 49 percent for the seven high schools that feed into the program. Additionally, 83 percent of the ACE/ACE+ participants go on to attend postsecondary institutions both in and out of state.

Another Arizona college conducted a survey of previous concurrent enrollment students who had just completed their first year of college (Finch, 1997). Questionnaires were sent to four hundred students, asking for feedback on their preparedness for subsequent college coursework and their current academic status, and copies of transcripts were requested as well. Respondents had earned an average of 25 credit hours during their first two semesters at local and out-of-state colleges and universities, including Columbia, Notre Dame, Pepperdine, University of Washington, Arizona State University, the University of Arizona, and Sacred Heart. The most frequently declared programs of study included engineering, education, business/economics, biology, design fields, computer fields, nursing, music, law, journalism, mathematics, theater, and general studies.

Other findings from the survey indicate that concurrent enrollment students performed better during their first semester or year at the university than did typical community college transfer students. For Arizona State University (ASU), specifically, studies show that MCCD students dropped in median grade point average (GPA) from 2.85 to 2.32, whereas concurrent enrollment students entered with a median GPA of 3.22 and finished at 3.41. This was not a controlled sampling; the students may have had very different abilities or levels of preparation. Students who were concurrently enrolled for high school credit only and elected to take the advanced placement test out-performed their national counterparts. For those students scoring grades of 5 and 4 (the highest grades), respectively, on the AP test, the national average was, respectively, 13 percent and 18 percent, whereas the percentage for high school students in the concurrent enrollment class (not enrolled for college credit) was, respectively, 14 percent and 27 percent. In addition, respondents to the survey reported advantages in their ability to think analytically, formulate ideas, use quantitative skills, function independently, and assess their own work (Finch, 1997).

A recent study conducted by the University of Arizona (U of A) found similar results. Of 2,351 Fall 1997 Arizona-resident freshmen, 29 percent had earned community college credit through some form of concurrent enrollment. Between high school and the U of A, these students experienced an average drop in GPA of .56, compared with .78 for those with no community college credit and .53 for those with AP credit. The university determined that "when differences in high school grade point averages and SAT scores were accounted for, both AP and [concurrent] community college credit were associated with better university grades. This held true when changes in students' grade point averages between high school and university were calculated as well as in the regression analysis" (Richardson, 1999, p. 2).

The growth spurt in concurrent enrollment between 1993 and 1998 could not have been predicted. According to a status report from the state board of directors for Arizona Community Colleges (Puyear, 1998), just under nine thousand (unduplicated headcount) high school students statewide enrolled in concurrent enrollment classes during the Fall 1996 semester. Extrapolation places this figure at well over twelve thousand for Fall 1999. The types of courses provided in the Arizona programs range from general studies to the humanities and fine arts, and from the social and behavioral sciences and the natural sciences to literacy and critical inquiry. The primary model for program delivery was high school-based, with a community college–certified high school instructor providing the instruction during the regular high school day. However, there were college districts that sent college faculty members to the high school campus to teach the course as an augmentation of a high school course, or to provide the course at a location other than the high school, to a mix of high school and non–high school students. Some colleges charge tuition and fees to concurrent enrollment students and provide financial stipends to the high schools in amounts equivalent to adjunct faculty salaries. Other colleges employ what is called a balanced-exchange financial arrangement, in which the college invoices the high school for tuition and fees, and the high school invoices the college, in the same amount, for instruction and facility usage. Invoices are exchanged but money is not.

Not everyone in the state understands the benefits of the concurrent enrollment program; program proponents have faced some significant challenges in the state legislature and sometimes in their own districts. On October 28, 1999, the newspaper *Arizona Republic* ran a front-page article entitled "Colleges May be Double Dipping." The article espoused that "the state is paying twice for high school students to take dual enrollment classes that earn them college and high school credit . . . [and that] college professors are questioning whether the classes even provide a college level of instruction" (Jones, 1999, p. A-1). The article states that both the high school and the participating community college receive funding for the same students in a concurrent enrollment arrangement and that "double dipping has the Arizona Tax Research Association (ATRA) and the governor's office looking at how dual enrollment programs are funded" (p. A-1). In addition to this commentary in the press, several other activities have contributed to a year-long political battle. These have included the airing of a debate on the state's public television station between a key ATRA representative and a community college president about funding and quality concerns in concurrent enrollment programs. Along with the negative perception of double dipping, at issue was the practice of having mixed classes—students enrolled for concurrent college credit in the same class with students enrolled only for high school credit—and whether or not a distinction between a high school–level and a college-level curriculum could be made in certain occupational courses, such as keyboarding. In addition, some community college faculty members objected to high school teachers, rather than full-time college instructors, teaching these courses.

Along with all of the press and media attention, the state representative who served as the chair of the House Education Committee "opened a file," which is the first step in initiating legislation on funding issues related to concurrent enrollment. Legislative research analysts requested follow-up meetings with college and high school administrators for purposes of sorting through what were misperceptions and what were realities. A legislative roundtable composed of the previously noted state representative, a high school concurrent enrollment teacher, college presidents, a parent, a high school district governing board member, community college faculty members, an ATRA representative, and others convened to determine whether legislative regulation was truly needed. The ultimate outcome of this public debate was the introduction of four bills into the Arizona 2000 legislative session. Although the thrust of the first three bills was to reduce, even eliminate if possible, state funding for concurrent enrollment and establish a state-level compliance officer for these partnerships, it was only the fourth bill that received any real consideration. This bill was initiated by the Arizona Community College Association and called for the formation of a joint legislative study committee on concurrent enrollment to do three things. First, the committee was to conduct an evaluation of current guidelines and determine minimum standards necessary to ensure the highest level of quality instruction; second, it was charged with identifying and reviewing the current state funding formula and examining the long-term cost benefit of concurrent enrollment programs to

Arizona; and third, it was to examine the effect of dual enrollment courses on student success in school, high school retention rates, and the number of students who go on to postsecondary education. Two of the bills died and one was held, but the bill calling for the establishment of a study committee passed both the House and the Senate and was signed by the governor.

Simultaneous with these legislative activities, community college officials throughout Arizona attempted to address issues and concerns at both the state and local levels in order to avoid future legislative action. The Arizona Community College Presidents' Council formed a committee to propose revisions to the state board rule governing concurrent enrollment. One significant change would be the requirement that students be enrolled in four regular high school courses while taking a concurrent enrollment course, unless they are seniors who can at that point satisfy graduation requirements by taking fewer than four more high school courses. This stipulation is intended to address the "double dipping" concern, as high schools incur the costs but do not receive additional funding for students who remain on their campuses beyond four periods a day. The second change focuses on the quality issue of "mixed classes" and would require that all students in a dual enrollment class be enrolled for college credit unless designated as advanced placement or honors students. Obviously, the quality recommendation addresses only part of the concern; the issue surrounding the appropriateness of providing some of the occupational courses is still being discussed. However, there is a consensus that not all high school students are college-bound and that students who earn some college credit while still in high school have the potential of increased marketability upon entering the workforce.

Concluding Thoughts (Necessary Compromises)

Concurrent enrollment issues have consumed large quantities of high school and community college administrators' and staff members' time over the last five years, but these programs will be stronger and of higher quality as a result. There was, in fact, some inconsistency in the way different colleges went about setting up concurrent enrollment courses. There were, as well, variations in the financial arrangements between colleges and even between a given college and different high schools. These inconsistencies and variations in basic procedures created a climate of doubt regarding the manner in which the concurrent enrollment programs were being administered. Refinement of state board rules to address these inconsistencies is therefore necessary. Those responsible for educational policy must ensure that concurrent enrollment programs are administered in such a manner that the benefits to individual students and to the state are not clouded by questionable practices. It must be clear that concurrent enrollment courses are of high quality, meet rigorous academic standards, are taught by fully qualified faculty members, and are consistently administered.

A recent session of the Arizona town hall addressed higher education in the state. The town hall strongly endorsed the concept of concurrent enrollment programs as a positive step toward bridging the gaps between secondary education and higher education. Town hall participants saw this and other collaborative efforts between high schools and colleges as essential if the state is to successfully address the challenges of the emerging information-based economy.

References

Collins, J. J. "Summer Scholars: A New Program at Jamestown Community College." *Community College Frontiers,* 1980, *8*(3), 35.

Edmonds, G. S., Mercurio, J., and Bonesteel, M. *Syracuse University Project Advance and the Advanced Placement Program: Comparing Two National Models for Curricular Articulation and Academic Challenges.* Syracuse, N.Y.: Syracuse University, Mar. 1998.

Finch, P. "Intervention Assessment: The Status of Concurrent/Dual Enrollment." Prepared for submission by the Phoenix Think Tank. Phoenix, Ariz., Fall 1997.

Greenberg, A. *High School-College Partnerships: Conceptual Models, Programs, and Issues.* Washington, D.C.: George Washington University, Mar. 1992. (ED 34 956)

Jones, M. L. "Colleges May be Double Dipping: Dual Enrollment Sparks Questions." *Arizona Republic,* 1999, *110*(163), 1. [http://www.azcentral.com/]

Osborn, J. W. *Overlapping and Omission in Our Course of Study.* Bloomington, Ill.: Public Schools Publishing Company, 1928.

Puyear, D. "Concurrent and Dual Enrollment of High School Students in Arizona Community Colleges." A report prepared for the State Board of Directors for Community Colleges of Arizona. Phoenix, Ariz., Aug. 7, 1998.

Richardson, R. M. "Community College and AP Credit: An Analysis of the Impact on Freshman Grades." A report prepared for the University of Arizona. Tucson, Ariz., June 10, 1999.

Virginia Community College System. *Virginia Plan for Dual Enrollment.* Richmond: Virginia Community College System, 1988.

Wilbur, F. P., and Lambert, L. M. *Linking America's Schools and Colleges: A Guide to Partnerships and National Directory.* (2nd ed.) Washington, D.C.: American Association for Higher Education, 1995.

DONALD E. PUYEAR is executive director of the State Board of Directors for Community Colleges of Arizona, Phoenix.

LINDA M. THOR is president of Rio Salado College in Tempe, Arizona.

KAREN L. MILLS is senior associate dean of instruction for academic programs at Rio Salado College, Tempe, Arizona.

5

Although concurrent enrollment activities provide an opportunity for cooperation between a community college and local high schools, they are not the only opportunity. This chapter examines concurrent enrollment in the context of a larger working relationship between one community college and the high school districts it serves.

Concurrent Enrollment and More: Elements of a Successful Partnership

Steven R. Helfgot

Local high schools are valuable partners with community colleges and should be seen and treated as such. Cerritos College in Norwalk, California, has a history of that kind of relationship with its local high schools—a relationship that has in recent years yielded a highly successful concurrent enrollment program. Cerritos College has spent ten years cultivating multi-faceted partnerships with local high schools. These partnerships have resulted in substantial benefits for Cerritos College, including increased visibility for the college among potential students, promotion of the college as a place for real academic engagement, and a small source of income for the college's own programs. The high schools have benefited from the partnership by being able to provide high-quality college-oriented programming, such as an enhanced and cost-efficient College Fair and Senior Preview Day.

The College and Community

Cerritos College is located in southeast Los Angeles County and enrolls close to 23,000 students each semester. The college district encompasses eight cities, each with a population of more than 450,000. These eight cities are highly diverse, both ethnically and socioeconomically. The population in each city is relatively stable, with a large number of long-term residents, many of whom have had a long relationship with the college over its nearly forty-five-year history.

Four unified school districts serve the eight cities, with eleven high schools feeding a significant number of students to Cerritos College.

NEW DIRECTIONS FOR COMMUNITY COLLEGES, no. 113, Spring 2001 © Jossey-Bass, A Publishing Unit of John Wiley & Sons, Inc. 43

The Impact of Free Flow

Until the late 1980s there was a legislatively mandated in-district attendance policy for community colleges in California. Students were required to attend their local community college, though they found any number of ways to get to another college if they wanted to. Nonetheless, the college assumed that it had a captive population in the high schools and therefore made only minimal outreach efforts to those high schools.

The situation began to change in the late 1980s, in part because of economic conditions. Community college enrollments dropped and enrollment fees (tuition) were introduced for the first time into a system that had previously been tuition-free. Competition for students developed and the colleges—Cerritos included—started to recruit more actively in local high schools.

This trend continued to accelerate throughout the 1990s. The California legislature enacted free-flow legislation that allowed students to attend any community college in the state. That situation remains in place today, causing a highly competitive environment in which community colleges compete aggressively for high school graduates.

For a college like Cerritos, the competition is especially intense. There are three other community colleges within a fifteen-minute drive from the Cerritos campus, and four more are within less than a half hour's drive. Add to that four campuses of the California State University in the Los Angeles Basin, as well as two campuses of the University of California, and it is easy to see why competition for students is so intense.

An Effective Relationship: More Than Recruiting

High school teachers and administrators are interested in sending their graduates to college and they are thus receptive to recruiting visits from both two- and four-year colleges. However, their ability to act on this interest is limited by their circumstances. High school principals have schools to run, counselors have a variety of duties to perform, and teachers have classes to teach. Frustration develops when high school staff perceive that their relationship with the colleges and universities is less than equal: recruiters come at their convenience but not to events to which they are invited by the high school. When enrollments are low or when diversity goals can be achieved by actively recruiting students from certain schools, recruiters are available, calls are returned, and information is provided. But when the applicant pool is large and meeting diversity goals is not a problem, college and university recruiters are nowhere to be seen. Simply put, high school staff at times perceive that high schools are important to colleges and universities only when their graduates are needed and can be ignored when there is no such need.

It was against the backdrop of these perceptions—shared among college administrators in any number of formal and informal meetings—that Cerritos College began to formulate a new relationship with its local high schools.

Building a Partnership. Cerritos College leaders determined that if their recruiting efforts were going to be taken seriously in local high schools and, even more, if they were going to be actively supported by principals, counselors, and teachers, they would have to develop a balanced and equitable relationship with local high schools. In short, college officials were determined to build real partnerships with local high schools.

Meeting Principals. The first step in establishing effective relationships with high schools involved an individual meeting with personnel from each high school. Each principal received a letter from the coordinator of high school relations (now called the executive director of school and community relations) requesting a meeting at the high school to discuss how the college could be of service to the high school and its students and staff members. The letter was followed by a phone call from the recruitment technician (today called the school relations specialist—a reflection of the changed relationships with high schools) to schedule a meeting with the principal and his or her staff.

The coordinator of high school relations and the recruitment technician went to all the meetings together. They heard a variety of requests from the high school staff for information, for services from the college staff, and for materials, as well as for regular contact with the college. Two points were made in virtually every meeting. First, each principal wanted a single contact person at the college—someone whom they would know and could call and from whom they would get a timely response; second, each principal wanted to know what other principals were saying, what other high schools were doing, and what the college was doing with those schools.

Three things occurred as a result of those meetings. First, the specific requests for information, material, and service were met immediately; second, a thank-you letter went to the principals, identifying the coordinator of high school relations as their contact; and third—and over time, the most important—the high school principals' council was established. These initial high school visits were so successful that they are now conducted on a regular basis.

The High School Principals' Council: A Vehicle for Cooperation and Collaboration

In Fall 1990, the principal of each of Cerritos College's in-district high schools was invited to a two-hour breakfast meeting on the college campus. These principals chose both the time and the location for these meetings. Key administrators from the college also attended. The first forty-five minutes of the meeting was a period for people to get acquainted and engage in informal discussion. The goal was for the principals to feel that this time was to be devoted to addressing their concerns and meeting their needs.

The formal meeting was cochaired by the college's coordinator of high school relations and the vice president for academic affairs. The early part of the meeting continued the informal discussions. The principals introduced themselves individually and talked about current priorities, problems, and programs in their schools. Each principal also offered items for a common agenda and suggested ways in which the college and the high schools might work together.

Ten years later, the principals' council remains the foundation of Cerritos College's relationship with its local high schools. The group meets four to five times a year and the format remains unchanged. Meetings are chaired by the college's executive director of school and community relations— although his role is by design mostly that of a facilitator. Relationships and friendships among the principals and between principals and college administrators have grown strong. As principals have moved on, their successors have joined the group, as have administrators from the school district offices. Trust and confidence are high and allow for extensive cooperation among the districts and between the districts and Cerritos College. Indeed, the principals' council has spawned a number of cooperative programs, including an extensive dual enrollment program.

Activities to Meet High School Needs

Three specific activities illustrate the way in which the principals' council has spawned programs to meet high school needs, resulting in the building of trust and confidence between Cerritos College and local high schools. These activities are the Peer Power Conference, College Night, and Senior Preview Day. Experience with these programs has allowed for easy introduction of the college's new concurrent enrollment program.

The Peer Power Conference. In the early 1990s, peer counseling programs were popular in a number of high schools in the Cerritos College service area. Cerritos also had a well-established peer counseling program. At principals' council meetings, several principals lamented that tight budgets prevented them from sending their peer counselors to state and national conferences. Responding to the concern, the school relations and counseling departments at the college offered to provide a low-cost one-day conference for high school peer counselors.

The conference was held annually for seven years (and ended only because peer counseling programs were being replaced by mediation and conflict resolution programs). It drew between 250 and 600 students from up to thirty high schools. The program was always substantive and fun— and received rave reviews.

Each year's program began with a keynote presentation delivered by a motivational speaker. For example, one year, Olympic gymnast and actress Cathy Rigby, who spoke about her struggle with eating disorders, delivered the keynote speech. Workshops covered topics ranging from AIDS and STDs (sexually transmitted diseases) to substance abuse, from interpersonal communications to basic helping skills, and from domestic violence to gang violence. Members of the college faculty and staff often served as workshop leaders. The conference ended each year with a performance (drama or dance) with a socially relevant theme.

Evaluations were always positive. They praised the straightforward way in which the workshops addressed important issues, as well as the quality of the workshop leaders. They also contained favorable comments about the way in which the program validated high school peer counselors and the work they did. And the high schools were thrilled with the opportunity to send sometimes as many as forty students to the conference.

The conference had positive results for the college, as well. A number of high school students have chosen to attend Cerritos after graduation on the basis of its own strong peer counseling program. And the money generated from the conference fees was sufficient to support an annual two-day retreat for the college's peer counselors.

College Night. Another frustration that has emerged in the principals' council concerned the "college nights" that each district—and in some cases each high school—held annually. The principals and counselors found them to be an administrative burden. Attendance lagged, especially when one high school in the district sponsored the night for all the schools in the district. Participation by universities, whose recruiters were stretched very thin in the wake of statewide budget cuts, was minimal. And both students and parents were dissatisfied with the events. At a principals' council meeting, the college was asked if it could sponsor one college night on the Cerritos campus for all eleven in-district high schools. The school relations office eagerly agreed.

Joint College Night is now an annual event. In 1999, nearly three thousand students and parents attended and visited with representatives from nearly seventy universities. They also had the opportunity to attend financial aid workshops in either English or Spanish. Students and parents get to preview a large number of universities. The universities are delighted with the "economy of scale" and the resulting decrease in individual school visits. Cerritos College draws a large number of potential students to its campus, collects a fee from each school for managing the event, and earns enormous good will from the high schools.

Senior Preview Day. Senior Preview Day is the third example of a program that originated in the principals' council to meet a need in the high schools.

Although a number of community colleges with which Cerritos competes have held Senior Days for a number of years, Cerritos has not. Principals have reported that many of these events were without substance and were little more than a college tour, a picnic, and a concert. When Cerritos decided to introduce a Senior Preview Day, concepts and ideas were discussed in the principals' council as well as with counselors, and a substantive program was designed. As a result, the event that was developed includes academic program presentations and tours, mini-classes, and a program fair. High school counselors preregister their students for the event and students preselect mini-classes and presentations. The program grew from seven hundred students in the first year to a thousand in the second. High school counselors are enthusiastic participants and believe that the day is truly well spent for students.

As these examples illustrate, by working in partnership with high schools and being responsive to their needs, Cerritos College has been able to implement programs and services that are of mutual benefit. The college's concurrent enrollment program, though relatively new, is another highly successful example.

Concurrent Enrollment: College Classes on High School Campuses

High school juniors and seniors have been enrolling in classes at Cerritos College for years. Several hundred typically register each semester and a larger number do so during the summer session.

In Spring 1998 the college's board of trustees changed policy by waiving the enrollment fee (tuition) for any high school student enrolled in a Cerritos College class and awarded dual credit. The cost for a course was thus reduced to the price of the textbook and some nominal fees. Credit would be awarded by both the high school and the college.

This change was received enthusiastically in the principals' council. One principal asked if a course could be taught at his school. The college agreed, the logistics were worked out, and the course was offered. It filled easily and was a great success. Not surprisingly, a flood of requests followed. Multiple courses are now offered in some half-dozen high schools and the number of students enrolling is growing, as Table 5.1 indicates. That growth alone is evidence of the program's success.

There have, however, been some unanticipated benefits as well.

Employing High School Faculty Members. One of the unanticipated benefits of this program has been the opportunity to employ high school faculty members who meet the college's minimum qualifications to teach some of the classes on the high school campuses. Often among the best and most popular teachers in the high schools, these instructors draw students into the college classes they teach. Beyond that, in becoming part-time

Table 5.1. Enrollment of High School Students in Cerritos College Courses

	Spring	Summer	Fall
1996			73
1997	221	468	85
1998	298	1,088	356
1999	670	1,595	692
2000	1,006	2,643	880

instructors at Cerritos College, these individuals develop a relationship with the college. The result is a group of high school teachers who know about the college, have a positive association with the college, and pass those positive feelings on to the students.

Sending Outstanding Instructors to Teach at High School Locations. Cerritos College, like most, if not all, community colleges, suffers from certain myths that exist about community colleges—such as that community colleges are just like high school, only without all the restrictions; that they are just for dummies; and that classes are not "real" college classes; the list goes on. These myths are often passed on from generation to generation of high school students. Offering college credit courses in high schools has given Cerritos a chance to attack these myths head-on. The college does this by inviting some of its very best faculty members to teach these courses. Most often, these teachers eagerly agree to do so. Thus, high school students (including those at the most academically rigorous high schools in the district) have experienced great teaching from great professors. They know it and tell others. Word of mouth is powerful, and positive words from academically talented students do much to enhance the college's image and reputation.

Increased Enrollment for the College. Bringing college credit classes with dual credit to the high schools has had a positive impact on Cerritos College's enrollment, which results in increased funding as well. The enrollment of high school students in the fall and spring semesters has increased from a few hundred each semester to more than nine hundred a semester. And summer enrollment has grown from 468 to 2,643. The numbers speak for themselves.

A Big Win for the High Schools—and the College. The high schools provide classroom space for the courses, recruit the students, and take care of the paperwork. Without leaving school, students can earn college credit at almost no cost. Some students are graduating from high school with more than a semester's worth of college credit. They are pleased, their parents are ecstatic, and the high school is seen as providing a tremendous service— with minimal cost and effort.

Conclusion

The success of Cerritos College's concurrent enrollment program is based on the hard work invested in building an honest and mutually beneficial relationship with local high schools and with their principals, teachers, counselors, and students. If there is a lesson to be learned from the Cerritos College example, it may be that it is worth investing in and building those relationships consistently and over an extended period of time.

STEVEN R. HELFGOT *is executive director of school and community relations at Cerritos College, Norwalk, California.*

6

*This chapter traces the ten-year history of the dual enroll-
ment program in Virginia, highlights its successes, and
identifies issues that will be examined for the future. It
also identifies how dual enrollment can serve the needs of
rural as well as urban communities.*

Dual Enrollment in Virginia

Rhonda K. Catron

Dual enrollment programs have been offered formally in Virginia since
1988. At that time, Donald Finley, secretary of education, S. John Davis,
superintendent of public instruction, and Jeff Hockaday, chancellor of the
Virginia Community College System (VCCS), signed the *Virginia Plan for
Dual Enrollment* (Virginia Community College System [VCCS], 1988), the
document governing partnership agreements between public schools and
community colleges in Virginia (Donald Finley, interview, Oct. 20, 1997; Jeff
Hockaday, letter to the author, Nov. 20, 1997). The agreement itself resulted
from the work of a task force on dual enrollment, which included representatives from both public instruction and the VCCS. The *Virginia Plan for
Dual Enrollment* outlines basic parameters for dual enrollment program
offerings but does not serve as an official policy; instead, the VCCS dele-
gates authority for the implementation of the plan to each of its twenty-
three community colleges. This allows each community college to structure
its own program to meet the needs of its constituency.

Rationales for Dual Enrollment Programs

In Virginia, the impetus for a dual enrollment program seems to have been
an outgrowth of increased emphasis on articulation between public schools
and colleges during the 1980s. At that time, public schools and colleges
were developing and implementing 2 + 2 programs and Tech Prep programs.
The 2 + 2 programs sought to establish agreed-upon curricula that allowed
students to complete two years of a vocational degree in high school and
the subsequent two years of the degree at a community college. The two
institutions cooperatively worked out details to avoid unnecessary duplication of material. The Tech Prep program was based on a similar premise,

with the additional rationale that many educational programs primarily catered to the most academically successful college-bound students and that there was a need for a program for the larger number of "average" students who might desire some education beyond high school but were unlikely to pursue a bachelor's degree. As these programs developed, administrators apparently began exploring the possibilities of offering some of the college-level courses to those high school students who were prepared and who had time available in their high school schedules that would allow them to get a head start on their college degrees. Parents and students became increasingly enthusiastic about dual enrollment, and community colleges welcomed this emerging program as a new student recruitment tool.

Development of the Virginia Plan for Dual Enrollment

Deborah DiCroce, president of Tidewater Community College, chaired the task force on dual enrollment. In addition to DiCroce and other signers of the agreement, Edward Barnes, president of New River Community College, and Dewey Oakley, from the Virginia Department of Education, also played key roles in developing the plan. DiCroce noted that the VCCS was in the best position to provide the courses because its course offerings, as well as its colleges' geographic distribution, were designed to serve all regions of the state (interview, June 27, 2000). Donald Finley, secretary of education and task force member, pointed out that dual enrollment programs were expected to be particularly beneficial to rural school systems that often did not have the resources to offer a wide range of advanced courses, especially for their gifted students. The community colleges often had advanced courses already in place, so it seemed logical to make these courses available to qualified high school students. Not only did sharing resources make sense financially, but it also helped eliminate the unnecessary duplication of courses for students who had sometimes been required to take very similar courses in both their high school and college programs (interview, Oct. 20, 1997).

Components of the Virginia Plan for Dual Enrollment

The 1988 plan addressed the relevant aspects of the program through flexible requirements.

Course Offerings. As part of the agreement, the dual enrollment task force established certain parameters for the types of courses that could be offered, stating that these could include "academic, fine arts, and vocational subject areas" (VCCS, 1988, p. 1). Initially, it was expected that vocational courses would be the most popular dual enrollment offerings, particularly with the 2 + 2 and Tech Prep programs already fairly well established in the mid-1980s. During the first decade, however, academic courses in the transfer area came to dominate dual enrollment offerings.

Ironically, as the program has continued to evolve, several community colleges have reported an increased interest in occupational/technical dual enrollment courses, thus indicating that the pendulum may be swinging back toward the initial expectation. Regardless of whether courses are for transfer or are occupational/technical, all dual enrollment courses must be part of a degree, certificate, or diploma program at the community college but may not include developmental courses or health and physical education courses (VCCS, 1988).

Student Eligibility. Once course eligibility was established, the task force on dual enrollment addressed the issue of student eligibility. Although some people wanted courses to be available to any high school student who could meet the placement criteria, regardless of the student's age, the task force decided that only qualified high school juniors and seniors who were sixteen or older would be eligible to participate. Even though the task force recognized that some younger students might have mastered the prerequisite skills for certain courses, members believed that students younger than sixteen might not have the necessary level of maturity to handle collegiate material and the college environment. Beyond the age requirement, high school students would also have to be recommended by the public school and meet the admission requirements established by the community college. Community colleges in Virginia do have open-door admissions policies, but students must take certain English and math placement tests to determine if they will be required to complete developmental courses. There are also prerequisite requirements for enrollment in specific courses. Dual enrollment students are not to receive special consideration for admission but are instead held to the same admissions standards as any other student seeking to enroll at the community college.

Credit Awarded. If students are admitted to and successfully complete the dual enrollment courses, accrediting standards dictate the credit to be awarded, as noted in the plan's section titled "Credit Awarded."

The award shall be in compliance with state and regional accrediting standards. High school credit shall also be awarded to participating high school students upon successful completion of the course. The award shall be based on the college credit hour, with one high school unit equivalent to six semester hours of college credit (VCCS, 1988).

Faculty Selection. Although both high school and community college accrediting agencies govern admissions requirements and credit awarded, the Southern Association of Colleges and Schools' (SACS) criteria for accreditation (1998) for community colleges take precedence in terms of policy on teacher selection. All dual enrollment faculty members must meet the minimum requirements of all community college teachers.

Assessment. At the time the *Virginia Plan for Dual Enrollment* was signed (in 1988), it did not include a section on assessment—perhaps because, at the time, outcomes assessment was just being developed. This may well have been the weakest component of the dual enrollment arrangement. In fact, lack of assessment measures initially left the program open to criticisms about quality, which in turn led to initial problems with transferability of dual enrollment courses to other institutions. As the program has evolved, regular assessment has become an integral component, with SACS having added criteria specifically designed to assess the quality of dual enrollment programs. The VCCS now requires all community colleges to include reports on dual enrollment programs as part of their overall annual assessment reports. Increased efforts in assessing dual enrollment programs have certainly contributed to the transferability of dual enrollment courses to most public four-year institutions in Virginia.

State Funding. Even more challenging than the issue of transfer articulation has been the issue of state funding for dual enrollment. This issue has come under more scrutiny and attack than any other single component of the *Virginia Plan for Dual Enrollment* (VCCS, 1988) because of the state-approved credit funding for both public schools (in terms of average daily membership credits) and community colleges (in terms of full-time equivalent student credits). Some critics consider this to be "double-dipping" because both institutions benefit financially. However, Finley pointed out that from his perspective money was not a major issue; the purpose of the program was to provide student access to expanded course offerings. Ned Swartz, who represented the Virginia Department of Education on the dual enrollment task force, and who is currently a dean at Lord Fairfax Community College, pointed out that such funding provided necessary incentives for participation by both institutions (interview, Nov. 21, 1997).

Tuition and Fees. In terms of payment of tuition and fees, the *Virginia Plan for Dual Enrollment* (VCCS, 1988) states that "schools and colleges are encouraged to provide high school students the opportunity for dual enrollment at no tuition cost to them or their families. In addition, neither the public school nor the community college shall be penalized in their respective state appropriations for developing and implementing the dual enrollment agreement" (p. 2).

However, even though the agreement "encouraged" that courses be offered at no tuition cost to the student, it was not a requirement, and under some agreements, students do pay their own way. The initial plan was deliberately vague in terms of tuition and fees. Members of the task force believed that individual colleges should negotiate their own agreements with the public schools in their service regions because those colleges were already aware of the dynamics involved. Dual enrollment agreements between public schools and community colleges, particularly in rural areas, have been developed whereby the colleges pay the high schools for facilities usage and the dual enrollment portion of the faculty member's salary; the high school then pays the tuition costs for students. Regardless of whether the students or the school systems pay, tuition and fees are meant only to cover costs of instruction.

Dual Enrollment in Rural and Urban Areas

The *Virginia Plan for Dual Enrollment* (VCCS, 1988) has succeeded in its purpose of increasing high school student access to college-level courses, with dual enrollment full-time equivalent students (FTES) accounting for 3.8 percent of total FTES in the VCCS in 1999–2000 and as much as 17 to 21 percent of total FTES at some individual colleges.

Finley's contention that dual enrollment programs would likely benefit rural areas has generally proved to be correct. Recent statistics show that community colleges that serve predominately rural areas tend to have the largest dual enrollment programs in the VCCS (Catron, 2000). The success of these programs may well be attributed to cooperative efforts between public schools and community colleges. In many rural areas, per capita income is generally low and, undoubtedly, financial agreements that allow students to participate in dual enrollment courses at no direct cost have increased the popularity of such courses. Also, some community college administrators speculate that community colleges may well be considered a first choice of higher education in more rural areas, thereby attracting larger numbers of students to dual enrollment programs (D. Boyce, interview, June 28, 2000; T. Suarez, interview, June 27, 2000; and B. Wyles, interview, June 27, 2000). Another factor contributing to larger programs in rural areas may be geography. Because many of the public schools in rural areas are located some distance from community college campuses, it may not be possible for students to physically attend on-campus courses. Most of the dual enrollment courses are taught in the high school setting, thus making these courses more accessible to students.

Community colleges in the more metropolitan areas of Virginia, especially the larger institutions, tend to have smaller dual enrollment programs. In each of these cases, campus administrators cite competition from well-established advanced placement (AP) programs as a key factor. Despite the guaranteed college-level credit from successful completion of dual enrollment courses, parents and students tend to consider AP courses to be more prestigious; therefore, public school officials typically favor AP programs.

Benefits and Issues

Regardless of the size of each community college's dual enrollment program, these programs provide numerous benefits. Most students cite their ability to earn college credits while still in high school as a primary advantage. Dual enrollment allows students to accumulate credits and ultimately shorten the time required to complete a college degree. It also often serves as an excellent recruitment tool for community colleges when successful dual enrollment students, who might not otherwise consider pursuing a college degree, see that they are capable of doing college-level work. Most parents are extremely supportive of dual enrollment programs because their children are able to accumulate college credits while still in high school. Parents also like the cost-saving feature of the program because, in most cases, the participating high school districts pay the cost of tuition through their articulation agreement with community colleges.

In completing the annual survey of dual enrollment students at Wytheville Community College, students and graduates consistently rate their dual enrollment experience as either "excellent" or "good" (Dual Credit Evaluation Survey, 1995, 1996, 1997, 1998, and 1999). Data on the transfer success of students and their success following graduation are limited and do not provide specific information regarding students who have completed dual enrollment courses. Students' self-reporting of success during recent qualitative interviews regarding Wytheville Community College's dual enrollment English program indicated that students believed that the dual enrollment English courses they completed had prepared them for subsequent college-level work at transfer institutions. These graduates also self-reported earning A's and B's in most of their college-level courses.

Despite the popularity and obvious benefits of dual enrollment programs, some concerns do exist. Some faculty members and administrators continue to express philosophical concerns about combining (if not virtually replacing) junior and senior high school courses with college-level courses, particularly in terms of dual enrollment English courses. Faculty members also question whether or not high school students are mature enough to handle some college material.

In addition, administration of dual enrollment programs creates special challenges. The coordination of placement testing and registration is time-consuming for both high schools and community colleges. Scheduling courses can also be a challenge, particularly if high school students are traveling to college campuses for the dual enrollment courses, because the high schools and colleges generally operate on different time schedules. Travel time must also be considered. Even if the majority of dual enrollment courses are being taught in the high school setting, scheduling can be problematic, particularly with block scheduling. In situations where students complete an entire year of a high school subject in one semester, some administrators have wanted to offer the entire year of a dual enrollment sequence in a single semester. Although the number of required contact hours can be met, faculty members express serious reservations about student success in accelerated courses of study that combine a year of high school and college instruction into one semester.

Another issue related to dual enrollment programs involves faculty time commitments. In most cases, community college faculty members are responsible for developing appropriate course outlines, selecting textbooks, and working with dual enrollment faculty members, but receive no additional compensation for such efforts. This can be a burden to instructors who are already teaching fifteen credit hours per semester, advising as many as fifty to a hundred advisees, serving on committees, sponsoring student clubs and activities, and participating in professional development activities. High school teachers are also often asked, if not required, to devote additional efforts to dual enrollment programs. In some cases, because of the accreditation criteria for faculty selection, it is not unusual (particularly in small rural schools) to find only one faculty member per discipline certified to teach dual enrollment courses. He or she may be assigned to teach the course, regardless of desire or willingness.

Another concern with dual enrollment courses centers on the physical settings of such courses. In Virginia, only a small number of courses are generally offered on the community college campus. More often, dual enrollment courses are taught in the high school setting. Some four-year colleges and universities question whether the high school setting can provide an environment equivalent to that of a classroom on a college campus. Critics argue that high school class time is often interrupted with announcements and other extracurricular activities. Also, dual enrollment students do not have the same opportunities to interact with the wider range of peers that they might if they took courses on the college campus. This issue of setting and its effect on the quality of dual enrollment courses is one that must be addressed. Only if community colleges and participating high schools can guarantee comparable quality will dual enrollment programs continue to flourish.

Advances in technology and increased emphasis on distance education may well affect dual enrollment offerings. Some community colleges have begun delivering dual enrollment programs via distance education and this trend will likely continue. Such delivery may well expand dual enrollment programs but will also create new challenges.

Conclusion

Dual enrollment course offerings have become an integral part of offerings at many community colleges in Virginia. The popularity of these programs continues to increase, and though dual enrollment courses may continue to compete with AP courses, increased emphasis on occupational/technical dual enrollment courses and distance education opportunities will likely ensure continued growth of the program. The VCCS and participating public school systems are committed to providing strong, high-quality dual enrollment programs that meet the needs of a wide range of constituencies.

References

Catron, R. K. *Dual Credit 1999–2001, VCCS Student Summary 2000*. Richmond: Virginia Community College System, 2000.

Dual Credit Evaluation Survey. Wytheville, Va.: Wytheville Community College, 1995, 1996, 1997, 1998, 1999.

Southern Association of Colleges and Schools. *1998 Criteria for Accreditation.* Decatur, Ga.: Southern Association of Colleges and Schools, 1998.
Virginia Community College System (VCCS). *Virginia Plan for Dual Enrollment.* Richmond: Virginia Community College System, 1988.

RHONDA K. CATRON *is associate professor and coordinator of college development and public information at Wytheville Community College, Wytheville, Virginia, and a doctoral student at Virginia Polytechnic Institute and State University.*

7

In Miami, a unique collaboration of three educational sys-
tems has created New World School of the Arts. Talented
young students study with professional artists, and in the
process they earn high school and college credits and pre-
pare for careers in dance, music, theater, and the visual
arts.

New World School of the Arts: Creativity Across the Curriculum

Nancy M. Wolcott

For twenty years the state of Florida has been committed to providing high school students with a range of opportunities to accelerate their education. In 1980, the state legislature mandated "articulated acceleration . . . to shorten the time necessary for a student to complete the requirements associated with the conference of a degree, broaden the scope of curricular options available to students, or increase the depth of study available for a particular subject. Articulated acceleration mechanisms shall include, but not be limited to, dual enrollment, early admission, advanced placement, credit by examinations, and the International Baccalaureate program" (Florida statute 240.116).

Dual Enrollment at Miami-Dade Community College

In response, Miami-Dade Community College and Miami-Dade Public Schools established an agreement of cooperation for the support of dual enrollment programs. Through that agreement and through similar agreements with private schools, Miami-Dade Community College (MDCC) provides a wide range of options for advanced high school students to earn college credit: dual enrollment courses taught by qualified high school or college instructors in high school facilities during regular class hours, select college courses offered on campus as part of the regular college program, a special summer program for advanced students, and an early admissions program through which high school students attend the college in lieu of their senior year in high school. Dual enrollment students represent close to 2 percent of the total MDCC student population. Whatever the variations in institutional funding formulas, no dual enrollment student in the public school system is charged for tuition or textbooks. (Private school fee arrangements vary; students are responsible for textbooks and materials.) Upon successful completion of high school, MDCC dual enrollees wishing to continue at the community college simply present a copy of their final high school transcript and continue to enroll in college courses. State articulation agreements ensure that dual enrollment credits are generally accepted throughout the Florida public university system.

PAVAC: Dual Enrollment and More

For a select group of talented young students, there is yet another dual enrollment option: the New World School of the Arts (NWSA). New World, a unique cooperative venture of Miami-Dade County Public Schools, Miami-Dade Community College, and the state university system, evolved from a pioneering collaboration sparked by state mandates for magnet schools and dual enrollment. In 1981, two performing and visual arts centers (PAVAC) were created under the joint sponsorship of the school district and Miami-Dade Community College. Quickly expanding from a successful summer pilot program, PAVAC provided artistic training to talented tenth- through twelfth-graders in the county's twenty-four high schools, who earned high school and college credit for classes in dance, music, theater, and the visual arts. Every morning during the school year, PAVAC students attended academic classes at their regular high school, and then traveled by school bus to a MDCC campus to spend three hours in arts studios. The PAVAC curriculum was developed by both college and high school faculty members, and both systems provided the program's faculty members and administrators. Adjunct instructors were hired to meet the specialized needs of the arts program, and outstanding guest artists were brought in for master classes.

PAVAC received national recognition for the achievements of its students, many of whom went on to professional careers in the arts. Seniors scored impressively in the National Foundation for Advancement in the Arts (NFAA) high school competition and earned scholarships to prestigious colleges and conservatories. This striking and rapid success was made possible by the innovative dual-system structure; however, that structure posed its own problems. With academic courses at one location every morning and intensive studio work at another location every afternoon, the school day was necessarily fragmented. Identities were fragmented as well, as students' ties with their high schools weakened. In addition, some high school arts instructors and administrators at the home schools resented the loss of their strongest students to PAVAC.

Creation of New World School of the Arts

The logical next step was taken by the Florida legislature in 1984. Responding to community enthusiasm for PAVAC and the program's demonstrated value to students, the state established a new high school and college: "a center of excellence for the performing and visual arts, to serve all of the State of Florida [with] a program of academic and artistic studies in the visual and performing arts [for] talented high school and college students" (Florida statute 240.535). During the next three years, while PAVAC continued to thrive, its administrators and faculty members, community leaders, and academics from the community college and local universities worked in consultation with national arts educators to develop a new school where all classes could be taken at one site.

New World School of the Arts opened with grades ten through twelve on the MDCC Wolfson campus in downtown Miami in September 1987, offering programs in dance, instrumental and vocal music, theater, and the visual arts. Most PAVAC students transferred to the new school, which graduated its first high school class in June 1988. As the school district changed its middle school pattern, NWSA added a ninth grade, in September 1991. By design, enrollment has remained constant at about 460 students.

The first college freshmen enrolled at NWSA in September 1988. College students take all their arts courses at NWSA, and complete general education requirements at Miami-Dade Community College. Upon completion of their NWSA programs, students are awarded the associate in arts degree by MDCC and the bachelor of fine arts degree or the bachelor of music degree by the University of Florida. Many students, because of the rigor of the conservatory-style programs, take four years to complete their 36 general education credits and receive their associate's and bachelor's degrees at the same time. College enrollment is currently at 350 and is projected to grow to 600.

The New World High School

Structure. As one of Miami-Dade County's magnet high schools, New World School of the Arts requires that students be residents of the county. They attend the school without charge. In contrast, the college program recruits nationally and internationally, and students pay community college and public university fees. A full range of academic courses is taught by twenty-five Miami-Dade County Public School faculty members during the first five periods of the school day. Students spend three periods in intensive arts classes in the afternoon and often stay late for rehearsals and other arts activities. Students in grades 10 through 12 earn eight dual enrollment credits a year for college-level arts courses.

Mission. The curriculum of the high school is designed to develop both the academic and artistic skills of talented students to prepare them to be practicing artists in the changing context of contemporary society. Problem solving and creativity are encouraged through independent studies, workshops, master classes, and collaborative cross-disciplinary student projects. Development of practical business skills related to the management of professional work in the arts is a complementary objective. These goals were outlined in the legislation that created the school (and that were set forth in the school's mission statement) and have been refined and expanded through ongoing internal and external review.

Faculty. Central to the school's success is a corps of arts instructors who bring their own experience as practicing artists to the high school and college students. Five arts instructors come from the K–12 school system and eighteen are tenure-track faculty members employed through Miami-Dade Community College, the school's fiscal agent. About eighty adjuncts, also employed through the community college, teach high school and college arts courses. The deans who direct the arts divisions are themselves artists of national reputation, with extensive experience as arts educators.

A Record of Success. Like PAVAC before it, New World School of the Arts achieved almost immediate success. As early as its second year, NWSA placed first among high schools throughout the country in the number of first- and second-place awards received in the NFAA Arts Recognition and Talent Search, an achievement frequently repeated over the years. To date, eight NWSA students have been honored at the White House as President Scholars in the arts. The school was honored by *Redbook* magazine as one of five outstanding arts high schools in 1992, and as "best of the state" in 1994. New World has been recognized as a Blue Ribbon School of Excellence by the U.S. Department of Education.

Standardized test scores are consistently among the highest in the district, though students are selected only on the basis of artistic talent. In 2000, New World was designated by the Florida Department of Education as an "A" high school—one of only three in South Florida. The state rating was based primarily on outstanding reading, math, and writing scores received on the Florida comprehensive assessment tests.

The high school's success factors were analyzed in a 1996/1997 research project, in partnership with the Leonard Bernstein Center for Education Through the Arts. A report based on questionnaires, extensive observation, and interviews concluded that New World's vitality and its demonstrable educational success are due in large measure to the creative interaction of its arts and academic curricula. Students are encouraged to use their artistic strength to express their academic knowledge, and the skills of analysis and synthesis they hone both in the arts and in academics are mutually reinforcing (Boston, 1998).

How Students Are Selected

To develop the most representative applicant pool possible, school representatives visit each of the county's middle schools to talk about the opportunities at New World. Special encouragement is given to exceptional education students and those for whom English is a second language. The arts faculty conducts outreach programs throughout the year, offering on-site demonstration classes for middle- and primary school students, bringing New World students to inner-city schools, and bussing younger students in to see performances by guest artists. The success of this broad effort is demonstrated by the nearly 1,100 applications the school received for 130 available slots in 2000.

The NWSA application, widely distributed in English, Spanish, and Creole, details audition requirements for the respective disciplines and asks for basic student information and the recommendation of an arts teacher. Applicants are not required to submit academic records or test scores. Simply indicating interest by completing the application entitles all applicants to an audition or portfolio review by the faculty and the dean of the arts division in which they are interested. These individual auditions are preceded by open audition workshops to familiarize applicants with the process.

Admission to the school is determined by the arts faculty solely on the basis of talent, with particular care given to identifying students with raw potential who may not have had the advantage of private training. The volume of applications makes the process a highly competitive one, and the number of qualified students invariably exceeds the number of openings available.

New World has a strong relationship with its arts feeder schools. Each year, admissions results are analyzed carefully to determine patterns of application and acceptances from those schools. Where weaknesses appear, the New World staff works with the feeder school faculty and administration to strengthen the middle school arts programs.

Once accepted, students are placed in the appropriate arts courses, based on the results of the audition and on evaluative juries that take place twice a year. In academic areas, incoming students are assessed through prior test scores, individual conferences, and teacher recommendations. To maintain continued enrollment, students need a 3.0 grade point average in all arts courses each semester, a 2.0 overall grade point average, and a satisfactory attendance record.

New World Strengths

Diversity. New World School of the Arts serves as a model of the balanced enrollment that can be achieved in a metropolitan area when students are recruited solely on the basis of artistic talent. The student body is representative of the wide socioeconomic range of Miami-Dade County, a diverse population that includes many recent immigrants, particularly from Latin America and the Caribbean. Multiculturalism is not a value layered on top of other lessons that the school teaches. Appreciating diversity is the core of what the school is about—because it is in Miami, because the student body mirrors the complexity of the larger community, and because the arts are predicated on that appreciation. As the arts programs at the school have matured, they have increasingly reflected community traditions. In dance, for instance, students learn Caribbean, African, and Spanish dance, tap, and jazz, as well as modern dance and classical ballet. In all the arts, ensemble work teaches students not just to tolerate differences but also to appreciate how they enrich and strengthen the whole.

A Learning Climate. New World is an informal and open place, but there is nothing casual about the intensity and discipline with which students work. Clear expectations and unstinting faculty support result in a consistently high level of achievement, not only in the arts but also in academics. In studios and workshops, students develop creativity and mastery, and the resulting self-assurance and awareness are evidenced in the academic classroom. Arts faculty members provide a secure framework within which students can experiment, create, and take chances without risking ridicule or disapproval. Class scheduling that creates a full, uninterrupted afternoon arts period, used in different ways within each arts discipline, provides for both flexibility and intensity.

Development of Adaptive Skills. Faced with long commutes, demanding arts and academic classes, and evenings and weekends spent in studios and theaters, New World students learn to manage their time effectively and to focus on what is important. Intensive arts training helps develop concentration, discipline, and perception—qualities key to academic as well as artistic success. In both the arts and in academics, they learn that mastery of fundamentals through repetition and exercise provides the grounding for individual expression and creativity. And throughout, instructors emphasize that learning is a process, a way of approaching the world.

Community. Faculty and staff members meet frequently—formally and informally—to coordinate approaches and goals. Parents are actively involved in the school. Both faculty members and students provide mentoring and peer support. Students collaborate not only in classrooms and studios, but also in counseling groups, class meetings, service and social organizations, and community projects. They learn to appreciate all art forms by seeing their classmates' work in progress as well as polished performances and exhibitions. The school reaches out to other schools in the district at every level, works closely with established and fledgling arts groups, and networks with other arts schools throughout the country.

Professional Preparation. New World prepares students for the workplace by giving them mastery of basic skills, training for professional careers, tools for continuing learning throughout their lifetimes, and role models who have taken many different routes to their current positions. The arts instructors provide a realistic sense of the competitive world that students anticipating professional arts careers will encounter. And both the arts and academic faculty members prepare students to be responsible, competent, and flexible adults whose creativity and sense of appreciation will serve them well in every aspect of their lives.

New World School of the Arts Alumni

More than 95 percent of New World School of the Arts graduates go on to colleges and conservatories, where they continue study in the arts, explore other interests, or combine fields in innovative ways. One valedictorian completed a double major in music and psychobiology at Oberlin College, then enrolled in medical school. A visual arts alumnus, told in junior high that his dyslexia ruled out college, went on to graduate from Maryland Institute College of Art, building on the skills and confidence he gained at New World. About 10 percent of New World high school students stay on for the college program, particularly in the visual arts and dance. Thirteen years after the school began, its graduates are making a mark in a significant way. Alumni currently dance with Mikhail Baryshnikov's White Oak Project and Alvin Ailey, play jazz with Wynton Marsalis, sing with the Houston Grand Opera, exhibit at the Whitney Museum, and act on Broadway and television. The 2000 high school graduation speaker was a 1990 visual arts graduate who is currently vice president for Disney Interactive in Burbank, California.

Challenges

New World School of the Arts' innovative partnership with its sponsoring institutions has made possible a fully integrated academic and artistic program that offers high school students college credit, provides a faculty of professional artists not ordinarily available even to magnet schools, enables students to take advantage of the science and library facilities of the community college, and brings high school and college students together to perform and to learn from one another.

The complexity of the structure, however, carries some costs. Although there is consistent agreement about the school's mission and pride in its successes, issues of institutional governance and leadership require ongoing discussion and refinement. External changes that might have an impact on any school are multiplied by the number of partner institutions. And meshing the systems of two very large bureaucracies—the largest community college in the country and the fourth-largest school district in the country—can sometimes seem daunting.

What is known about the high school graduates of New World is primarily anecdotal. It is clear that the many students who go on to Florida universities benefit from dual enrollment as the legislature intended; their college programs are significantly accelerated. No formal analysis has been done of acceptance of dual enrollment credits in the arts by schools outside the state. It is the general sense of New World administrators that as the school has gained recognition and plaudits, other prestigious arts programs are increasingly willing to recognize New World instruction as equivalent to their own.

There is a widely expressed need for an alumni office, though resources are not currently available. It would be helpful to study the experience of high school graduates as they proceed through their education, particularly their initial academic placement. Although faculty and staff members share news about outstanding professional achievements of individual students, there is no repository of alumni history. And the school's story will not be complete without some analysis of how many high school alumni continue study in the arts or earn their living as professional artists.

Summary

New World School of the Arts has developed from an innovative dual enrollment pilot to a mature eight-year-old institution that is nationally acclaimed and emulated. It is a source of pride to the pioneers who developed it. It is an energetic, enthusiastic community in which students have an opportunity to work full strength at what they love, with adults who offer both challenges and support. Students who might be at risk elsewhere thrive in a small school created to value and nurture their gifts.

Reference

Boston, B. O. "What Color Is Flavor? Success Factors at the New World School of the Arts." Unpublished report commissioned by Leonard Bernstein Center for Education Through the Arts and the New World School of the Arts. Miami, Fla.: New World School of the Arts, May 20, 1998.

Florida Statute 240.116. *Articulated Acceleration Act,* 1980.

Florida Statute 240.535. *The New World School of the Arts Act,* 1984.

NANCY M. WOLCOTT *is executive assistant to the provost at New World School of the Arts, Miami, Florida.*

8

The dual enrollment program at Santa Monica College facilitates the school-to-college transition and improves access to college for diverse populations. Traditionally underrepresented students, whose college options have suffered in light of a hostile political climate evidenced by the Hopwood decision, Proposition 209, and Proposition 187, may gain access to college curricula and develop a positive academic self-image based on successful participation in a dual enrollment program.

Dual Enrollment for Underrepresented Student Populations

Esther B. Hugo

As a result of strong commitment to working collaboratively toward the goal of developing partnerships, the Santa Monica College (SMC) dual enrollment program has established articulation with the K–12 system and has enhanced the high school curriculum of feeder high schools. High school students attend transferable classes, taught by Santa Monica College professors, on their own high school campus. Students have access to college-level courses such as astronomy, ballet, geography, advanced drawing, and psychology.

When it began in Spring 1998, the program enrolled 676 students from seventeen Los Angeles–area high schools. Now in its sixth semester, it has served over five thousand students in more than thirty Los Angeles–area high schools. The program is administered by three Office of School Relations outreach counselors. Courses are offered after school and do not interfere with the students' high school class schedule. The goal is to engage them in learning activities beyond the regular school day.

Students enrolled in the program are primarily in the eleventh and twelfth grades, and some tenth-graders have access to the performing and visual arts classes. Students come from a range of socioeconomic backgrounds throughout Los Angeles County, and most of the students served come from low-income and historically disadvantaged, minority backgrounds.

The end of affirmative action, brought about by the University of California regents, has challenged the university to continue expanding the pool of eligible minority students. Proposition 209, approved in November 1996, says that state and local governments cannot discriminate against or give preferential treatment to any individual or group on the basis of race, sex, color, or ethnicity. Outreach programs have proliferated and the University of California

NEW DIRECTIONS FOR COMMUNITY COLLEGES, no. 113, Spring 2001   © Jossey-Bass, A Publishing Unit of John Wiley & Sons, Inc.   67

(UC) campuses have extended their reach to the middle- and elementary schools with such organizations as the Los Angeles Basin Initiative (LABI). LABI represents the collaborative effort of eight UC campuses to expand the pool of students from educationally disadvantaged schools. Eligible students must earn a minimum grade point average (GPA) of 2.8, complete 15 units of high school coursework, and take appropriate standardized exams. The UC system now provides $60 million annually for new outreach and partnership efforts with school districts in areas with historically low higher education participation rates (Adelman, June 1999). The SMC dual enrollment program provides academic enrichment for these populations; participating students are able to list more college preparatory courses on their applications for college.

Surveys conducted by the National Association for College Admission Counseling (1999) cite the paramount importance of the student's academic record; the student's academic program in college preparatory courses is the single most important factor in the college admissions process. The dual enrollment program provides a curricular means for disadvantaged students to augment their academic portfolio. Students are able to take—at no cost except for books and supplies—college-level courses that will enhance the academic profile they present for college admission. For students in schools where elective and supplemental academic opportunities are meager, such as inner-city schools, the program provides substance and academic capital. The more quickly students gain access to challenging courses, the more likely they are to complete a degree program (Education Trust, 1999).

Enhanced Curriculum

Students in the dual enrollment program have the chance to preview college-level classes in an environment less threatening than that offered by the College Board advanced placement (AP) program, which requires a rigorous examination upon completion. For example, at Crenshaw High School, located in South Central Los Angeles, students enroll in SMC chemistry and physics classes. Successful students in this program are subsequently inspired to enroll in AP chemistry and AP physics, which historically have had low participation in South Central Los Angeles. Students who did not consider themselves "AP-eligible" are now able to enroll in these demanding science courses, which underscores the importance of building an infrastructure of access and capacity (Oakes, 2000).

The dual enrollment program appeals to those students who are often neglected in their high school—the students "just below" the level of the advanced placement student. Dual enrollment courses offer the opportunity to experience college-level coursework in a smaller group setting than is traditionally offered in their schools. The majority of dual enrollment courses boast an enrollment of twenty-five or fewer students—a formula that has proven successful, as small class size enhances student-faculty interaction. With preliminary data collected (Santa Monica College, 1998), students perform well in the class and enjoy a high percentage of success (73 percent) and a strong average GPA of 3.21. On average, the grade point averages of dual enrollment students are higher than those of the regular college students.

Dual enrollment provides a long-term strategy to improve the preparation of minority students so that they will be competitive for college admission. The program also enhances their college and graduate school prospects. One such example is the Saturday Science Program. With the Center for Educational Achievement, Santa Monica College offers Introduction to Cell Biology and Human Biology. Students attend classes for six hours a day (on Saturdays!) for nine weeks. The goal of the program is to increase the participation of African American and Latino youth in science fields. The college sponsors high school students to come on campus and participate in a college biology class team-taught by SMC and Drew Medical Center faculty members. The students' exposure to two years of basic biology provides them with greater potential for academic success in science-related fields. Among other things, it teaches them diagnostic skills. The instructor, Al Buchanan, finds that the students are the "most highly motivated I've ever seen in fifteen years in education." He describes the students as enlightened, committed, and keenly aware of the potential benefits offered through dual enrollment. The students are fiercely ambitious, competitive, and enjoy the support of their parents, some of whom take the class as well. Buchanan points with pride to the several students who have earned scholarships to selective colleges as pre-med majors and who have gone on to medical school. Buchanan says that the real benefit is that students are exposed to the rigors of college life, and this instills in them the awareness that they are capable, erudite individuals who can achieve a great deal. He says that the program "undoes some of the real harm done to their self-esteem by an uncaring, unsympathetic educational system which seeks to relegate them to the obscurity of menial jobs."

Buchanan reflects on the students' behavior: "They put on a lab coat and the transformation is totally gratifying. They walk differently, they hold their heads erect, they acquire confidence. In a way, it sums up what we can do with society if we provide an opportunity" (interview, Mar. 2000).

An enhanced curriculum does more for students than any other factor in the admissions process (Adelman, June 1999). What students are required to take in high school turns out to have decisive, long-term implications for their future. Indeed, recent research conducted by Adelman at the U.S. Department of Education makes the extent of those implications painfully clear. "Among all of the factors in college success," he says, "the single most important by far is the quality and intensity of the high school curriculum" (p. 84).

Adelman (1999) adds that the impact of a high school curriculum of high academic intensity and quality on degree completion is far more pronounced for African American and Latino students than any other precollege indicator of academic success.

At the same time, many of the attitudes and educational experiences associated with college attendance are not typical for many low-income students.

Indeed, exposing all students to rigorous college preparatory courses in high school and encouraging them to aspire to higher education has only lately come to be commonly viewed as good educational practice (King, 1996).

Proponents of Proposition 209 argued that college admission should be based solely on merit as defined by grades and scores on standardized tests. The dual enrollment program takes advantage of the power of the curriculum to facilitate the transition to college and increase minority completion rates in college.

For Fall 2003, the UC system will expand its general education course requirements to include a year of fine arts (*California Notes,* 1999). The dual enrollment program boasts an offering of about twenty-five visual and performing arts classes, thereby removing the burden from the high school to offer these specialized courses. The program offers classes in ballet, watercolors, drawing, design, ethnic dance, jazz, and Mexican dance, which not only will enhance the students' academic profiles but will also help make more underrepresented students UC-eligible.

Santa Monica College art professor Tony Beauvy, who teaches drawing at Manual Arts and Los Angeles High Schools, sees his role as an instructor and counselor. He tries to get the students to see themselves as college material.

Beauvy acknowledges that the students are adolescents dealing with lots of pressure. They face many challenges unique to their urban background. They may not have role models; they may not have developed the skills it takes to be a good student. Beauvy takes seriously his job to provide the "bridge" to go to college. Through his art classes, he tries to give students more tools to further their education. "What this program provides is a forum to find the talent and encourage the students to pursue their studies. They don't even have it in their imagination until we bring it to them. When they see themselves as college material, they are at first stunned, then very eager to learn" (interview, Apr. 10, 2000).

Orientation to Higher Education

A significant component of the dual enrollment program is the offering of the human development course "Orientation to Higher Education," taught by Santa Monica College counseling faculty. In many cases, the classes are taught by the high school college counselor who has been hired as a part-time instructor by the SMC counseling department. This one-unit course holds significant advantages for the student and the counselor. The counselor interacts positively and regularly with the student, thereby creating a foundation of knowledge and insight. The student is able to explore the college search process in greater, guided detail. In this class, students complete mock applications, research colleges, write college essays, and compile student résumés to be used for the college admissions process during the senior year. The students are able to gather current information and focus on college preparation, including test-taking strategies and programs, as well as learn about career options.

The counselor is able to get to know students in a client base that often numbers in the thousands. For the most part, enrollment in the class is composed of minority or first-generation students (first-generation students are those whose parents' highest level of education is a high school diploma, and who are often not aware of college possibilities and options). Venice High School students met a Latina admissions counselor from Yale, who turned out to be a pivotal person for them. After her presentation, several of the students who had never considered attending an East Coast college are now interested in applying to one next year. Ann Keitel, human development instructor, remarked that this presentation had done much to open students' eyes to their options.

Students whose parents did not attend college face significant barriers to attaining a postsecondary education. They lack knowledge of postsecondary education in general, and of the admissions and financial aid processes in particular. First-generation students are generally less prepared academically and less likely to pursue college preparatory courses and take college entrance exams. They also frequently delay enrollment in postsecondary education. The human development class provides a valuable jump start to students in their postsecondary options, as it is focused on the first year of college. Students are able to earn high school and college credit, satisfy the graduation requirement of an education and career planning course, and acquire significant skills in college research.

Undocumented Students

Because of their rapid population increase and very low median age, Latinos are expected to be the largest minority in this country within ten years. However, in the western states, the high school graduation rate of Latinos is among the lowest in the country. Fifty-four percent of Latino students who continue their education after high school begin in community colleges, a ratio far larger than that of any other race or ethnic group (Adelman, 1999). The large number of undocumented students in California were adversely affected by Proposition 187, which denied financial aid for higher education to undocumented students. Although a student without U.S. documentation does have the right to attend college and pay full tuition or nonresident fees, he or she does not qualify for federal financial aid or resident fees.

Students enrolled in high school have a "presumption of residence," which stipulates that students under nineteen years of age shall be presumed to have the intent to make California their home for other than temporary purposes if they and their parents have continuously maintained a home in the state of California for the last two years. For the dual enrollment program, all students are treated as residents in the sense that they are not charged fees or tuition. For students under nineteen, therefore, immigration status is not an issue. Students could theoretically begin taking up to two classes each semester as early as the tenth grade. Upon graduation from high school, students could have completed at least a year toward an associate in arts degree. Through this program, students may earn advanced training before their immigration status becomes an issue. Also, in this program, the admissions counselor refers students to immigration specialists so that their immigration status can be resolved before high school graduation.

Santa Monica College's registration and enrollment coordinator, Rosa Martinez, says, "We try to make a concerted effort to get all the paperwork in for these students. If they have a green card or visa, we want to make sure we can establish residency, so when the students are ready to enroll full-time, they will pay resident tuition" (interview, Apr. 18, 2000).

Conclusion

Dual enrollment is one strategy for building closer links between high schools and colleges. It supports the establishment of a long-term dialogue that strengthens the ties between the K–16 sectors and leads to more partnerships and stronger collaborations. Ultimately, these classes will be instrumental in assisting more minority students in qualifying for competitive colleges and universities.

The dual enrollment program administered through the Santa Monica College Office of School Relations highlights the reality that outreach must be an academic and not just a public relations function. The overall goal of the program is to make a concerted effort to increase the pool of eligible students through better teaching and counseling.

The dual enrollment program provides an opportunity for minority and first-generation students to learn about colleges and improve their study skills, and it gives them more information about the process of attending college. The dual enrollment program provides the best kind of outreach available—outreach that offers academic enrichment and inspires students to excel.

References

Adelman, C. Answers in the Tool Box: Academic Intensity, Attendance Patterns, and Bachelor's Degree Attainment. Washington, D.C.: U.S. Department of Education, 1999.

California Notes, 1999, 45(3).

Education Trust. Thinking K–16: A Newsletter of the Education Trust, 1999, 3(2).

King, J. E. "The Decision to Go to College: Attitudes and Experiences Associated with College Attendance Among Low-Income Students." Washington, D.C.: College Board, 1996.

National Association for College Admission Counseling. Admission Trends Survey. Alexandria, Va.: National Association for College Admission Counseling, 1999.

Oakes, J. "Unequal Opportunities for Successful Participation in Advanced Placement in California High Schools." Paper presented at Advanced Placement Conference, sponsored by State Senator Martha Escutia at the Whittier, Calif., Hilton Hotel, Apr. 7, 2000.

Santa Monica College. "Santa Monica College Grade Report." Santa Monica, Calif.: San Monica College, Fall 1998.

ESTHER B. HUGO is an outreach counselor at Santa Monica College, Santa Monica, California.

9

Ohio Senate Bill 140 was enacted in 1989 to allow dual
enrollment. The legislative intent and components are
reviewed in this chapter, followed by an overview of criteria and procedures at Columbus State Community College. Methods that foster student success and growth are
also discussed.

Dual Enrollment Options: Columbus State Community College Model for Successful Implementation

Tammi C. Jordan

Ohio's dual enrollment program has a legislative history that began over ten years ago. The Postsecondary Enrollment Options (PSEO) program was orig-inally enacted in 1989 in response to Ohio Senate Bill 140, Sec. 3365.011 (1989), which applied to eleventh- and twelfth-grade students. An amended bill (House Substitute Bill 215, Sec. 3365.01, 1997) permitted PSEO to include ninth- and tenth-grade students and unchartered private schools. Per Ohio Revised code, Sec. 3365.02 (1999), PSEO now includes community schools, and it is stipulated that a student may not enroll in any specific col-lege course through the program if he or she has taken high school courses in the same subject area as the college course and failed to attain a cumula-tive grade point average of at least 3.0 on a 4.0 scale, or the equivalent, in the completed high school courses. This chapter reviews the structure and func-tion of Ohio's dual enrollment programs.

Structure

The PSEO program was established to provide appropriately qualified high school students with the opportunity to take college-level courses and expe-rience a college-level environment while receiving both high school and col-lege credit. Institutions may not design courses specifically for PSEO students, and all these courses must be open to the institution's general stu-dent population. Students may attend either day or evening classes. Any high school student accepted into the PSEO program at a higher education institution should be expected to perform at the same level as any other student at that institution. The program was designed not to substitute but to enhance the high school curriculum. Students must be enrolled in a public school, a chartered or unchartered private school, or a community school (henceforth known as "high schools") registered in the state of Ohio. Home school learners are not eligible to participate.

Options Available for Dual Enrollment

Students may choose one of two options for dual enrollment. Under option A, a student can determine at the time of enrollment to receive only college credit for a course. The student is responsible for all fees, textbooks, and materials associated with the course, and upon successful completion of the course, is awarded college credit. He or she will not be awarded high school credit for the course.

Under option B, a student can decide at the time of enrollment into the program to receive both high school and college credit. The district school board or the state board of education, in the case of a student attending a private school, reimburses the college for the cost of student fees, textbooks, and materials. After successful completion of the course, both high school and college credit will be awarded. A student may not choose option B if he or she is already taking the full amount of credits permitted in the high school during a particular term.

Rules Governing PSEO

The legislation defines general parameters for PSEO programs across Ohio.

Notification. School districts and high schools shall provide information regarding the program before March 1 of each year to all students enrolled in grades eight to eleven. No further guidelines are given regarding this notification process, so various methods of notification are used. Sponsoring special PSEO information sessions for students and parents, sending letters to each home explaining dual enrollment options, and making announcements in the school newsletter or over the public address system have all been used.

Student-Parental Response. A student or at least one of his or her parents is required to inform the appropriate governing body by March 30 of the intent to participate in the program the following year. Any student who fails to provide this notification by the deadline may not participate in PSEO during the following school year without the written consent of the district superintendent or governing body.

Counseling Services. Secondary schools are required to provide counseling services to students and their parents before participation in the program to ensure that they are aware of the possible risks and consequences of participation. After the counseling session, the student and his or her parents must sign a form provided by the school stating that they have received counseling and that they understand the responsibilities they will need to assume. The counseling session must cover the following:

- *Program eligibility.* Every college that implements PSEO has been given authority by the state of Ohio to set its own acceptance criteria. Students must meet the criteria set by their chosen institution to participate in the program.
- *Process for granting credit.* School districts or private schools must award comparable credit for high school graduation in terms of quantity and quality of courses successfully completed under option B, using the conversion that 7.5 quarter hours equals one Carnegie unit.
- *Financial arrangements—tuition, books, materials, fees.* Private school administrators must at this time inform students that funding is limited, which may prevent some from participating. Each year, $1 million is set aside to fund PSEO for all students who attend private high schools. Students attending public or community schools are not limited by funding issues, with the exception that students will only be funded for 7.5 college credits for each free period in high school. Federal legislation does not permit financial aid, and students are required to pay the regular rate of $57.95 per credit.
- *Criteria for transportation aid.* Only students eligible to receive free and reduced-priced lunches may be reimbursed for transportation from the high school to the college.
- *Available schedule support services.* High school services are still available to students; therefore, high school guidance counselors will still assist students in selecting appropriate courses to meet graduation requirements.
- *Consequences of failing.* Students who fail because of nonattendance or failure to complete required assignments may be required to reimburse the district board all fees associated with the course. In addition, failing a college course used for high school requirements may jeopardize high school graduation.
- *Grade calculation for high school transcripts.* The district board or high school determines whether a grade is listed for a college course and whether a grade counts toward the high school grade point average.
- *Graduation requirements.* No graduation requirements will be eliminated or reduced to allow a student to participate in PSEO.
- *Academic and social responsibilities of students and parents in the program.* In high schools, a parent can discuss a student's performance with the teacher. The parent receives the student's grades and can intervene for the student in various situations. In colleges, parents and students do not sign agreements to allow parents to discuss anything with instructors. Therefore, parents are encouraged to assist students with difficulties in the classroom or throughout the college; however, they should not make contact with college instructors without written consent of the student.

College students are expected to perform the same as all other students at the institution. This change in responsibility lessens parental influence and control at the institutional level.
• *Other college services.* Students are encouraged to take full advantage of all college support services and activities, with the exception of intercollegiate sports.

College Notification. A college must provide written notice of acceptance into the program to the student and his or her school district within ten days after acceptance. Within ten days after each term, the college must also send to the student, the student's high school, the school district, and the superintendent of public instruction a written notice indicating the courses, number of credit hours, and option (A or B) selected by the student.

Columbus State Community College

Located in central Ohio, Columbus State Community College has a four-county service district. The college serves as a catalyst for creating and fostering linkages between the community, business, and educational institutions (Columbus State Community College, 1999). It offers more than sixty degree programs, including two transfer programs, with courses on the main campus—located in downtown Columbus, at seven off-campus centers—located throughout its county service districts, and via distance learning, which includes video and Web-based courses.

The PSEO program is administered by the college's K–12 initiatives department. This department is charged with enhancing the educational opportunities of all youth in the college's service area, while fostering the development of lifelong learning. Besides administering the PSEO program, the department facilitates "adopt a school" activities, literacy programs, and Tech Prep, and it sponsors numerous programs and activities for young people.

Columbus State has established two sets of criteria for admission into PSEO. By the first set of criteria, twelfth-grade students must possess a 2.7 cumulative GPA (3.0 for eleventh-graders) and they must have successfully completed Ohio's ninth-grade proficiency examination. By the second (alternative) set of criteria, students must have achieved an ACT score of 22 or higher or an SAT score of 1150. A high school guidance counselor may request that the college waive the preliminary criteria for a student who has the ability to complete college-level work but does not meet the minimum GPA requirement. A tenth- or ninth-grade student must be able to demonstrate advanced academic skills and a high level of maturity. The type of high school classes completed and standardized test scores are used to determine advanced academic skills. Other factors taken into consideration for a ninth- or tenth-grade student are his or her GPA and a recommendation from the high school guidance counselor or chief administrator. Students are also interviewed to determine their intent for participation in the program and their readiness to handle the social and emotional ramifications of enrolling in a college course.

Once students have met the preliminary criteria for PSEO at Columbus State, they are invited to complete the COMPASS/ESL placement exam. COMPASS/ESL is a comprehensive computerized adaptive testing system that helps place students into appropriate courses (http://www.act. org/compass/ index.html). On the placement exam, students must test into a freshman college-level writing course and Algebra 2, and they must demonstrate the ability to read above the developmental reading level. These criteria for PSEO applicants are higher than the actual placement results achieved by recent high school graduates. In 1995, 42 percent of the traditional-age freshmen entering Ohio's two-year community and technical colleges tested into at least one developmental course (Secondary and Higher Education Remediation Advisory Commission, 1997). Meeting the standards set by the placement criteria demonstrates that a student has the ability to comprehend a college-level textbook, possesses college entry-level writing skills, and has met the basic math requirements to graduate from high school. State legislation permits each institution to set its own admissions criteria for PSEO, with the understanding that the state will not pay for developmental coursework. Other community colleges in Ohio use similar requirements for PSEO.

Students who do not meet COMPASS/ESL criteria may repeat the placement exam one time for a fee to achieve higher scores. Students who fail to meet COMPASS/ESL criteria may also opt to take courses at Columbus State at their own expense if they meet individual course prerequisites. If a student passes the course(s) in the area of deficiency (as indicated by COMPASS/ESL results) with a grade of "C" or higher, he or she is eligible for PSEO the following quarter.

PSEO Process at Columbus State

After students are accepted into the PSEO program at Columbus State Community College, they must attend a mandatory orientation session with their parents. The session leaders teach students how to select and register for courses that meet high school graduation requirements, are transferable to local four-year institutions, or meet requirements for an associate's degree at Columbus State. Students also receive instruction in determining future career goals and obtaining course-related books and supplies. Students have the opportunity to share their expectations of the college experience. After PSEO policies have been reviewed, students and parents sign documentation, thereby indicating their understanding of all the policies regarding the PSEO program and their agreement to abide by Columbus State regulations, as outlined in the college handbook. Parents are also required to sign a medical release form, which is filed in the College Health Office and the Office of Public Safety at Columbus State.

In fall 1999, 259 students participated in dual enrollment at Columbus State Community College. The average cumulative grade point achieved this quarter was 3.08. Twenty percent of these students attended Columbus State full-time. Since fall 1999, the number of dual enrollment students has increased by 13 percent. The vast majority of these students are in the twelfth grade. As in the previous year, several students are attending college full-time and intend to obtain an associate's degree during the same quarter as their high school graduation. Through participation in the PSEO Program, at least one student each year accomplishes this goal.

Records Restriction. All PSEO students have "blocks" on their academic records that prohibit them from registering for courses or changing their course schedules without approval by the program adviser. By having this restriction system in place, the adviser is able to notify the high school of any changes in the students' course schedules that may affect the high school graduation requirements. This also gives the adviser the opportunity to help the students select the most appropriate courses to meet their needs and to remind them of the risks involved in withdrawing from courses.

PSEO Course Request Form. To have the records restriction block temporarily lifted, students must complete a PSEO Course Request Form. The high school guidance counselor must approve this form, and then the student submits it to the college. This creates a dialogue between the student and the high school guidance counselor regarding the student's progress in college, and it gives the counselor the opportunity to check the student's transcript to ensure that he or she meets the 3.0 GPA requirement.

Unsatisfactory Progress. A student who fails a course but has completed all assignments and exams is permitted to repeat the course at the expense of the school district, state private school funds, or community school. Columbus State does not permit students to continue taking new coursework until the failed course is completed successfully. This policy encourages students to master the subject as well as improve their college transcript. Students who fail courses because of attendance issues or who fail to complete assignments or exams may be charged by the district board, state, or community school and are dismissed from the PSEO program immediately.

Progress Reports. Each quarter, Columbus State instructors are asked to identify those students who are in jeopardy of receiving an unsatisfactory grade in a course, because of either attendance problems or low assessment scores. The PSEO adviser then contacts all PSEO students listed on the report. These students are able to receive the assistance needed to be successful in the courses via individual tutoring, personal counseling, or study groups.

Counselor Meetings. Columbus State hosts an annual PSEO Counselor Breakfast to inform the high schools of revisions to state legislation, review policies and procedures regarding the college's implementation of the program, and solicit suggestions for improving the program and its processes. The PSEO Course Request Form, previously mentioned, was developed as a result of the comments received during one of these breakfast meetings.

Courses Offered at the High School. The college may offer courses taught by Columbus State faculty members on-site at a high school. Under state law, these courses must be open to the general population but are scheduled at times convenient for the high school. High school students must meet PSEO criteria to enroll in the Columbus State College course. These courses may also be taken for option A or B.

Support Systems. PSEO students have the opportunity to experience a college environment with the support of the systems in place at Columbus State to assist them. Students may receive assertiveness training to assist them in speaking to instructors and other administrators; instruction in time management skills to learn how to juggle attendance at two schools, part-time employment, and household responsibilities; and career guidance to help them determine which fields fit their abilities and interests.

Home School Learners. Although the state of Ohio does not allow home school learners to participate in the PSEO program, Columbus State Community College does permit them to enroll as students at their own expense. Unfortunately, federal regulations prohibit them from receiving financial aid. Home school learners may take any course for which they meet the prerequisites. They also have a record restriction that will be lifted prior to registration after they receive appropriate academic advisement.

Final Words

Ohio views dual enrollment as a program for the student who has completed the majority of required courses in high school, desires to explore more challenging coursework, or is interested in enhancing his or her own high school experience. Columbus State Community College provides the opportunities for students to build upon their knowledge base, and it encourages social growth and development.

References

Columbus State Community College. "Columbus State Community College 1999 Report to the Community." Columbus, Ohio, 1999.

Ohio Revised Code, Sec. 3365.01–3365.10. *Baldwin's Ohio Revised Code Annotated.* Eagan, Minn.: West, 1999.

Ohio Senate Bill 140, Sec. 3365.01. *Baldwin's Ohio Revised Code Annotated.* Eagan, Minn.: West, 1989.

Ohio Substitute House Bill 215, Sec. 3365.01. *Baldwin's Ohio Revised Code Annotated.* Eagan, Minn.: West, 1997.

Secondary and Higher Education Remediation Advisory Commission. *Improving College Preparation in Ohio: A Total System Approach Executive Summary.* Columbus, Ohio: Secondary and Higher Education Remediation Advisory Commission, 1997. [http://www.act.org/compass/]

TAMMI C. JORDAN is an academic adviser in the K–12 initiatives department at Columbus State Community College, Columbus, Ohio.

10

This annotated bibliography presents exemplary con-current enrollment programs, discusses controversies about student outcomes, and recommends steps for establishing partnerships with local schools.

Sources and Information: Creating Effective Collaboration Between High Schools and Community Colleges

Gigi G. Gomez

The following publications discuss impressive concurrent enrollment programs, student outcomes in several states, and lessons learned from establishing collaborative partnerships between high schools and institutions of higher education. Overall, concurrent enrollment programs vary from one another, but their benefits are similar. Students earn college credit while in high school, students are better prepared for college, students and their families save on education costs—which also saves the state expenses, and administrators and faculty members are satisfied that they are improving students' educational opportunities and quality of life. The resources included in this chapter may augment the understanding of concurrent enrollment programs for community colleges and high schools preparing to undertake such a venture.

Most ERIC documents (publications with ED numbers) can be viewed on microfiche at over nine hundred libraries worldwide. In addition, most may be ordered on microfiche or on paper from the ERIC Document Reproduction Services (EDRS) by calling (800) 443-ERIC. Journal articles are not available from EDRS, but they can be acquired through regular library channels or purchased from one of the following article reproduction services: (1) Carl Uncover, Internet: http://www.carl.org, e-mail: uncover@carl.org, telephone: (800) 787–7979; (2) UMI, e-mail: orders@infostore.com, telephone: (800) 248–0360; and (3) ISI, e-mail: tga@isinet.com, telephone: (800) 523–1850.

New Directions for Community Colleges, no. 113, Spring 2001 © Jossey-Bass, A Publishing Unit of John Wiley & Sons, Inc. 81

Exemplary Programs

These documents illustrate the range of concurrent enrollment programs, which are tailored by community colleges and high schools for their students' needs.

Brown, J. L. *The High School Partnership at Kansas City Kansas Community College*. Paper presented at the Annual International Conference of the National Institute for Staff and Organizational Development on Teaching Excellence and Conference of Administrators, Austin, May 1993. (ED 362 244)

The Kansas City Kansas Community College's Partnership Program serves ten of the seventeen high schools in its service area. Established in 1987, the program allows high school senior students to begin earning both high school and college credit for college-level courses taken at their own high schools. Almost all of the courses offered meet the general education distribution requirements for a liberal arts education. The high school faculty members who teach in the partnership program are recommended by their districts and approved by college personnel. The program has helped the college create positive connections with its feeder high schools, which has diminished the image of the cold and distant academy that the larger community has had of the community college.

Report on Community College Classes Offered in Conjunction with High Schools (R7–1–709) FY 1998–1999. Phoenix: Arizona State Board of Directors for Community Colleges, 1999. (ED 440 686)

This publication presents the 1998–99 report on community college classes offered in conjunction with Arizona high schools. Eight of the ten community college districts in Arizona currently provide dual enrollment programs, which offer more than six hundred courses to 11,236 high school students. The report breaks down the individual courses provided in each community college by district. Statewide, it appears that the most popular courses are from the traditional academic disciplines, such as college algebra, physics, general chemistry, composition, history, biology, and foreign languages. However, computer courses are the most commonly offered courses by the community colleges. Vocational and personal development courses in nursing, welding, hospitality management, air traffic control communication, weight training, photography, and problem solving are also available through dual enrollment.

Postsecondary Enrollment Options Program. St. Paul, Minn.: Program Evaluation Division, 1996. (ED 405 771)

The program evaluation division provides a comprehensive report on Minnesota's Postsecondary Enrollment Options program. Through interviews and surveys of enrolled students, their parents, and participating high school and college administrators, the authors found that 6 percent of Minnesota public school juniors and seniors took part in the accelerated program during the 1994–95 academic year. In addition, many of the study's respondents reported that the main reasons they enrolled in the program were to get a head start on college and to cut down on college costs. Perhaps a more intriguing finding is that program participants generally received higher grades than did regularly admitted college students, except for program participants who enrolled at technical colleges, who performed below those regularly admitted.

Student Outcomes

These documents present general student outcomes for concurrent enrollment programs in Washington, California, and Florida.

Crossland, R. *Running Start: 1996–1997 Annual Progress Report.* Olympia: Washington State Board for Community and Technical Colleges, 1998. (ED 416 921)

Running Start is a concurrent enrollment program that allows eleventh- and twelfth-grade high school students to take college-level courses tuition-free at thirty-two participating community and technical colleges in the state of Washington. To be enrolled in Running Start, students must pass a standardized test to determine whether they have the skills needed to succeed in college. The average grade point average (GPA) of Running Start students in 1996–97 was approximately 2.70, which is slightly higher than the average entering freshman GPA. A follow-up research study on those Running Start students that transferred to the University of Washington shows that 41 percent of them graduated in four years, in comparison with the 31 percent graduation rate of its traditional students. In addition, the average graduating GPA of the Running Start students at the University of Washington is higher (3.42) than that for the traditional students (3.14). Overall, the follow-up research study finds that the program is well received by students and parents, but the counseling time and costs are substantially more for them than for regular students, and the funding formula does not recognize the extra workload.

Progress Report on the Effectiveness of Collaborative Student Academic Development Programs. Sacramento: California State Postsecondary Education Commission, 1996. (ED 407 900)

This study examines the progress of nine collaborative student academic development programs in California, which aim to improve the college preparation of high school students. These programs share the common goals of increasing enrollments for groups that have a historically low college-going rate, creating and maintaining collaborations between public schools and higher education, enhancing direct service to students and collaborative partners, and focusing on streamlining the transition from high school to college.

Among the 1994 high school graduates, program participants attend a college or university at a rate of 65 percent, which is higher than the statewide rate of 43 percent for students who have backgrounds similar to those of the program students. Overall, this study finds that the partnership programs are effective in helping students prepare for college.

Windham, P. *High School and Community College Dual Enrollment: Issues of Rigor and Transferability.* Tallahassee: Florida State Board of Community Colleges, 1997. (ED 413 936)

One issue concerning concurrent enrollment programs is the need for students to retake the courses because these courses do not meet the academic standards at another university. In 1993, the University of Florida issued a report stating that a large majority of students who had taken chemistry courses in concurrent enrollment programs at a community college had to retake chemistry at UF. In response to the UF report, Pensacola Junior College and Tallahassee Community College created a study of their 1991–92 concurrent enrollees. The study shows that the grade point averages of the dual enrollees are either the same or slightly higher than those of traditional transfers. Systemwide, of the fifty thousand–plus dual enrollments for 1991–92, only 140 classes had to be retaken by students between 1992 and 1995, indicating that the program is providing an effective acceleration mechanism for the students.

Windham, P. *Academic Career Benchmarks by Ethnicity.* Tallahassee: Florida State Board of Community Colleges, 1997. (ED 441 525)

This report on student academic outcomes from the Florida Community College System focuses on a comparison of white, black, and Hispanic students. A comparison of the percentage distribution of major ethnic groups at different points in their academic careers shows that not all groups are progressing consistently and equally. For instance, the concurrent enrollment programs have the largest percentage concentration of white students than of any other racial group considered. In terms of attaining degrees, blacks are more likely to attain a vocational credit certificate than any type of award, whereas Hispanic students are more likely to attain an associate in arts degree. Yet all in all, white students tend to increase or maintain their degree process, whereas underrepresented students lose ground.

Windham, P. *Fast Facts 1–25.* Tallahassee: Florida State Board of Community Colleges, 1999. (ED 440 713)

This report contains twenty-five facts on the Florida Community College System. Frequently, the state requirements for high school courses and the course competencies for college-level courses do not differ much from each other. Where there is similarity, dual credit can avoid repetition and duplication of time and money at the high schools and colleges. Hence, the partnership provides a practical and very cost-effective approach to education for the students, parents, taxpayers, and community at large. Many of Florida's members are able to reap the benefits from Florida's dual credit program. For instance, the college credits earned by a student are placed into the equivalent of an escrow account that can be cashed in once the student enters college after high school. In 1992–93, nearly twenty thousand students were enrolled in dual enrollment courses. Four years later, the enrollment in this program grew to 26,672 students, an increase of 38 percent. Because these students are not assessed fees, the participating students and their families have a combined savings of almost $7.1 million.

Challenges to Program Maintenance

After establishing a concurrent enrollment program, administrators are challenged to better strategize for future concurrent enrollment programs or other collaborative partnerships, and to enhance current concurrent enrollment programs for effectiveness.

Tafel, J., and Eberhart, N. *Statewide School-College (K–16) Partnerships to Improve Student Performance. State Strategies That Support Successful Student Transitions from Secondary to Postsecondary Education.* Denver: State Higher Education Executive Officers, 1999. (ED 434 611)

This report describes the efforts of three states—Georgia, Maryland, and Ohio—to develop comprehensive K–16 partnerships to achieve two goals: (1) the alignment of K–12 reform efforts with college admissions and (2) the reduction of postsecondary remediation through better student preparation. Georgia's P–16 initiative aims to implement and adapt state-level student performance standards from preschool to postsecondary education by the year 2001. The state of Maryland sets itself as an example that uses good data from SOAR (Student Outcome and Achievement Report) to create effective and good educational policies. To battle its remediation problems, Ohio uses a "total system approach" that is designed to increase performance expectations of students, build capacity, engage with the public, and provide quality teacher education. All three states focus their K–16 approaches on promoting successful transitions for all students. However, some common lessons have been learned. K–16 partnerships should establish clear and explicit goals, create a statewide organizational framework, find incentives to sustain partnerships, develop informative, comprehensive data systems, establish a communication system with the public, and identify substantive issues requiring immediate attention.

Fincher-Ford, M. *High School Students Earning College Credit: A Guide to Creating Dual-Credit Programs.* Thousand Oaks, Calif.: Corwin Press, 1997. (ED 403 665)

This handbook offers a dual enrollment template, but cautions that the suggested strategies and tips may not be applicable to all because of varying resources, levels of accountability, and specific needs of the constituents. Nonetheless, this "how-to" book, based on empirical data, was created for practitioners, administrators, and teachers involved in developing, implementing, maintaining, and evaluating a dual credit program between high schools and community colleges. Perhaps the most useful portion of the book is its attention to the importance of the faculty. Faculty cooperation can determine the success or failure of a dual credit program. The author stresses to administrators that because faculty members must design, develop, and implement the program, faculty members must be involved in programmatic planning. Hence, the handbook lays out a model that includes issues the faculty will need to address when attempting to develop a dual credit program. The school administrators should be available to answer faculty questions and reassure the faculty members that their active participation in the program will not render teaching positions less secure.

Gips, C. J., and Stoel, C. F. (eds.). *Making a Place in the Faculty Rewards System for Work with K–12.* Washington, D.C.: American Association for High Education, 1999. (ED 441 391)

This report describes the collaboration of four universities with high schools to create a coherent K–16 experience for both teachers and students by giving faculty participation a place in the faculty reward system. The Public Schools Rewards Project, a three-year plan project, asked four campuses to do a self-study of their current faculty reward system, create a pilot to change the reward system, and disseminate the new reward system. The goal of the project was to include faculty work with K–16 schools in the formal faculty rewards systems at each campus. More specifically, the aim of the project was to rewrite the university personnel policies pertaining to the criteria by which faculty members are awarded tenure, promoted, and given merit salary increases. However, the project's plans did not go as smoothly as planned. Engagement in changing the reward system to include K–16 work was a long, arduous, and complex undertaking. The crusaders of the project learned that they were trying to bring together several different worlds with conflicting values, different styles of working, and even different languages. The report presents lessons learned through personal essays written by faculty members and administrators at Temple Texas at El Paso, California State University at Northridge, and southern Colorado universities. Finally, the report offers strategies for honoring faculty K–16 work and incorporating it into academe.

Gigi G. Gomez is a student in the Graduate School of Education and Information Studies at the University of California, Los Angeles.

INDEX

Back Issue/Subscription Order Form

Copy or detach and send to:
Jossey-Bass Inc., 350 Sansome Street, San Francisco CA 94104-1342

Call or fax toll free!
Phone 888-378-2537 6AM-5PM PST; Fax 800-605-2665

Back issues: Please send me the following issues at $28 each
                (Important: please include series initials and issue number, such as CC90)

1. CC _____

_____

$ _____ Total for single issues

$ _____ Shipping charges (for single issues *only;* subscriptions are exempt
from shipping charges): Up to $30, add $5^{50} • $30^{01}–$50, add $6^{50}
$50^{01}–$75, add $8 • $75^{01}–$100, add $10 • $100^{01}–$150, add $12
Over $150, call for shipping charge

Subscriptions   Please ❑ start ❑ renew my subscription to *New Directions
for Community Colleges* for the year ___ at the following rate:

U.S.:	❑ Individual $63	❑ Institutional $115
Canada:	❑ Individual $63	❑ Institutional $155
All Others:	❑ Individual $87	❑ Institutional $189

NOTE: Subscriptions are quarterly, and are for the calendar year only.
Subscriptions begin with the Spring issue of the year indicated above.

$ _____ Total single issues and subscriptions (Add appropriate sales tax for
your state for single issue orders. No sales tax for U.S. subscriptions.
Canadian residents, add GST for subscriptions and single issues.)

❑ Payment enclosed (U.S. check or money order only)

❑ VISA, MC, AmEx, Discover Card #_____ Exp. date_____

Signature _____ Day phone _____

❑ Bill me (U.S. institutional orders only. Purchase order required)

Purchase order #_____

Federal Tax ID 13559 3032   GST 89102-8052

Name _____

Address _____

_____

Phone_____ E-mail _____

For more information about Jossey-Bass, visit our Web site at:
www.josseybass.com   **PRIORITY CODE = ND1**

OTHER TITLES AVAILABLE IN THE
NEW DIRECTIONS FOR COMMUNITY COLLEGES SERIES
Arthur M. Cohen, Editor-in-Chief
Florence B. Brawer, Associate Editor

Hello Kitty®
Little Angel

By Paul Coco
Illustrated by Sachiho Hino

SCHOLASTIC INC.

ISBN 978-0-545-50210-8

12 11 10 9 8 7 6 5 4 3 2 1   12 13 14 15 16 17/0

Printed in the U.S.A.   40
This edition first printing, December 2012
Designed by Angela Jun

Hello Kitty was the star of
the winter play.
She couldn't wait to get
to school.

Mama brought Hello Kitty her costume.

She had forgotten it!
Hello Kitty laughed.

HONK! HONK! HONK!
The school bus arrived!

Hello Kitty hugged Mama.
Then she got on the bus.

Joey, Fifi, Jodie, and Thomas were
on the bus already.

They were practicing for the play.
Hello Kitty sat down with her friends.

Hello Kitty and her friends got
to school.
They all sat in their seats.

Today was the day of their class play.
Everyone was excited!
The whole class cheered.

Mr. Bearly read the class
a story that morning.
Then he collected everyone's
homework.

Everyone was very excited
to start the play.
But first they had to go
to lunch.

Hello Kitty and her friends ate
their lunch.
Then Jodie gave each of them
a cookie.

They all wished one another
good luck.
Now it was time for Hello Kitty's
class to set up the play.

Everyone worked very hard.
Thomas and Jodie lined up the chairs.
Joey and Fifi made fake snowflakes
by ripping up paper.

Hello Kitty and the rest of the class
got the stage ready.

Finally everything was done.
The stage looked wonderful.

Mr. Bearly thanked everyone for helping.
Then Hello Kitty and her friends changed
into their costumes.

The auditorium was soon packed
with people.
Papa, Mama, Mimmy, Grandma, and
Grandpa sat in the front row.

Everyone quieted down.
The play was about to start!

The stage was a snowy forest.
Joey, Jodie, Fifi, and Thomas were
playing happily.
Then the forest became dark.

WHOOSH! The ripped pieces of paper blew around the stage.
It looked like a snowstorm!

Joey, Jodie, Fifi, and Thomas
were lost!
They couldn't find their way
through the wind and snow.

Uh-oh! A very scary cardboard snow monster came onstage!

Hello Kitty appeared suddenly.
She was a pretty snow angel
with shiny wings.

Hello Kitty made the snow stop
with her wand.
She made the monster go away, too.
Hello Kitty saved the day! YAY!

The play was over.
The audience stood up and
clapped.

Hello Kitty and her friends held
hands and bowed.
Everyone thought it was a great play!

Mama and Papa took Hello Kitty
and her friends for ice cream.

Mama and Papa were very proud.

Mama tucked Hello Kitty into bed
later that night.
She always would be Mama's little angel.
Hello Kitty hugged Mama.

MARCO POLO

KU-390-792

HAMBURG

North Sea
Sylt
DENMARK
Baltic Sea
Helgoland
Fehmarn
Rügen
Schleswig-Holstein
Hamburg
Mecklenburg-Western Pomerania
THE NETHER-LANDS
Bremen
Lower Saxony
Elbe
POLAND
Hanover
Saxony-Anhalt
Berlin
Potsdam
Weser
Magdeburg
North Rhine-Westphalia
Brandenburg

with **Insider Tips**

> I shall always be glad that I live in such a fantastic city. The quality of life in Hamburg is better than in any other German city.
> **MARCO POLO author**
> **Dorothea Heintze**
> (see p. 151)

HAMBURG

> SYMBOLS

Insider Tip

MARCO POLO INSIDER TIPS
Discovered for you by our author

★ **MARCO POLO HIGHLIGHTS**
Hamburg top tips at a glance

☼ SCENIC VIEW

📶 WI-FI HOT SPOT

▶▶ TRENDY MEETING PLACES

> PRICE CATEGORIES

HOTELS
€€€ over 180 euros
€€   120–180 euros
€   under 120 euros
Prices are for two persons in a double room, breakfast not always included

RESTAURANTS
€€€ over 20 euros
€€   12–20 euros
€   under 12 euros
Prices given are for a medium-priced main course without drinks

> MAPS

[122 A1] Page numbers and coordinates refer to the Hamburg Street Atlas

[0] Site located off the map

For your orientation, co-ordinates are also given for places, which are not marked in the street atlas. Please refer to pp. 140/141 for an overview of Hamburg and the surrounding area. A plan of the public trans-port system can be found inside the back cover

CONTENTS

DISCOVER HAMBURG!

Our top 15 highlights point out the most wonderful places and the most fascinating sights

The highlights are marked on the map on the back cover

 Jungfernstieg
Hamburg's recently renovated chic promenade can now be admired in all its glory (p. 29)

 Kunsthalle
One of Germany's most important museums – and not only when there is a special exhibition on (p. 29)

 Rathaus
Planned over a thirty-year period, the result is a feast for the eye: The people of Hamburg are proud of their grand Town Hall (p. 30)

 Landungsbrücken
Ships' captains, tourists, commuters: there is always something going on down on the quayside (p. 35)

 Michaelskirche
The spire of St. Michael's Church – referred to by everyone simply as 'Michel' – is and always will be the city's most loved landmark with a special place in the hearts of the locals (p. 35)

 Miniaturwunderland
The biggest model railway in the world, made with incredible attention to detail, guaranteed to make everyone happy – from fathers and mothers to children and grandparents (p. 42)

 Hafen City Viewpoint
You might find that the viewing tower is not where you expect it to be – a reflection of how the 'Hafencity' area is continuously changing: the tower is moved to a different site each month (p. 44)

> # THE BEST
MARCO POLO
HIGHLIGHTS

 Jenischhaus/Jenischpark
Hamburg arguably has the most parks of any city in Germany. In this park, with its mansion and view of the Elbe, you can find out why (p. 47)

 Övelgönne
On the right, the Elbe, on the left, quaint captains' houses – where a lot of people would like to live (p. 48)

 Ohlsdorfer Friedhof
The largest landscaped cemetery in the world – a vast oasis in the city (p. 55)

 Louis C. Jacob
A restaurant in which everything is just right: marvellous chef, marvellous river views, marvellous *petits fours* (p. 60)

 Schmidt Theater
A night out on the town – visit a musical in Schmidt's Theatre for example (p. 86)

Thalia Theater
Great programme of shows, great actors, great theatre bar (p. 87)

Strandhotel Blankenese
With the most beautiful bridal suite in town – in a white fairy-tale villa on the Elbe in Blankenese. And not just for honeymooners either (p. 94)

 Hagenbecks Tierpark
Germany's only privately-owned zoo celebrated its 100th birthday in 2007 – with the opening of a new tropical aquarium. Let the celebrations continue! (p. 98)

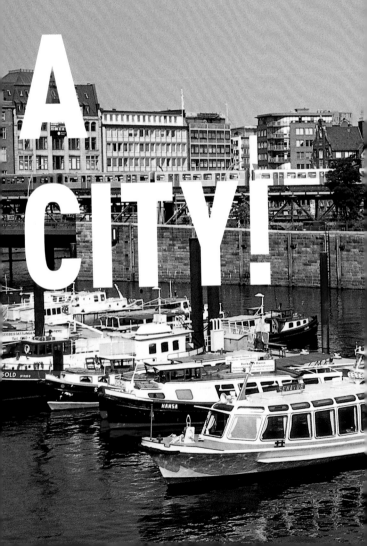

WHAT
A
CITY!

INTRODUCTION

> Wind and water – these are the elements that make up Hamburg. There's no better place on a summer's day than on the banks of the Aussenalster (Outer Alster basin): with swans and sailing boats against a backdrop of grand town houses. There's no more exhilarating place on a stormy autumn day either than down by the jetties: with waves, tugs and gigantic container ships in view. Hamburg – that always has been and still is the star of the north – with more bridges than Venice, with its brand new 'Hafencity' area, with beachclubs, superb museums, enthralling theatres, world-class restaurants and shopping arcades right across the city. And no other city in Germany can boast such an increase in the number of tourists. So that leaves just one question open: when are you coming?

BUENOS AIRES

CREMON IV

> Unlike any other major German city, Hamburg is conditioned by water and by the variety of things to see and do provided by the trading port, the media and culture. Explore the city from its most dominant element – the water – and chug around on the harbour ferries or take a paddle boat along the city's pulsating arteries. The people of Hamburg are proud of their city's skyline with its church spires, former counting houses, dock cranes, bridges, canals and merchants' houses – and look after them as well as they can.

The 'free and Hanseatic town of Hamburg' is the city's official title. But for the people of Hamburg, the 'free' has always been more important than the 'Hanseatic'. Free too from the power of kings, imperial chancellors and church dignitaries. Free from the merging of federal states and free from minister presidents. The fusion of the federal states of northern Germany remains as remote as ever before. And on top of the locals' love of their city is the dream of far-off lands: the sounding of ships' horns on foggy nights can

> *Freedom, a love of Hamburg and the call of far-off lands*

even be heard is those areas of the city where the cry of the seagulls is a rare occurrence and where the spring tides have never flooded the streets. The population of Germany's second largest city is growing year for year: in 2006 it reached the 1.75 million mark. And many are under 30 – Hamburg having become a metropolis for the young.

People enjoy living here and like to demonstrate it by sharing their

One of the flagships in Hamburg's theatre landscape is the Thalia Theater

good fortune. There are around 1,000 private charities and Hamburg's trust commission is there to help those in need: its members include students and millionaires who decide which projects are to receive sponsorship from their funds. Cultural initiatives also profit from generous benefactors. Ballet, 'Poets on the Beach' or the children's theatre – culture is very much part of everyday life and is closely intertwined with the city's maritime setting: the 'Elbphilharmonie' and the open-air theatre in the Warehouse District, or the international shipping and oceanic museum, for example. And on Veddel, an island in the Elbe, the 'Emigrant World Ballinstadt' museum opened its doors in summer 2007. The city has more than 60 theatres, many of which survive without subventions.

Hamburg is one of the greenest cities in Germany – which is not really surprising considering there are two rivers, the Alster and the Elbe, that flow through the city under countless bridges. With the combination of water from below and water from above the city cannot be anything but green and luxuriant. Rain and fog do

> **A cultural metropolis thanks to benefactors**

not deter the true northerner. After all, to make up for things, there are always wonderful sunny days when a refreshing breeze blows and the air is so clear that all you want to do is take one deep breath after another. On such days, the locals like to sit with a cool beer on the banks of the Elbe and enjoy the view across the water.

Most locals are open and friendly towards visitors and are anything but arrogant or stand-offish. Traders from the Hanseatic city have been crisscrossing the world's oceans, building up business, since time immemorial and their relationship with their British counterparts across the Channel has always been very close. And true to tradition, the genuine Hamburg citizen is liberally-minded – whether towards the eternal punks in the Hafenstrasse or the hip youngster from an advertising agency: live and let live. But everybody is expected to do one thing: keep a stiff upper lip. Hanseatic northerners faithfully uphold their local mentality – never to lose face and always to show a certain restraint. Those who are not from Hamburg would perhaps call this aloofness.

The sense of freedom that makes the city so proud that it doesn't take things too seriously, is – how could it be anything else – closely linked with the port. On 7 May, 1189, Emperor Friedrich 1st Barbarossa is reputed to have signed a charter granting the town permission to trade along the River

> The 'Harbour City' welcomes in a new millennium

Elbe. And that's reason enough for the city to celebrate the port's birthday every year in May. Even though it has been known since 1907 that this charter is a forgery, that doesn't stop the people of Hamburg from celebrating anniversaries as they come – and making a fat profit at the same time with the biggest harbour festival in the world, as befits a merchants' town!

The 'star of the north' is also the driving force behind the economy of a whole region. The port is expanding, unemployment figures are sinking and everywhere in the city something is being planned and built. The tourist office recorded a total of almost 8 million overnight visitors, more than ever before. Many guests are from abroad, especially from Asia. And it hasn't happened by chance that Hamburg has attracted so many people. In 2013 Hamburg will host the International Building Exhibition – and some of the first projects are already being started now. Hamburg's 'Hafencity', one of the largest construction projects in a European city, is likely to change attitudes to inner-city living on a permanent basis. Some of the architects – who are from all over the world – have already completed their projects, while others are still working on planning details. Many Hamburg citizens may only realize just how much the 'Hafencity' has changed the face of the city in hindsight. Whoever wants to stand out from the crowd is investing in a loft on Dalmannkai or moving his legal offices to one of the former warehouses on Alter Wandrahm in the

> LIKE A PANCAKE – HARDLY!
Hamburg's best view points

Hamburg doesn't have any hills – that's not true at all! The Süllberg in Blankenese is 75 m (245 ft.) high! And the view from the top can match that of any mountain peak in the Alps ... well, nearly. On the Stintfang above the jetties it seems like being 500 m (1,450 ft.) up – there is even a vineyard, it's so high and sunny up there! You can also view Hamburg from church towers: from 'Michel', the Petri and Jakobi churches and from the top of Nikolai church tower. From the viewing platform in the Planetarium in the City Park you can watch the planes taking off in Fuhlsbüttel. From the top floor inside Karstadt's sports shop on Mönckebergstrasse you can look straight across the Alster, and the Highflyer next to the Deichtorhallen goes up to a height of 150 m (490 ft.) *(daily, 10 am–midnight | Tickets 15 euros | not open in all weathers | Tel. 30 08 69 69 | www.highflyer-hamburg.de).*

'Speicherstadt' district. But not everything is perfect. Critics have been ranting about prestigious projects costing millions and boring office blocks. On top of this, there are too few affordable homes, too few schools and too few shops. Nevertheless, nobody denies that the 'Hafencity' and the new 'Elbphilharmonie' have catapulted centuries, a slowly evolving city centre of historical importance has been preserved, of which the people of Hamburg are prouder than of any new building project.

Let yourself be taken in by the magic of the seaport. The absolute highlights can even be seen without any problem in just one weekend. Or

Planten un Blomen – perfect for a quite moment away from the hustle and bustle

Hamburg right to the top of rankings for international cities. However, the most sensational thing about Hamburg is and always will be the city as a whole. The mighty Town Hall, the Baroque 'Michel', the villas on the Alster, the Art Gallery, the Jungfernstieg, the former Counting Houses, Hamburg's museums and its theatres. Despite all the fires and wars that Hamburg has had to endure over the take a trip to Veddel to see the port museum under construction. At weekends volunteers can often be watched working on old boats and cranes. Listen to their tales of what things were like in the past, in the old seafaring days. And then go to the tip of the quay at Hansahöft and look across the water: that's where the 'Hafencity' is taking shape. Past, present and future, all in one place.

▶▶ HAMBURG TREND GUIDE

Katrin Wienefeld steers you through the scene jungle to the hottest finds and coolest hot spots!

Our scene scout

Katrin Wienefeld loves her flat right on the Fischmarkt. From there it's just a hop, skip and a jump to the numerous music clubs and to the heart of Hamburg's nightlife, which she explores with friends at the weekend. In her free time, the journalist likes to box; for her job she delves into Hamburg's trendy scene as she writes for various travel guides and local city magazines.

▶▶ INDIE CONCERTS

Live and spontaneous

Hamburg's active subculture scene is worlds apart from mainstream music and beyond the realms of established music clubs. Whether hip-hop or electro – the most startlingly innovative concerts are the spontaneous performances on the pavements outside the bars. Up-and-coming musicians are also taking the stages by storm. The places to look out for are *Kulturhaus 73 (Schulterblatt 73, www.dreiundsiebzig.de)*, the wacky pub *Hasenschaukel (Silbersackstr. 17)* and of course the subversive *Hafenklang (Grosse Elbstr. 84, www.hafenklang.org)*.

▶▶ GAY & LESBIAN

St. Georg – flying the rainbow flag

Anything goes in St. Georg. Ever since the bookshop *Männerschwarm (www.maennerschwarm.de)* moved to Lange Reihe 102, the district has become more and more a gay and lesbian hotspot. At the advice bureau *Hein&Fiete (Pulverteich 21, www.heinfiete.de)* you'll find plenty to talk about and a useful network. If you want to natter over tea and cake with a colourful crowd, drop in at *Café Gnosa (Lange Reihe 93, www.gnosa.de, photo)*.

SCENES

▶▶ ART PIONEERS

Art vs. redevelopment

Low-budget artists have brought new life to a whole district and have made it mushroom culturally. In Grosse Bergstrasse in Altona, so-called 'gentrification' can be experienced first hand. The concrete former shopping arcade from the 1960s is due for redevelopment – and low rents attract artists. The scene's forums  can be found at *Kultwerk West*, where political discussions and cultural events are held *(Grosse Bergstr. 162, www.kultwerkwest.de, photo)* and *Quartiersladen,* where a documentary history of the city can be seen *(Grosse Bergstr. 156, www.konsalt.de)*.

▶▶ COOKERY COURSES

Tie that apron tightly

This is where you have to cook yourself! But no, not everyday meals: aubergine ravioli with red pesto, blanched zander in a crab sud with tender spinach – gourmet food is served here. The cookery courses held at the 'in' restaurants *Nil (Neuer Pferdemarkt 5, www. restaurant-nil.de)* and *Atlas (Schützenstr. 9A, www.atlas. at)* are very popular. And the bookshop *Koch Kontor* is following suit – Martina Olufs has turned a passion of hers into a wonderfully sensual experience: recipes in the books in her shop are put to the test every week in a cookery session *(Karolinenstr. 27, www. koch-kontor.de, photo)*.

▶▶ BEAUTIFULLY BONKERS

Fashion and design

Tomorrow's trends are being created in the hip 'Karo' district *(www.karolinenviertel. de)*. The designer Anna Fuchs has made a name for herself among German fashion stars with her feminine outfits for the more self-confident woman *(Karolinen- strasse 27, www.annafuchs.de)*; *Andreas Linzner* makes the hearts of lifestyle freaks beat faster with cool designs made of terry cloth *(Marktstr. 6, www.andreaslinzner. com)*. The motto in *Lockengelöt,* the most innovative store in St. Pauli, is 'nothing is useless': washing machine drums have been turned into bedside cabinets, old records into clocks, and even Lufthansa had a lamp designed here, made from parts of an old aeroplane *(Wohlwillstr. 20, www. lockengeloet.org)*.

▶▶ PUNCHY

Boxing workouts

Boxing is booming. That's not really surprising considering that Hamburg is the home of world champions: most of the boxers at the Universum stable emerge as stars. At the public training sessions every Monday and Friday you can watch fighters such as Felix Sturm or Susi Kentikian, or spot the talent in the up-and-coming stars. Bring your own  autogram cards *(Am Stadtrand 27, www.boxing.de,* photo). In many sports clubs and gyms people sweat it out during fitness boxing – and the ultimate kick is 'manager fighting' *(www.white-collar-boxing.de)*. One manager against another! The *crème de la crème* can get rid of their surplus energy. Well, that can only be good for their colleagues!

▶▶ POETRY SLAMS

Literature on the forefront

Hamburg is 'Slamburg'! Following America's example, writers in the *Macht-Clubs (www.macht-ev.de)* present their works to the public. Crossover events and interdisciplinary networking with performances and music are both wanted and in demand. The public poetry slam in the music club *Molotow (Spielbudenplatz 5, www.molotow club.com,* photo) can get crowded and hot. Ingeniously good and ingeniously spine-chilling poetry can be heard at the late-night slam in the *Zeise-Kinos (Friedensallee 7–9, www.zeise.de).* Anything can happen here: young aspiring authors have even landed contracts with publishers. The precursors of this unconventional literary event are members of the *Writers' Room;* 'Poets-on-the-beach' meet in the summer for a read-in near the beach on the Elbe *(Schulberg 2, for dates see www.writersroom.de).*

▶▶ DESIGNER BARS

Where to party: Hamburg's hotel bars

The 'in' crowd has discovered the bars in the designer hotels for itself. *Yakshi's Bar* in *East-Hotel (Simon-von-Utrecht-Strasse 31, www.east-hamburg.de)* has become everybody's darling, not just thanks to its breath-stopping decor but also due to its list of 250 different drinks. Relax over sushi and longdrinks in the retro chic bar in the popular *Twenty Five Hours Hotel Hamburg (Paul-Dessau-Strasse 2, www.25hours-hotel. com,* photo), or join the 'in' crowd for a sundowner in *Le Ciel* with a fantastic view over the city. The atmosphere on the ninth floor of the *Le Royal Meridien* hotel is low key – and you're not that far from heaven either *(An der Alster 52–56, www.starwoodhotels.com/ lemeridien).*

> 'PEPPER-SACKS', SHIPS AND THE HANSEATIC PEOPLE

Characteristics and noteworthy features of Hamburg

AIRBUS

Hardly any other subject has caused such a stir in the past few years in Hamburg as this. A booming economy may be good, but woe betide anything that spoils the view of the Elbe. And it was not just the view that was in peril but the Mühlenberger Loch – the freshwater mud flats, too. Part of the nature reserve was filled in for the A380; northern shovelers and common teals will now have to make their nests elsewhere. The Hamburg Senate subsidized this prestigious project in Finkenwerder with millions and thousands of jobs were created. When Airbus skidded off course into its own internal crisis in 2006, the whole discussion bubbled up to the surface again. Was all this trouble for nothing? The apple farmers in Neuenfelde, who protested against extending the runway in the first place, are deeply embittered.

Above: Stilwerk near the Fish Market

HAMBURG
IN CONTEXT

HANSE

HH – these are the first two letters on the index plate of every car registered in Hamburg and they stand for 'Hansestadt Hamburg'. From the 13th to the 15th century, Hamburg was part of the 'Hanse' guild of merchants – the most powerful league of cities in the world at that time. There is little left now in the city to remind us of that time, unlike in Rostock, Bremen and Lübeck. But one quality

of times gone by is still very much present: the Hanseatic mentality – "A Hanseatic merchant has many virtues: he is proud of his tradition, is honest and direct, but never short-tempered. A true Hanseatic citizen doesn't look back ('what's gone is gone …'), but forward." And this can be seen in the 22,684 new companies registered at Hamburg's Chamber of Commerce in 2006 – more than ever before in the history of the city.

The Globushof counting house

FLOODING

Had there been no flooding in 1962, Helmut Schmidt – who was Minister for Internal Affairs in Hamburg at the time – would not have been able to show that he had the makings of a future German Chancellor. When the banks burst in Wilhelmsburg, the decisive action he took saved the lives of thousands of people. The subject has now become more a myth than a fact: the plaques that commemorate the great flood in Övelgönne and in Blankenese tell of a certain pride – 'look at us now; we even survived that'. The subject is, however, deadly earnest. Climate experts reckon that the water level in Hamburg will rise by 30 cm (12 in.). The 103 km-long (64 mls.) embankment in the city has been or is still being raised to 8.5 m (28 ft.). The planned dredging of the

shipping passage in the Elbe has come under strong criticism: the water will flow more swiftly and the floodwaters will come in faster and with greater force. This somehow all seems to be such a contrast to the 'Hafencity' project. While all the new buildings have been constructed on artificially raised banks, terraces, parks and underground garages have been planned so casually as if this were a lake. What really might happen if and when those living in the Hafencity have to flee the floodwaters, is not something that people like to talk about when there is so much euphoria for this major undertaking.

'PEPPER SACKS'

This derogatory term ('money bags' or 'money grabbers') for the enterprising merchants of Hamburg, found in conjunction with any conceivable subject in Hamburg, has a long tradition. It was first used by Denmark's King Christian IV (1577–1649). A quotation from one his letters about the citizens of Hamburg tells it all: "Arrogant skinflints and pepper sacks, slimey fishmongers and lazybones …"

QUEEN MARY & CO

When the Queen Mary comes in, the people of Hamburg as well as tourists line the banks of the Elbe in the thousands. They wave and dance around, there is a special coverage of the event on television, bakers bake breadrolls in the shape of a ship and guests from the Rhine area feel at home: it's party time on the Elbe. In mid 2008, the cruise liner hype will reach a new peak: the Cruise Days event will see seven huge ocean liners being prepared for their voyages, all moored in Hamburg at the same time. That's never happened before and has never been seen anywhere in the world. Even the old cruise centre on Grosse Elbstrasse is being reopened for the occasion. Hamburg awaits the cruise passengers of the world!

red tiles" and, please, "no columns, ornament or timber framing". Brick buildings are a feature of the city and can be found everywhere, from detached houses in Ohlsdorf to housing estates in Barmbeck, from the old warehouse district down on the harbour to 'Hafencity'. A few years ago a bitter dispute broke out: 'glass or

The 'Queen' in St. Pauli: the luxury liner in port

BRICKS

As Fritz Schumacher, the head of the city's building department back in the Roaring Twenties, said: "Brick makes constructing new buildings that much easier in the best possible way." The director of the Art Gallery, Alfred Lichtwark, described his ideal building as follows: "Simple bricks with a network of light joints" with a "roof of

brick' was the question. Architects such as Hadi Teherani were making the people of Hamburg furious with their new glass palaces. Modern is fine – but in brick please! That's how it was in the past and that's how it should stay. And by the way, the fascinating annual publication brought out by the local literature crowd is called 'The Hamburg Brick' – and there's nothing dowdy about that!

SPORT, SHIPS & CULTURE

The people of Hamburg create their own reasons to celebrate

> The locals love their festivals: the tri-annual Dom fair in Heiligengeistfeld, the show jumping derby in Klein Flottbek and the tennis championships at Rothenbaum, as well as countless marathons, half-marathons, cycling and skating races, for which week for week half the city is closed off. But most of all they love their street parties and ship festivals: be it to celebrate the 'Queen Mary 2', the 'Aida Diva' or any of the other beautiful ships that call in from around the world – all hell is let loose on such occasions at the passenger liner terminal at Grosser Grasbrook. (For dates see *www.hamburg.de*).

PUBLIC HOLIDAYS

These are the usual holidays in Protestant areas of Germany: **1 Jan; Good Friday; Easter Monday; 1 May; Ascension Day; Whit Monday; 3 Oct; 25/26 Dec.**

EVENTS

April
Marathon: Almost 20,000 participants, every year, 42 km right through the city

May
Tennis championships at Rothenbaum: Game, set and match to the best tennis aces. *Rothenbaumchaussee | U 1, Hallerstrasse*
The Long Museums' Night: Visit the museums deep into the night (and pay only once), free shuttle buses. *Meeting point: Deichtorhallen | U 1, Messberg*
★ *Harbour Birthday:* A huge knees-up along the landing jetties with tall masts' parade and the 'tug dance'. *Over one weekend at the beginning of May*

May/June
Japanese Cherry Blossom Festival: The best fireworks display in the city around the Alster
German Spring Derby at Klein Flottbek: One of the world's best-known derbies. *Derbypark | S 1, Klein Flottbek*

June/July
Jungle Nights at Hagenbeck: The zoo is turned into a jungle – on several different Saturdays. *Lokstedter Grenzstrasse 2 |*

> FESTIVALS & EVENTS

Tel. 53 00 33 0 | U2, Hagenbecks Tierpark
Altonale: Art and culture in the Ottensen/
Altona district
Derby week: Fast horses and pretty hats
at Hamburg Horn. *Rennbahnstr. 96 | U3,*
Horner Rennbahn
Hamburg Ballet Days: John Neumeier's
ballet never fails to fascinate.
Staatsoper | U 1, Stephansplatz | www.
hamburgballett.de

July/August

Hamburger Jedermann: Spectacular
open-air theatre in the warehouse district, held on seven weekends. *Auf dem*
Sande | Metrobus 6, Auf dem Sande
Schleswig-Holstein Music Festival: Europe's
largest classical music festival takes
place in barns and halls throughout the
neighbouring federal state
Vattenfall-Cyclassics: Thrilling cycle race
for professionals and amateurs alike
through the city and out into the suburbs
Christopher Street Day: Originally mostly
for the gay/lesbian community, today it
is a colourful procession and street

party. *St. Georg/Landungsbrücken*
Hamburg Jazz Open: Open-air jazz in
Planten un Blomen, on one weekend at
the end of August. *No entrance fee |*
S-Bahn Dammtor
Alster Party: Hot-dog stands, music and
amateur theatre performances around
the Inner Alster basin
Hamburg City Man: Triathletes swim
across the Inner Alster, cycle and run –
watch from the Alster Arcades

September/October

Hamburg's International Film Festival:
Essential viewing for film fans.
www.filmfesthamburg.de

November/December

Markt der Völker: Special Christmas
market in the Museum for Ethnology
with gift items from around the world.
U 1, Hallerstrasse
Christmas Market on the square in front
of the Rathaus (Town Hall)
New Year's fireworks display on the
harbour. *S-/U-Bahn Landungsbrücken*

> BETWEEN THE ALSTER AND THE ELBE

The green metropolis on the water: cosmopolitan, sporty, cultural and business-like

> One thing is clear for anyone visiting Hamburg: first of all, it's off to the Landungsbrücken – the jetties. This is where you can feel the heartbeat of the city. From here, it is not far to the Rathaus (Town Hall) and there you are standing on the banks of the Alster – the next highlight.

The Hafencity (Harbour City) project is becoming increasingly important for both the locals and tourists. And: cultural events are also becoming more important. Hamburg's museums were always good but they did not sell themselves well. Today, magnificent exhibitions attract hundreds of thousands of visitors. New houses, such as the *Ballinstadt* on the Veddel or the *Maritime Museum* in the Speicherstadt (Warehouse District) which open in mid-2008, are being opened. Particularly the warehouse district is – and remains – Hamburg's pearl on the banks of the Elbe. Hamburg's city fathers (and mothers) want it to be included

Above: The Alster Arcades on the Kleiner Alster

SIGHT SEEING

on UNESCO's World Heritage list – and this wish is completely justified. The fantastic ensemble of red brick warehouses which were created in one fell swoop is absolutely unique.

Leave your car where it is. The entire inner city can be easily covered on foot. Take advantage of what the Tourist Office has on offer, such as the *Hamburg Card* which lets you use public transport free of charge (*information under www.hamburg-tourismus.de*). And, if you have a little more time, discover the great variety Hamburg has to offer in its various districts: Eppendorf, St. Georg, Altona, Winterhude, Eimsbüttel and Blankenese all used to be villages and small towns independent of Hamburg and have all preserved their own charming characteristics. It is well worthwhile getting to know them. There are wonderful pubs, boutiques, cheerful shops, theatres and cinemas.

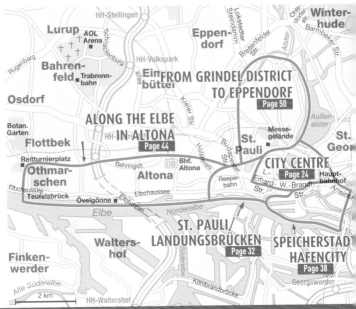

The map shows the location of the most interesting districts. There is a detailed map of each district on which each of the sights described is numbered.

CITY CENTRE

> There is one major activity in the city centre: spending money. One shopping passage follows the next; there are luxury boutiques and cheap outlets, department stores, jeans shops, expensive restaurants and affordable snack bars. With all this magnificent commercialism you should still give culture a chance. Some of the most beautiful museums are located in the heart of the city. Even if you only have little time, a visit is worthwhile. And then, of course, there is the magnificent Town Hall with the inscription high above the portal: *Libertatem quam peperere maiores digne studeat servare posterias:* 'May

future generations preserve with dignity that which the older achieved.' The perfect motto to remember when strolling through the town!

◼ BINNENALSTER
(INNER ALSTER)   [123 D–E3]

You are in the heart of the city. Sit down on the lovely new benches near the Jungfernstieg moorings and enjoy the view. The white Alster steamers cast off in front of you, a few swans between them; the fountain shoots up in the middle of the Inner Alster – and, at Christmastime, the lights of the giant Christmas tree glitter across the water. The former mill pond, which took on its present form after the great fire of

1842, covers an area of 18 hectares (around 45 acres). During the Second World War, the Inner Alster was built over with cardboard dummies to disorientate enemy bombers. The technically complicated construction of the public transportation system started in 1967 and took 15 years. Today, the underground and district lines run deep beneath the Inner Alster. *S-/U-Bahn Jungfernstieg*

▣ BISCHOFSTURM/
DOMPLATZ   [123 E5]

You can see the remains of the Bishop's Tower, which used to be next to the Hammaburg, in the exhibition rooms in the basement of the Petri-Kirche *(Mon–Fri 10am–1pm, 3–5pm, Sat 10am–1pm | Entrance fee 1.50 euro | Speersort 10)*. The excavations opposite on Domplatz (Cathedral Square), a carpark which the city council neglected for decades, are interesting. This was once the site of the Johanneum scholarly institution and, later, the great Catholic cathedral which the citizens of Hamburg irreverently demolished brick by brick between 1804 and 1807. More remnants were found during recent excavations. Was this the site of the Hammaburg? There are now lively discussions among the residents of Hamburg about what should happen to the square. Maybe a modern citizens' centre? Or, one more museum? *U 3, Mönckebergstrasse*

▣ BUCERIUS KUNST FORUM [123 D4]

What would Hamburg be without its generous patrons? Gerd Bucerius, the founder of the weekly newspaper 'Die Zeit', was one of them. In 2002, the

MARCO POLO HIGHLIGHTS

★ **Rathaus**
Gold, splendour and Hanseatic pride (p. 30)

★ **Michaeliskirche**
The 'Michel' is the city's landmark (p. 35)

★ **Hafencity View Point**
This is where a brand new district is being created (p. 44)

★ **Jenischhaus/Jenischpark**
Mansion and surrounding park on the Elbchaussee (p. 47)

★ **Jungfernstieg**
Hamburg's glamourous boulevard on the Alster (p. 29)

★ **Kunsthalle**
A must for all art fans (p. 29)

★ **Landungsbrücken**
Like a station on the water (p. 35)

★ **Miniaturwunderland**
This is where everyone feels happy: the largest model railway in the world (p. 42)

★ **Ohlsdorfer Friedhof**
A wonderful park for those who are no more (p. 55)

★ **Övelgönne**
This is how lots of people would like to live: in one of the old ship-pilots' houses on the Elbe (p. 48)

CITY CENTRE

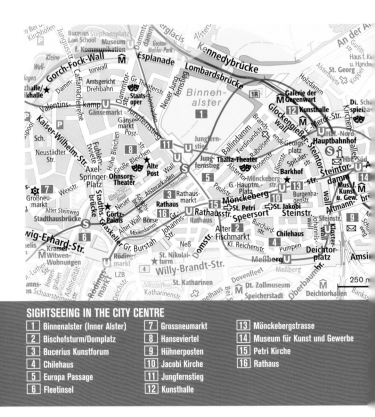

SIGHTSEEING IN THE CITY CENTRE

1. Binnenalster (Inner Alster)
2. Bischofsturm/Domplatz
3. Bucerius Kunstforum
4. Chilehaus
5. Europa Passage
6. Fleetinsel
7. Grossneumarkt
8. Hanseviertel
9. Hühnerposten
10. Jacobi Kirche
11. Jungfernstieg
12. Kunsthalle
13. Mönckebergstrasse
14. Museum für Kunst und Gewerbe
15. Petri Kirche
16. Rathaus

Zeit Foundation, which he financed, established an exhibition centre in the former Reichs Bank on Rathausmarkt. The curators have a real knack for organizing sophisticated exhibitions which also appeal to a wide audience. *Open every day 11 am – 7 pm, Thurs to 9 pm | Entrance fee 5, Mon 2.50 euros | Rathausmarkt 2 | Tel. 360 99 60 | www.buceriuskunstforum.de | U 3, Rathaus*

4 CHILEHAUS [123 F5]

The Chilehaus was regarded as a 'wonder of world architecture' when construction was completed in 1924. Stand directly beneath the stone eagle at the top and you will be able to understand the fascination. The architect Fritz Höger used more than 4 million red clinker bricks for this construction which was commissioned by the merchant Henry B. Sloman who had made his fortune importing saltpetre from Chile. The construction of this building was regarded as a signal of Hamburg's revival after the First World War. *U 1, Messberg*

5 EUROPA PASSAGE   [123 D–E4]

The eastern and western halves of the city were separated for decades. Now, pedestrians can walk through passages from Gänsemarkt to Mönckebergstr. And, they do that in droves; the passage is often packed. Whether the passage was a good idea is a matter of opinion seeing that the concentrated purchasing power (110 shops!) draws customers away from other parts of the city. The passage was built by Hamburg's architectural darling Hadi Teherani. *S-/U-Bahn Jungfernstieg*

6 FLEETINSEL   [122 B–C5]

A piece of old Hamburg, which is particularly popular today with art lovers, has been preserved around the Admiralitätsstrasse surrounded by the 'fleeten' (channels). Thanks to a generous patron, some of the best galleries in the city are located in the preserved merchant houses as is the wonderful bookshop *Sautter + Lackmann* and the tiny theater ▶▶ *Fleetstreet (Admiralitätsstr. 71 | Tel. 39993883 | www.fleetstreet-hamburg.de)*, where young actors often give magnificent performances for little money but with great passion. There are also some delightful restaurants and, in summer, an artistic street festival. *S1, 3, Stadthausbrücke*

Insider Tip

7 GROSSNEUMARKT   [122 B4]

The 'Big New Market' (it got this name because there was already a smaller 'New Market' near the Nicolai-Kirche) was once the assembly point for Hamburg's militia. Today, there are many good inns on Grossneumarkt; and in summer you can have a romantic meal under the lights. Take a stroll away from the square through the 'New City' (the

Expressionistic: the Chilehaus

'Old City' is located around Nikolai-fleet). There are some renovated half-timbered houses on Valentinskamp and an entire row of magnificent baroque buildings has been reconstructed on Peterstrasse. Not all preservationists are satisfied with the ensemble ('like Disneyland'); but the likes of us are happy that, once again, a patron took the initiative. In this case, it was Alfred C. Toepfer. *Metrobus 3, Bus 112, Johannes-Brahms-Platz*

CITY CENTRE

⑧ HANSEVIERTEL [122 C4]

No matter what you think about the Europa Passage, this district is still the queen in Hamburg's passage landscape. The mixture of bourgeois Hanseatic attributes (bricks, coats of arms, medals) and luxurious affectation (scampi and champagne stands) is remarkable. The Hamburg GMP architectural office (von Gerkan, Marg and Partners) made their international breakthrough in 1980 with the construction of the spectacular glass dome. Shopping passages have a long tradition in the city: the first was 'Sillem's Bazar' a passageway constructed in 1845 which was later replaced by the pompous new construction of the Hamburger Hof Hotel (today, this is also a passage). The Colonnaden, Hamburg's most beautiful shopping street, was also constructed in the middle of the 19th century. The representative house façades with their magnificent arcades create an Italian flair – recently, money has also been invested here and there are a few nice restaurants. *S-/U-Bahn Jungfernstieg*

⑨ HÜHNERPOSTEN ▶▶ 📶 [137 E5]

A cheerful place for tourists to warm up, surf or read a newspaper – this is the site of the *Central Library*. The Hühnerposten is a trendy party location and attracts dancers at weekends. The two striking bronze figures on the forecourt were created by the sculptor Stephan Balkenhol. *Library: Mon 2–7pm, Tues–Fri 11am–7pm, Sat 11am–4pm | Entrance free | Hühnerposten 1 | Tel. 42606215 | www.buecherhallen.de | S-/U-Bahn Hauptbahnhof*

Sturdy walls for the fine arts: Hamburg's Art Museum

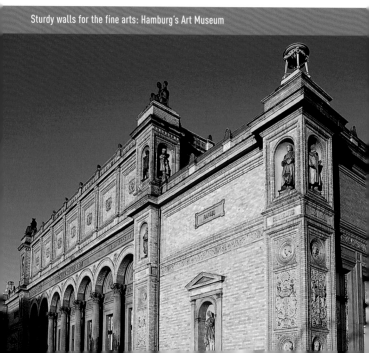

SIGHTSEEING

10 JACOBI-KIRCHE [123 E4]

The Jacobi Church is one of the five main churches in the Hanseatic city. It was severely damaged during the war. However, its most precious possession, the Arp Schnitger organ with 60 stops, survived unscathed. There is an organ recital every Thursday at noon. *Mon–Sat 10 am – 5 pm | Tower open at irregular times | Jakobikirchhof 22 | www.jacobus.de | U 3, Mönckebergstrasse*

11 JUNGFERNSTIEG ⭐ [123 D3-4]

The people of Hamburg call this 'the most beautiful shopping street in the world'. This might be a bit exaggerated but the recent renovation produced miraculous things: where pedestrians previously had to give way to traffic, they now play the main role once again. Unfortunately, commerce has the street completely in its grip. In summer, there is a never-ending series of festivals with booths. What would Heinrich Heine have written if he had seen such colourful goings-on? He really liked to make fun of the Hanseatic 'pepper sacks' while drinking his coffee in the Alster Pavilion. The pavilion (Café Alex) still exists. However, it is no longer a meeting place for intellectuals but for visitors from the suburbs. In any case, the view from the terrace is still overwhelmingly beautiful! *S-/U-Bahn Jungfernstieg*

12 KUNSTHALLE ⭐ [123 E-F3]

The people of Hamburg have an ambivalent relationship to the fine arts. On the one hand, they consider culture to be 'prime importance' to the State but, on the other, many do not seem to realize that their Kunsthalle is one of the most important art museums in Germany. Of course, there are queues reaching out onto the street for the major exhibitions, such as Caspar David Friedrich in 2006. But, there is often nobody visiting the magnificent permanent exhibition even though a visit to the recently renovated rooms is always worthwhile. Go and see the Old Masters – in particular Master Bertram's altarpiece, and marvel at the masterpieces of Classical Modernism ranging from Max Liebermann, to Emil Nolde and Pablo Picasso. In the Contemporary Gallery – a cubic building by Oswald Matthias Unger – you will find works by Gerhard Richter, Jeff Koons and Georg Baselitz. Small-scale temporary exhibitions are displayed in the 'Hubertus-Wald-Forum'. Afterwards, relax in the *Café Liebermann. 10 am – 6 pm, Thurs to 9 pm | Entrance fee 8.50 euros | Sun 10 am – 2 pm, brunch with guided tour 25 euros | Glockengiesserwall | Tel. 428 13 12 00 | www.hamburger-kunsthalle.de | S-/U-Bahn Hauptbahnhof*

13 MÖNCKEBERGSTRASSE [123 D-F4]

The elegant curve of this 29-metre- (95 ft.)-wide street was cut through the Gänge district between 1908 and 1911. At the same time, the tunnel was made for the underground. Craftsmen, coachmen and workers were moved out. A few years before, cholera has spread through the streets around the Jacobi Church; office buildings were then constructed and Fritz Schumacher designed the Mönckeberg Fountain at the top of Spitalerstrasse to 'promote city life'. It is always lively – not to say packed – on Mönckebergstrasse. Previously, it was characterized by cheap shops, sausage stalls and loitering men with cans of cheap beer in their hands.

The Europa passage led to an upswing. But even more importantly: the sausages from the two stands opposite each other near C&A still taste great. *U 3, Mönckebergstrasse*

14 MUSEUM FÜR KUNST UND GEWERBE [137 E5]

The MKG is a must for any visitor to Hamburg interested in culture. It is currently undergoing a total renovation and some of the departments are closed. However, the building is so huge that there is always plenty to see. One must admire the first director of the museum, Justus Brinckman, for his foresight. In 1900 he purchased an entire Art Deco bedroom in Paris. The East Asian section is also rightfully famous. If you book in advance, you can take part in an original Japanese tea ceremony. The presentation of the porcelain and faïence collection has now been redesigned and spectacular photographic exhibitions always create a furore. You can regain your strength with one of the delicious salads in the museum's *Destille Café*. *Tues–Sun 10 am–6 pm, Thurs to 9 pm | Entrance fee 8 euros | Steintorplatz | Tel.* 42 81 34 27 32 | *www.mkg-hambur de | S-/U-Bahn Hauptbahnhof*

15 PETRI-KIRCHE [123 E-

Without any feelings for the pride the residents of Hamburg, Napoleon soldiers stabled their horses in th massive brick church. And, as if th were not enough, shortly before Chris mas 1813, the French commander o dered the citizens to stock up on pre visions for the coming months. Thos who could not do so were threatene with banishment. Thousand of thes poorest of the poor spent a night fu of fear and cold in the Petri-Kirch before being driven out of the cit through the Millern Gate on 25 Decen ber. A painting in the church recal this event. *Mon–Fri 10 am–6.30 p Sat 10 am–5 pm, Sun 9 am–9 pm Speersort 10 | www.sankt-petri.de | U Rathaus*

16 RATHAUS ⭐ [123 D4–

Take a tour of the Town Hall and a mire the gold and splendid architec ture – as in the large Emperor's Ha which got its name from Emperc William II who celebrated the oper

➤ TAKE IT EASY!
Sweating it out in a hamam

A long night out drinking? Bad weather? Then it's off the to Hamburg's hamam on the harbour. With the same sense of style and a good eye for detail, Selma and Coskun Costur have set up their second genuine Turkish steam bath in Hamburg in a former harbourside hospital. Sweat it out first of all on the mable benches before heading off for a soap massage. To finish it all off, sink into the thick cushions in the relaxatior area, and enjoy a glass of tea, all wrapped up in towels and a bath-robe. *Mon–Fri 10 am–10 pm, Sat/Sun 11 am– 10 pm | Book in advance | from 30 eurc | Seewartenstr. 10 | Tel. 311 08 39 90 | www.hamam-hamburg.de | S-/U- Bahn Landungsbrücken*

ing of the Kiel Canal there on 19 June 1895. Hamburg's luminaries have presented themselves to the world as honourable and dignified citizens every year in February since 1356: that is when they celebrated the Matthias feast along with the 'representatives of those powers friendly towards Hamburg'. During the Great Fire of 1842, the old town hall near the Trost Bridge was blown up in the hope that this would help curb the blaze. Subsequently, there were decades of quarrels and discussions about a new building. It was not until 1880 that the architect Martin Haller and his 'town hall builders' society' made a breakthrough. Technical problems made construction difficult. It was necessary to drive 4,000 pylons into the muddy, marshy ground near the Alster. Today, they still support the 113-metre-(367-ft.)-wide and 70-metre-(230-ft.)-long construction with its 112-metre-high central tower. Luckily, the Town Hall suffered only slight damage in the Second World War and, today, it is regarded as one of the most important buildings

Design classics in the Museum für Kunst und Gewerbe

in Germany in the Historicist style. The new restaurant in the rooms of the former town hall cellar is called *Parlament. (Open every day | Tel. 70 38 33 99 | €€). Visits to the Rathausdiele (Foyer) Mon–Fri 8 am–6 pm | Tours every half-hour Mon to Thurs 10 am–3 pm, Fri–Sun 10 am–1 pm | Tickets 3 euros (call in advance as tours do not always take place) | Rathausmarkt 1 | Tel. 42 83 12 47 0 (recorded information) | U3, Rathaus*

ST. PAULI AND LANDUNGS-BRÜCKEN

> The heart of Hamburg's harbour beats at the 'Landungsbrücken' (jetties). Enjoy the goings-on down on the water. Take a stroll

time to hear the trumpeters play a chorale from the tower? And then, off to the Reeperbahn at night.

■ **ALTER ELBTUNNEL** [136 A–B5]
It rattles and shakes and is a real adventure: a trip with the car lift under the Elbe, 24 m (29 ft.) deep. When the old Elbe tunnel was built in 1911,

Seafaring history live: the schooner Rickmer Rickmers and the cargo ship Cap San Diego

through the Alter Elbtunnel (old Elbe tunnel) and look back from Steinwerder at the silhouette of the city. **Sensational!** A tour of the harbour is a must for everyone – as well as a visit to Hamburg Museum and, of course, you simply have to climb Hamburg's landmark: the tower of the Michaeliskirche. Perhaps, in

it was considered a sensation worldwide. It is 448.5 m (1470 ft.) long and originally served the harbour workers on their morning way to the grind. The dome on the jetty was modelled on the Parthenon in Rome. The tunnel is closed to traffic at weekends. *Open to pedestrians and cyclists around the clock; cars only Mon–Fri 5.30 am – 8pm | Tickets 2 euros | S-/U-Bahn, Landungsbrücken*

2 BISMARCK-DENKMAL ☆ [122 A4]

This is the largest monument in Hamburg; the figure alone is 15 m (49 ft.) high. It was unveiled in 1906 but never found favour with anyone. Rolf Liebermann, the former opera director, thought it 'an unparalleled monstrosity'. Even today, you will not find many residents of Hamburg here, in spite of the magnificent view of the harbour. It has been in the process of renovation since 2007. The statue of Emperor William I experienced a similar fate to that of the disliked figure of the Chancellor. The equestrian statue from 1889 was actually planned for the Rathausmarkt but in 1930 it was moved to where it stands today, just as resolutely ignored as the good old Chancellor of the Realm. *S-/U-Bahn, Landungsbrücken*

3 CAP SAN DIEGO [136 B6]

White, proud and sleek, the former cargo ship lies moored at the Überseebrücke where, formerly, cruise ships docked. The Cap San Diego was launched in 1961 and is the largest functional museum ship in the world. You will really feel like a sailor if you spend a night in one of the (surprisingly roomy) cabins *(€)*. Book a place on the Cap San Diego for the parade of ships on the harbour's birthday – it doesn't get any better than that! *Open every day 10am – 6pm | Entrance fee 6 euros | Überseebrücke | Tel. 364209 | www.capsandiego.de | S-/U-Bahn, Landungsbrücken*

4 DEICHSTRASSE [122 C5–6]

'Fire! Fire on Deiekstraat!' This was the cry of the night watchman at one o'clock in the morning of 5 May 1842. What happened over the next three days had a greater effect on Hamburg's appearance than the Second World War bombings. Old Hamburg was razed to the ground by the Great Fire; one third of the population was made homeless. Alexis de Chateauneuf was responsible for the creation of an almost completely new city: the 'Venice of the north' with the Alster Arcades and Rathausmarkt. Deichstrasse looks (almost) exactly like it did around 1842. The 'Save Deichstrasse' Committee is to be thanked for this. You can walk through the narrow passageways down to the Fleet and have a meal there on the jetty. At low tide this is not quite so pleasant – the sludge stinks. *U3, Rödingsmarkt*

›LOW BUDGET

> A tour of the Elbe with Hadag harbour ferries is cheap: line 62 takes you from the jetties or from Altona to Finkenwerder, where you can change to line 64 to Teufelsbrück. From there take a bus to the city centre. Price: a day-ticket for the HVV costs 6 euros. *Insider Tip*

> The concert of coloured lights on the lake in the park in *Planten un Blomen* is romantic and free of charge [122 B1] *(May-Aug daily, 10pm, Sept 9pm)*.

> Almost all museums have reductions on entrance fees at certain times or on certain days. Just ring up and ask in advance!

ST. PAULI/LANDUNGSBRÜCKEN

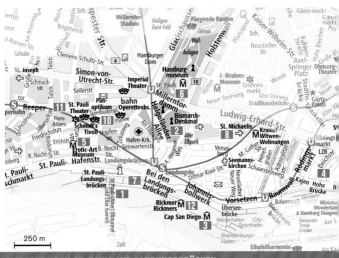

5 EROTIC ART MUSEUM [136 A5]

Eroticism between art and kitsch: this is the real thing, sometimes embarrassing, sometimes artistic, but always interesting. At the time of going to press, the museum was closed for renovation, but it is planned to be reopened as soon as possible. *Bernhard-Nocht-Str. 69 | Tel. 3178410 | www.eroticartmuseum.de | S1, 3, Reeperbahn*

6 HAMBURGMUSEUM [122 A4]

The façade itself is pure splendour and the interior of the museum, which was planned by Fritz Schumacher and inaugurated in 1922, impresses with it magnificent staircases and halls. Let

yourself be beamed back to the medieval age of knights in shining armour or to the Great Fire of 1842. You can look at the Hamburg Harbour the way it was in 1938 from the bridge of the steamship 'Werner', track down the 'pepper sacks' in original shops, or bring a model ship up through a lock. In a nutshell: here you can find everything relating to the history of Hamburg. There is even a model railroad (rides, four times daily). If you grow tired of culture, visit the *Café Fees* in the covered courtyard. *Tues–Sat 10am–5pm, Sun 10am–6pm | Entrance fee 7.50 euros | Holstenwall 24 | Tel. 4281322380 | www.hamburgmuseum.de | U3, St. Pauli*

7 LANDUNGSBRÜCKEN ⭐ [136 A–B5]

If one believes the statistics, these jetties or landing stages are – after the Brandenburg Gate in Berlin – Germany's second most visited tourist attraction. There is always something happening on the water. The pontoon installation was constructed between 1904 and 1910. There is the continuous coming-and-going of the harbour ferries, between them the catamaran to Helgoland or one of the two paddle-steamers (one Dutch, the other German). Construction work here is scheduled to continue until around 2009 and the flood protection dykes will be heightened in some sections. The bridges are numbered to help your orientation; for example, the Hadag line ferry 62 is stationed by Bridge 3. Don't be put off by the commotion made by the captains praising their harbour tours, the harried commuters and day-trippers with their bikes. Buy a fish sandwich, find a place on the steps and watch the action from above.
S-/U-Bahn Landungsbrücken

8 MICHAELISKIRCHE ⭐ [122 B5]

'Michel' – sorry, Michaeliskirche – is probably the city's most important symbol. No other church is held in such esteem by the people of Hamburg. If the church is in need, they rally and make donations. The present magnificent baroque building was planned by the architects Johann Leonard Prey and Ernst Georg Sonnin and completed in 1786. After a fire destroyed the church in 1906, the senate unhesitatingly decided to reconstruct it on the same site, using the original plans. You should not leave Hamburg without visiting 'Michel'. Wonderful

Uninhibited advertising for the Erotic Art Museum – in St. Pauli of course

concerts are held there; for example, during the Bach Weeks every year in autumn, and the Christmas concerts and church services are romantic when the white wood of the balustrades with its gold ornamentation is illuminated by candlelight. The ☀ tower is 132 metres (433 ft.) high and 452 steps lead to the top (there is also a lift). Visit the crypt, which was opened a few years ago, as well. Hamburg's former music director Carl Philipp Emanuel Bach (1714–88) is buried there. Johann Sebastian Bach's second son followed Georg Philipp Telemann in this position in 1767. The slide show *Hamburg History* takes you through 1,000 years of the city's past *(every 30 minutes | daily 12.30–3.30 pm, in winter only Sat and Sun). Church and tower: Open every day 9 am – 7.30 pm, Nov–April 10 am – 5.30 pm | Crypt, open every day 11 am – 4.30 pm (the times are subject to frequent changes, visits are generally not possible during services) | Tower chorale Mon–Sat 10 am and 9 pm, Sun at midday | Entrance fee for tower, slide show and crypt 5 euros | Englische Planke 1 a | Tel. 37 67 81 99 | www.st-michaelis.de | Schnellbus 37, Michaeliskirche*

9 **NIKOLAIKIRCHTURM** ☀ [123 D5]

The 147-metre-(182-ft.)-high tower was the only section of the church to survive the bombings of the Second World War and is now a memorial. The former main church was not very old at the time of its destruction: it was rebuilt in the style of a mediaeval-gothic cathedral after the Great Fire. The plans were drawn up by Gottfried Semper. The architect of the Semper Opera House in Dresden was born in Hamburg and earned his first laurels as a member of the 'Technical

The tower of the Michaeliskirche, called 'Michel', dominates the skyline of the city centre

SIGHTSEEING

Commission'. Buy the 4 euro ticket for both the glass lift and the war documentation centre. The breathtaking view is contrasted by impressive photos of the bombed city of Hamburg. *Open every day 10am–6pm, longer in summer | www.mahnmal-st-nikolai.de | U3, Rödingsmarkt*

10 PANOPTIKUM [136 A5]

Things are always changing on the Reeperbahn – but the Panoptikum stays the same. It is 125 years old and its 130 wax figures – including Harry Potter alias Daniel Radcliffe and Pope Benedict XVI – are waiting to greet you. *Mon–Fri 11am–9pm, Sat 11am–midnight, Sun 10am–9pm | Entrance fee 4.50 euros | Spielbudenplatz 3 | Tel. 310317 | www.panoptikum.de | S1, 3, Reeperbahn*

11 REEPERBAHN [136 A–B5]

Come on, admit it: you really are interested in the Reeperbahn! Where else can you so openly come into contact with a red-light district? Sex for money still plays an important role on Hamburg's sinful mile. There are several thousand officially registered prostitutes and a large number who are not. During the day, the area is quite dreary but it becomes more colourful at night with the lights and advertising signs. The 'Historical Whore Tour' can provide background information *(Thurs–Sat 8pm| Tel. 01805/125225 | Meeting point David-wache | 25 euros per person | reservations only | minimum age 18).* Don't get the wrong idea: the ladies are trained guides and absolutely respectable. Of course, they tell it like it is. But, that is only one side of St.

Pauli. The best bars and clubs in the city are located near the Reeperbahn; there are theatres, cabarets, musicals and readings. *Grosse Freiheit 36, D-Club* and *Molotow* are established, popular locations for live performances in the area. The club owners brought the music scene back to the district with the *Reeperbahn Festival* which they initiated in 2006: newcomer bands and stars play in the various clubs around the Reeperbahn on three days in September *(www.reeperbahnfestival.com).* The Beatles started their career in the *Starclub* on Grosse Freiheit and Little Richard and Bill Haley were also there. The club no longer exists; there is only a memorial stone commemorating these wild times in the back courtyard of the house at Grosse Freiheit 3. If Corny Littmann's plans are successful, the ardently longed-for Beatles Square will become reality in 2008. You can book a 'Beatles Tour' from *Stattreisen e. V. (May–Sept Sat 7pm | 16 euros | bookings: Tel. 4303481 | www.stattreisen-hamburg.de). S1, 3, Reeperbahn*

12 RICKMER RICKMERS [122 A6]

It is pretty tight in a sailor's bunk; and the cook had to be something of an acrobat in the galley. You can get a lively idea of how hard a sailor's life was on Hamburg's first museum ship. Since 1987, the sleek, green sailing schooner (sail area 3,500m^2; 4,185 yds.^{2}) lies moored at Bridge 1 on the 'Landungsbrücken'. Mail a post card from there, the ship is an official marine post office. *Open daily 10am–6pm| Entrance fee 3 euros | Landungsbrücken | www.rickmer-rickmers.info | S-/U-Bahn Landungsbrücken*

SPEICHER-STADT AND HAFENCITY

> The way the people of Hamburg have produced an entire district from scratch – or better, wrested it from the Elbe – is astonishing. Only a few years ago, this was the site of the free port; sheds and cranes stood where the first inhabitants of this area now look down on the Elbe from their loft apartments. It is a mere 800 metres (½ ml.) to Rathausmarkt but a trip to the Hafencity (Harbour City) and the Speicherstadt (Warehouse District) is a real adventure for many locals. There is no more exciting place in the city, although it is still really an enormous building site. There were similarly radical building activities here once before: in order to build the warehouses at the end of the 19th century, thousands of people were forced to leave their homes. The magnificent brick ensemble is one of the Hanseatic city's gems. Maybe, it will soon be included on UNESCO's World Heritage list. Deservedly so! The most important tip: walk! The Emigrant Museum *Ballinstadt* (see p. 54) is a new attraction in the multi-cultural district of Veddel.

■ DEICHTORHALLEN [123 F5]

This used to be the meeting place of the market women from the surrounding area, as they kept their vegetables fresh in underground cellars here. Today, that is where cars park and, above ground, art aficionados and photography fans get together. The F. C. Gundlach Collection has found a worthy home in the South Hall, along with the photo archive of the 'Spiegel' news magazine. Contemporary art is displayed opposite this in the North Hall. It is only a ten-minute walk to the main railway station along

Where there was once fruit and vegetables there is now art and photography: the Deichtorhallen

SIGHTSEEING

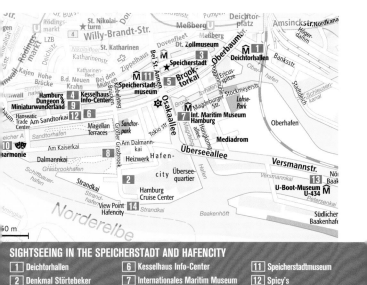

SIGHTSEEING IN THE SPEICHERSTADT AND HAFENCITY

1. Deichtorhallen
2. Denkmal Störtebeker
3. Dialog im Dunkeln
4. Hamburg Dungeon
5. HHLA-Zentrale, St. Annen 1
6. Kesselhaus Info-Center
7. Internationales Maritim Museum
8. Magellan und Marco Polo Terrassen
9. Miniaturwunderland
10. Neue Elbphilharmonie
11. Speicherstadtmuseum
12. Spicy's
13. U-Boot 434
14. View Point Hafencity

the so-called 'art mile': galleries, the art society and the Academy of Arts have all settled here without being able to make the public aware of the fact. The doors are often closed. You can find a lovely souvenir shop in the 'Abflugstelle' (Departure Lounge) of the hot-air balloon operation. The *Fillet of Soul* restaurant in the Deichtorhallen is one of the city's hot spots. *Tues–Sun 11am–6pm | Entrance fee 7 euros | Deichtorstr. 1–2 | www.deichtorhallen.de | U1, Steinstrasse*

2 DENKMAL STÖRTEBEKER [123 D6]

It is said that, shortly before his death, Klaus Störtebeker made a deal with his executioner: all of the fellow prisoners he walked past – headless – were

to come free. There are many legends dealing with the famous pirate who wreaked havoc in the Baltic Sea and Elbe in the 14th century. The memorial stood, unnoticed, near Brooktor (Brook Gate) for many years. It had to make room for the construction of the 'Harbour City' and its final resting place has not yet been determined. *Grosser Grasbrook | Metrobus 6, Am Dalmannkai*

3 DIALOG IM DUNKELN [123 E5]

What does a letter box feel like and how does one recognize the end of the pavement? The blind and partially sighted know that. Here, all visitors walk in total darkness – an enlightening experience. The financial survival of this especially worthwhile institution is permanently in danger. So: go there and support it! However, you do have to make an appointment and the tour lasts about one hour. *Tues–Fri 9 am–5 pm, Sat/Sun 11 am–5 pm | Tickets 14 euros |*

tors sometimes make the performance unintentionally more comical than frightening. *Open every day 11 am–6 pm | Entrance fee 16.50 euros | Kehrwieder 2 | Tel. 36 00 55 22 | www.hamburgdungeon.com | Metrobus 3, 6, Auf dem Sande*

Bold vision of the city of tomorrow: model of the 'Harbour City' in the Kesselhaus Info Centre

Alter Wandrahm 4 | Tel. 0700/44 33 20 00 | www.dialog-im-dunkeln. de | U1, Messberg

■4 HAMBURG DUNGEON [122 C6]

Here you will find a kind of modern ghost train dealing with the history of Hamburg: the Elbe flood, the Great Fire, the cholera epidemic – none of the catastrophes is left out. It is pretty drastic and definitely not for children under 10 even though the amateur ac-

■5 HHLA ZENTRALE, ST. ANNEN 1 [123 E6]

Towers, battlements, oriels: the building is more reminiscent of a fairy-tale castle than a company headquarters. This is the home of the HHLA – the Hamburg Harbour and Logistics Company. The Warehouse district, Altenwerder Container Harbour, Burchardkai and many other properties belonged to this organization which was founded by the city in

1885. The public was in uproar when the Hamburg Senate considered – for a short time – flogging off this original Hamburg institution to the German Railways. Now, a partial public offering is planned. If you ask the porter politely, he might let you into the roofed inner courtyard. *St. Annen 11 | Metrobus 3, 6, St. Annen*

6 KESSELHAUS INFO CENTRE [123 D6]

This is the ideal place to start your tour through the Warehouse district and 'Harbour City'. There is an 8×4-m^2 (26×13-ft.) model of the city in the former electricity works in the Warehouse district. 'Harbour City' will increase the area of Hamburg's inner city by 40 percent (!). More than 1.8 million square metres (0,7 square miles) of gross floor space – including 5,500 apartments, a school, a university, a science centre, etc., etc., etc. – will be created. The Boiler House provides a great deal of information, interactive frippery for young people and a café with delicious snacks. Free tours of the 'Harbour City' start here every Saturday at 3 *pm*. *Tues–Sun 10 am–6 pm | Am Sandtorkai 30 | Tel. 36901799 | www.hafencity.de*

On seven weekends in July and August, the square in front of the Info Centre becomes Hamburg's most beautiful open-air theatre where *Hamburger Jedermann* is performed. Death makes his entrance in a rowing boat and Everyman is a typical Hamburg 'money-bag' – a great production. Book in time! *Tickets 16–48 euros | Tel. 3696237 | www.hamburger-jedermann.de | Metrobus 3, 6, Auf dem Sande*

7 INTERNATIONALES MARITIM MUSEUM [123 E6]

In 1879, the B Silo was constructed on the Magdeburg Harbour. The brick colossus soon proved to be useless. At the beginning of 2008, the Hamburg International Maritime Museum opened its doors in the lavishly renovated building. The enormous collection was donated by Peter Tamm, the former head of the Springer publishing house. Critics feel the maritime aficionado's collection is too martial as there are so many warships. They are also annoyed that Hamburg financed this private museum with several million euros. However, the museum is the largest of its kind worldwide – a real superlative! *Metrobus 3, 6, Bei St. Annen*

8 MAGELLAN UND MARCO POLO TERRASSEN [137 D6]

When skaters discovered that the generously laid-out Magellan Terrace on Sandtorhafen and Marco Polo Terrace on Grasbrookhafen had perfect down hill slopes immediately after the opening, horrible little iron obstacles were put in. Now everything is peaceful and tidy. Is this the way to make the 'Harbour City' a lively new district? After the initial euphoria, scepticism is making itself felt: what is the use of having chic houses and squares when real life is excluded? But maybe a few ice-cream vendors will be allowed to set themselves up or, even better, mulled wine sellers. A brisk breeze usually blows through the 'Harbour City' and it is quite chilly most of the time. Don't forget your jacket! *Grosser Grasbrook | Metrobus 6, Am Dalmannkai*

9 MINIATUR-WUNDERLAND ⭐ [122 C6]

One superlative after the other – this time, justified! There is only one way to describe what the Braun brothers, along with their father and staff, have created in the Warehouse district: a great experience for the whole family. Interested in statistics? 12 km (7½ mls.) of tracks, 13,000 wagons, 200,000 figures, 3,500 houses ... The largest model railway in the world is run by 64 computers – and the enthusiasm of the team. The Alps were copied as well as the Grand Canyon, a football match between the rival local teams HSV and FC St. Pauli, the Kohlbrand Bridge and Las Vegas. A new Transrapid track is under construction. The four-millionth visitor was welcomed at the beginning of 2007. The best time to make a visit is in the early evening; the internet site provides up-to-date information on how long one currently has to wait. Another tip: take a tour behind the scenes. *Mon–Fri 9.30am–6pm, Tues 9.30am–9pm, Sat/Sun 8.30am–9pm (often open longer) | Entrance fee 10 euros | Kehrwieder 2 | Tel. 300 68 00 | www.miniatur-wunderland.de | Metrobus 3, 6, Auf dem Sande*

10 NEUE ELBPHILHARMONIE HAMBURG [136 C6]

The foundation which was called into life specifically for this purpose collected 64 million euros from private donators in just a few months to finance Hamburg's future symbol – usually called the Concert House. The picture of the wavy, futuristic glass palace on the former cacao silo

B, planned by the Swiss architects Herzog & de Meuron, can be seen on every street corner. What if the costs have risen from 186 to 241 million euros? Peanuts! No half measures in this case! What would the silo's builder Werner Kallmorgen think about this? The Hamburg architect was a representative of clear, purist lines and cube-like buildings just like the massive block of bricks where cars will soon park. The foundation stone was laid on 2 April, 2007, and the first visitors are expected in 2010. *Sandtorhöft | Metrobus 3, 6, Auf dem Sande*

11 SPEICHERSTADTMUSEUM [123 E6]

People like Henning Rademacher are those who keep the old Warehouse district alive. The harbour fan defends, with great commitment and smart ideas, the beautiful old museum warehouse against luxurious refurbishment plans. It is worthwhile going up to the third floor: here you can find out what the dockworkers used to do and where the electricity for the warehouse cranes came from (from what is today the Info Center in the boiler house). The *Kaffeklappe* offers small snacks. *Tues–Sun 10am–5pm, in summer Sat/Sun to 6pm | Entrance fee 3 euros | St. Annenufer 2 | Tel. 32 11 91 | www.speicherstadtmuseum.de | Metrobus 3, 6, Bei St. Annen*

12 SPICY'S [136 C6]

Another example of genuine enthusiasm: There was not much up when Viola Vierk moved to the warehouse district with her spice museum in 1993 – today, the house has become a long-established institution. You can poke around to your heart's content, sniff and taste or take part in one of the very special city tours – for example, with the historically costumed

13 U-BOOT 434 [137 E6]

It is a bit eerie, but very real: the original Russian submarine which you can visit at the somewhat remote Versmannkai is 92 metres (300 ft.) long. It

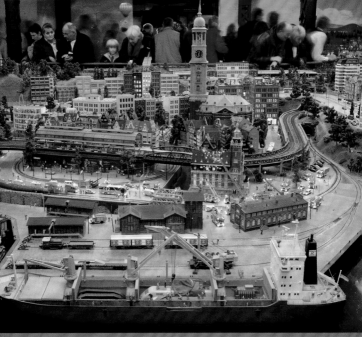

With an eye for detail: Hamburg's city centre in the Miniaturwunderland

night watchman Volker Roggenkamp. *Tues–Sun 10am–5pm | Entrance fee 3 euros | Am Sandtorkai 32 | Tel. 36 79 89 | www.spicys.de | Tours March to Sept, most Saturdays at 8.30pm | Meeting point: Baumwall underground station, Kehrwiederspitze exit | Tickets, incl. museum entrance 13 euros | Metrobus 3, 6, Auf dem Sande*

is included in some city tours. *April–Oct, Mon–Thurs 10am–6pm, Fri–Sun 9am–7pm, Nov to March, open every day 10am–6pm | Entrance fee 8 euros | Versmannstr. 23c | www.U-434.de*

14 HAFENCITY VIEW POINT ★ ☀ [136 C6]

At the moment, this is definitely one of the most exciting lookout points in the city! In the coming years, the mobile tower will be set up wherever there is something to be seen. Plans and maps can be found all over 'Harbour City' so you will be able to find the conspicuous, orange-coloured, contraption quickly. You might find yourself looking down into gigantic shafts – that is where the new U4 underground line is being built; one of 'Harbour City's' most disputed, immensely expensive, prestige projects. Or, giant piles of sand will spread out in front of you. One of the project's major logistic problems is finding a rational way of getting rid of them all. *Grosser Grasbrook | Metrobus 6, Am Dalmannkai*

Mobile tower: Hafencity View Point

SIGHTSEEING ALONG THE ELBE

1 Altonaer Balkon
2 Altonaer Museum
3 Altonaer Rathaus

ALONG THE ELBE FROM ALTONA TO TEUFELSBRÜCK

> Hamburg is one of the greenest cities in Germany. And precisely here, in the west of the city, you can find out why it is that way. One beautiful park leads into the next with villas and mansions – and, of course, the world famous Elbchaussee avenue – between them. Not only the upper class lives here. Many quite normal families still live in Övelgönne; they are the heirs of the captains and pilots who built these

SIGHTSEEING

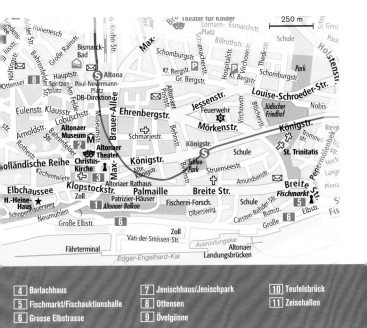

4 Barlachhaus		**7** Jenischhaus/Jenischpark		**10** Teufelsbrück
5 Fischmarkt/Fischauktionshalle		**8** Ottensen		**11** Zeisehallen
6 Grosse Elbstrasse		**9** Övelgönne		

charming houses on the Elbe. Ottensen also offers an attractive alternative programme: narrow streets, workers' houses, inns, many, many shops and a magnificent cinema tempt you to make an extended shopping spree well into the evening. Make a detour to the Altonaer Museum. And, if you fall out of bed early on Sunday morning: the fish market opens at 5 am in summer.

1 ALTONAER BALKON ☀ [135 E5]

This is a magnificent vantage point and a favourite meeting place for boules players and grill fans whenever the sun shines. The Köhlbrand Bridge spans the Köhlbrand shipping lane 54 metres (177 ft.) above the

water; the cable-stayed bridge is 500 metres (⅓ mls.) long – a technical masterpiece. The Altona Balcony is a good place to begin a stroll. To the right, you can walk along the Elbe to Wedel in a couple of hours and, to the left, you can make your way into the city. The 23 km (20 mls.)-long Elbhöhenweg makes all of this possible (not always sign-posted). *Palmaille/Klopstockplatz | Bus and S-Bahn station Altona*

2 ALTONAER MUSEUM [135 E5]

This is a charming building with barges, old fish cutters and figureheads. All this, along with North German landscape paintings from the 18th century to modern times.

Reconstruction and new concepts have brought a breath of fresh air into the old halls. An original, small cottage from the Altes Land was transferred to the museum and is now the site of the café. *Tues–Sun 10am– 6pm, Thurs 10am–9pm | Entrance fee 6 euros | Museumsstr. 23 | Tel. 428 11 35 82 | Bus and S-Bahn station Altona*

3 ALTONAER RATHAUS [135 E5]

This Danish suburb was once 'much too close' (all zu nah = Altona) to Hamburg. For centuries, this was the home of many religious refugees – the street names 'Grosse and Kleine Freiheit' (Greater and Lesser Freedom) remind one of this. In 1864,

Fischmarkt: always straight off the cutter

Altona became a part of Prussia. Between 1896 and 1898, the old train station was converted into a magnificent, white town hall with an equestrian statue of William I. Today, it is one of the most popular registry offices in the city. Incidentally, Altona was only incorporated into Hamburg in 1937 through the so-called 'Greater Hamburg law'. *Bus and S-Bahn station Altona*

4 BARLACHHAUS [133 F4]

This is probably one of the most beautiful small museums in Hamburg. Werner Kallmorgen's modest building in the centre of Jenisch Park is noteworthy for its clear lines. It now houses the magnificent collection of the Hamburg patron (and former tobacco king) Hermann F. Reemtsma. The sculptor Ernst Barlach was ostracized and persecuted by the Nazis. Reemtsma was not put off by this and continued to give him commissions. *Tues–Sun 11am–6pm | Entrance fee 5 euros | Baron-Voght-Str. 50a | Tel. 82 60 85 | www.barlach-haus.de | Bus 115, Hochrad*

5 FISCHMARKT/ FISCHAUKTIONSHALLE [135 F5]

It is said that some people in Hamburg have never visited the fish market; for others it is the ritual end to their parties or pub crawls. To be precise: this Sunday razzmatazz is nothing for those easily shocked. What the banana and eel sellers have to say is pretty direct and the hustle and bustle of tens of thousands of visitors at 6am is often overwhelming. In spite of all this: you should try it at least once. You won't find much fish these

SIGHTSEEING

Stately interior: the Jenischhaus

days – instead, big boats of green plants for 5 euros also make a nice souvenir. *(April–Oct 5–9.30am; Nov–March 7–9.30am).* The best thing to get your stomach back in order is have brunch in the *Fischauktionshalle* which was constructed by the Altona merchants in 1895 to be a 'cathedral to fish'. *Bus 112, Fischmarkt*

6 GROSSE ELBSTRASSE [135 D–F5–6]
Only a few years ago, streetwalking gave this road a bad reputation. To-day, with a series of new construc-tions, the Grosse Elbstrasse has been reborn as a 'row of pearls on the banks of the Elbe'. Start your stroll at the Fish Market. You can have a quick fish snack or a chic luncheon. The new beach clubs are located at the former cruiser terminal. The Dockland is the most spectacular building in the city; it was built in

2005 by Hadi Teherani. Go up to the 'commando bridge' – the roof. This is allowed and the view is sensational. *S1, 3, Königstrasse | Bus 112, 383, various stops*

7 JENISCHHAUS/ JENISCHPARK ⭐ [133 F4-5]
At an early stage, the western section of Hamburg became the preferred dis-trict of well-to-do merchants. Jenisch House is one of the most beautiful, English style, mansions from that time. Even Prussia's leading architect Karl Friedrich Schinkel was involved in the planning. The living rooms have been preserved in their original state and, today, form the core of the Museum of Art and Culture on the Elbe. *Tues–Sun 11am–6pm | En-trance fee 5 euros | Entrance with the neighbouring Barlach House 7 euros | Baron-Voght-Str. 50a | Tel. 828790 | Bus 115, Hochrad*

The park of the same name was also laid out in the English style. Baron Caspar Voght developed the huge area as an agricultural model estate around 1800 and had the magnificent park established at the same time. A lovely stroll takes you from the Teufelsbrück jetty to the New Botanical Gardens at the Klein Flottbek S-Bahn station.

8 OTTENSEN [135 D–E4–5]
This is a really colourful place. Punks hang around *Spritzenplatz*, organic food shops have found their home in the *Mercado* shopping centre and all of this is interspersed with fashion boutiques, jacket potato joints, Turkish snack bars and trendy pubs. For years, real estate agents have failed in their attempts to standardize this engaging

muddle to create boring new housing for yuppies. *Bus and S-Bahn station Altona*

9 ÖVELGÖNNE ⭐ [134 B–C 5–6]

Along with Blankenese, this is the spot most sought after by locals looking for some sun at the weekend. The picturesque row of old captains' and ship-pilots' houses on the banks of the Elbe is only a few hundred metres long. If you want to live here, you probably have to marry into one of the families – tradition is trumps, as is discretion: don't be caught pressing your nose too closely to the window panes! You will find wonderful old ships in the Övelgönne Museum and an old Hadag steamer has been converted into a café. Don't be afraid to speak to the people working away there – they enjoy it. *(Entrance free | www.museumshafen-oevelgoenne.de).*

The ☼ *café* on the roof of the Augustinum old people's home in the former cooling tower is open on Saturday and Sunday between 3 and 5 pm. The view is really worthwhile! A walk from here to Teufelsbrück will take around 1½ hours. *Bus 112 Neumühlen*

10 TEUFELSBRÜCK/ ELBCHAUSSEE [133 F5]

The former sovereign once sold this piece of land named 'Duwels Bomgarde' to a citizen of Hamburg. 'Düwels ok' is a Low German curse meaning 'the devil, too'. This wooded area with its marshy low-lying areas near Flottbek, was considered a bit eerie. Today, it is considered devilishly beautiful. The Teufelsbrück jetty is located at about the middle of Hamburg's most famous avenue – the Elbchaussee. In olden days, one

> BOOKS & FILMS
The flair of Hamburg on paper and on the screen

> **Hamburg: Architecture & Design** – This photographic guide of Hamburg by Christian Datz and Christof Kullmann (2006) will inspire a visit to one or two of the many stunning buildings going up in the city.

> **The Beatles In Hamburg: Photographs 1961** – Jurgen Vollmer recorded the young and completely unknown teenage band from Liverpool during their two-month gig in Hamburg in 1961, in their black leather jackets, pointed shoes and Elvis quiffs. Nostalgic stuff.

> **Inferno: The Fiery Destruction of Hamburg, 1943** – Keith Lowe

describes the 10-day period in July 1943 when British and American bombers dropped more than 9,000 tons of bombs on the German port city of Hamburg in powerful, sometimes sickening detail. Utilizing letters, diaries, and military reports from both Allied and German sources, he shows how vast areas of the city were obliterated by the bomb blasts.

> **Tomorrow Never Dies** – A certain gentleman called James Bond (alias Pierce Brosnan) paid homage to Hamburg in this film (1997): lovely views of the city as a film set for this action-packed thriller.

went by horse and carriage on an outing to the 'Café zum Bäcker'; today, a convertible is preferred and one drinks one's espresso on the terrace of the famous *Hotel Louis C. Jacob* (see pp. 60, 90). The poet Detlev von Liliencron once described the Elbchaussee as the most beautiful street on earth. However, recently Hamburg's top

the other side of the Elbe was completely booked out when the A380 landed for the first time! *Schnellbus 36, Metrobus 21, Bus 286, Hadagfähre 64, Teufelsbrück Landing*

11 ZEISEHALLEN [135 D4] Insider Tip

The former workshops of the Zeise ship propeller factory were converted

The steam ice-breaker 'Stettin' is one of the treasures in Övelgönne's harbour museum

address has been faced with a bitter image loss. The traffic – especially at the weekend with thousands of day-trippers – is terrible. In addition, uniform blocks of flats were thrown up in the old parks; some ugly, some pretentious, some both. And then came the Airbus – now the owners look at a runway from their expensive balconies. How annoying! But the tourists like it: the Hotel Jacob on

into a modern cultural centre with a cinema, galleries and restaurants as early as in 1988; at the time, this was a real novelty and served as a model for many similar projects in Hamburg. If you are interested in these things, go to the Otto-von-Bahren-Park. The enormous gasworks complex has been transformed (and that beautifully). *Friedensallee | Bus and S-Bahn station Altona*

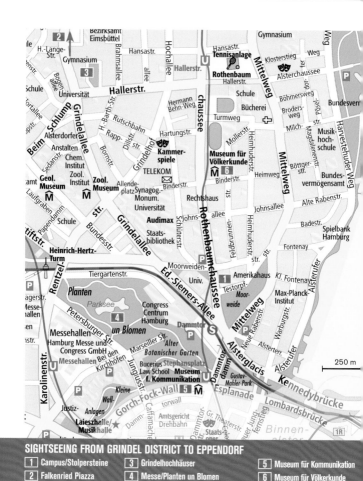

FROM GRINDEL DISTRICT TO EPPENDORF

> The districts described here lie on the west bank of the Alster. The green strip on the former ramparts, Planten un Blomen, is the green lung of Hamburg's city centre. You can have a quick beer with promising university students, get acquainted with foreign culture at the Museum of Ethnology, admire the Grindel skyscrapers as a part of Hamburg's building history or have a glass

of prosecco at one of the fashionable Italian bars in chic Eppendorf.

1 CAMPUS/STOLPERSTEINE [136 C2]

The University of Hamburg is located in the Grindel district. Forty thousand students enliven the inns and squares. Here, you can also find Germany's oldest repertoire cinema and many lovely old town houses. More than 30,000 Jews lived in Hamburg before the Second World War – one third of them in the Grindel district. The main synagogue was located on Bornplatz. It and many others in the district were destroyed by fire on the 'Night of Broken Glass' on 9 November 1938 and Jewish life in Grindel was eradicated, piece by piece. Be careful of the Stolpersteine (stumbling blocks), small, brass squares inserted into the pavement in front of the houses. They are in remembrance of those deported. Hamburg's most famous chief rabbi Joseph Carlebach lived at Hallerstrasse 76 until his deportation. *Grindelhof/Schlüterstr. | Metrobus 4, 5, Grindelhof | U1, Hallerstrasse*

2 FALKENRIED PIAZZA [128 B6] *Insider Tip*

Piazza? It sounds chic – just as chic as the apartments which were built on the site of an old tram terminus. Old and new have been combined prettily; there are inns and shops and even the old post office was moved. A successful example of urban planning and the Isebek Canal, a nice place to catch your breath, is nearby. Some old workers' houses still stand between Löwenstrasse and Falkenried. The alternative flair of their

The Stolpersteine are a reminder of the Jews from the Grindel district who were deported

common gardens and renters' action groups makes them quite special! *U3, Hoheluftbrücke, Eppendorfer Baum*

3 GRINDELHOCHHÄUSER [136 B–C1]
These were a real sensation: Hamburg's first post-war skyscrapers. Each of the twelve slender housing blocks is 200m (650ft.) long – the 'reincarnation of the buried ideals of the 1920s' is how they are described in the architecture lexicon. There is even still a paternoster lift in the district office *(Grindelberg 66)*. *Metrobus 5, Bezirksamt Eimsbüttel*

Insider Tip

4 MESSE/
PLANTEN UN BLOMEN [122 B–C1]
'Plants and Flowers' is the English translation of the name of Hamburg's green lung which is located next to the Messe (fairgrounds) which have recently been spectacularly extended all the way to the television tower. In the Middle Ages, the ramparts were

used to defend the city but they were transformed into green areas after the middle of the 19th century. The greenhouses are remnants of the time when this was Hamburg's only botanical garden. The New Botanical Garden is located in Flottbek but, with its plants, lakes, Japanese garden, miniature golf and trampoline area, Planten un Blomen still has a lot to offer. It is wonderful to be able to rest on the wooden chairs in summer. There is a large ice-skating rink behind the Hamburg Museum (in summer, for in-line skaters); there are fantastic playgrounds scattered throughout the park – the best (with pony rides in summer and a lot of ponds to get good and dirty in) is located at the corner of Marseiller Strasse and St. Petersburger Strasse. *May–Sep, Open every day 7am–11pm, Oct–April 7am–8pm | www.plantenun blomen.hamburg.de | U1, Stephansplatz | U2, Messehallen*

> BLOGS & PODCASTS
Interesting weblogs and files on the Internet

> There are a number of blogs and podcasts in English. Take a look at some of the following or brush up you German by reading the others!

> http://www.blogcatalog.com/ blogs/visit-hamburg.html – A blog about Hamburg, its sights, hotels, restaurants, museums and other interesting things to do when travelling to Hamburg. Serious comments regularly updated.

> www.tventy.de – Ultra short films, podcasts and weblogs can be found on this internet site, which has a direct link to the 'Hamburger Morgenpost', Hamburg's second most important daily newspaper.

> http://www.zimbio.com/Hamburg – A community portal about Hamburg with blogs, videos and photos.

> www.hamburg-tonight.de – Podcasts, weblogs and news on Hamburg's night life.

MARCO POLO does not take any responsbility for the contents of the blogs & podcasts

SIGHTSEEING

5 MUSEUM FÜR KOMMUNIKATION [122 C2]

Everything about the history of communications – from the tideland post runners to the internet. This institution belongs to the Post's Museum Foundation and is appropriately located in the old telegraph office built

building, constructed between 1907 and 1910, is imposing. The massive entrance hall impresses with its Jugendstil ornamentation. The somewhat old-fashioned exhibition concept is being modernized room by room. The Egyptian exhibition has become really stunning: Be careful, you are go-

An institution in Hamburg is being spruced up: the Museum für Völkerkunde

in 1882. Its many interactive stations make it particularly suitable for children; they can even send pneumatic dispatch letters themselves. *Tues–Fri 9–17, Sat/Sun 10 am–6 pm | Entrance fee 3.50 euros | Gorch-Fock-Wall 1 | Tel. 357 63 60 | U 1, Stephansplatz*

6 MUSEUM FÜR VÖLKERKUNDE [136 C2]

This is one of the largest ethnological collections in Germany; even the

ing down into a pyramid! The treasures of the Andes have also been given a new presentation. There are usually interesting special exhibitions as well and the museum gets incredibly crowded when there is an Easter or Christmas market. *Tues–Sun 10 am–6 pm, Thurs 10 am to 9 pm | Entrance fee 5 euros (extra fee for special exhibitions) | Tel. 01805/30 88 88 | www.voelker kundemuseum.com | Rothenbaum- chaussee 64 | U 1, Hallerstrasse*

ALSO WORTH A VISIT

BALLINSTADT   [141 D3]

The new Emigration Museum on the Vedde brings back memories of the 5 million people who left Hamburg between 1901 and 1914 for the New World. It was named after the ship owner Albert Ballin who had terminals for the emigrants constructed here. The museum cost 12 million euros and is a joint venture between the City of Hamburg and a private operator. It remains to be seen if it can match the great expectations expressed by Ole von Beust in his inaugural speech in July 2007. The loveliest way to get to the museum is to take the launch from the Landungsbrücken (Bridge 10) to the Ballinstadt pier. *Ticket approx. 5 euros (stops at several stations in the harbour) | Info: Tel. 31 22 88 | www.maritime-circle-line.de | Museum: Open every day 10 am–5 pm | Entrance fee 9.80 euros | www.ballinstadt.de | S3, 31 Veddel-Ballinstadt*

Insider Tip 50ER-SCHUPPEN   [141 D3]

The Harbour Museum – with a floating crane, dredges and other old work ships – is under construction here. There is an exhibition on harbour work in the shed. You look directly across at 'Harbour City' from the point of the quay – it seems just a stone's throw away. *Easter to Oct Tues–Fri 2–6 pm, Sat/Sun 10 am–6 pm | Entrance fee 3 euros | Australia-strasse | www.museum-der-arbeit.de | S Bahn Veddel, dann Fußweg*

HSH NORDBANK ARENA/ HSV MUSEUM   [126 B–C5]

You can get a good idea of the ups and downs of real fans in the HSV Museum and you can also book a tour of the stadium. *Open every day 10 am–8 pm | Entrance fee 6 euros | Tours at varying times | Sylvester-allee 7 | Tel. 41 55 15 50 | www.hsv-museum. de | Shuttle bus from S-Bahn station Stellingen, only on event days*

JARRESTADT   [129 F5]

In 1909, Fritz Schumacher became Hamburg's building director. In the years to follow, the then 39-year-old made a greater impact on the cityscape than any other person. Far-sighted, he planned for the need of millions of people and built the model estate Jarrestadt between 1927 and 1930. It is still a very popular residential area. It was partially destroyed in the War but was skilfully reconstructed by 1974. If you want to find out more, take a tour with the A-Tour's architecture experts. *(Group tours, only with reservation | Tel. 23 93 97 17 | www.a-tour.de). Between Jarrestr., Wiesendamm and Goldbekufer | Bus 172, Jarrestrasse*

MUSEUM DER ARBEIT   [130 B5]

Participation is what makes this labour museum so special: on the premises of the former 'New York Hamburg Rubber Goods Company' you (and your children) can active involve yourselves – in a printing shop, for example. *(Mon 6–9 pm). You can reach the museum by ship from the Jungfernstieg (End of March–end of Oct Sat/Sun four times from Jung-fernstieg | single trip 6.50 euros |*

Tel. 3574240). Mon 1–9pm, Tues to Sat 10am–5pm, Sun 10am–6pm | Entrance fee 4 euros | Wiesendamm 3 | Tel. 4281330 | www.museum-der-arbeit.de | S-/U-Bahn Barmbek

OHLSDORFER
FRIEDHOF ⭐   [124–125 C–F 4–5]

The largest park cemetery in the world is much more than a resting place for Hamburg's dead – it is also an excursion destination. The benches under the big old trees are perfect for pondering over the sense of our worldly existence. The *Crematorium (Talstr. | near the main entrance)* built by Fritz Schumacher between 1930 and 1932

by Hugo Lederer in Ohlsdorf Cemetery

is architecturally outstanding. One year later, Hamburg's building director was booted out by the Nazis. Many prominent Germans have found their final resting place here. With 200,000 graves and an area of 400 hectares, there is plenty to see. There is an information centre, a small museum and you can download tips for tours from the internet. *April–Oct open every day 8am–9pm, Nov–March 8am–6pm | Main entrance Fuhlsbütteler Str. 756 | www.friedhof-hamburg.de | S-/U-Bahnhof Ohlsdorf*

STADTPARK/PLANETARIUM   [129 E4]

The Stadtpark (city park) was also developed by Fritz Schumacher who planned the grounds with military precision. The intention was to create an 'open-air home for the people' out of the former hunting estate of the big landowner Adolf Sierich. It has remained that to this day: on Sundays, leisure-time sports enthusiasts get together on the large meadow, there is a beer garden, an open air pool, an enormous playground and, of course, the *Planetarium*. Here, you can find out anything you want to know to be able to explain the starry skies of Turkey to your children, for example, as well as many other things; after all, it is one of the most modern planetariums in Europe. Call before you come, it is often booked out. *Ticket office and observation platform Tues–Sun from 9am, different closing times | as many as ten shows daily | tickets from 7.50 euros | Plattform 1 euro | Hindenburgstr. 1b | Tel. 42886520 | www.planetarium-hamburg.de | U3, Borgweg | Bus 179, Stadtpark*

> PLAICE WITH A VIEW

Hamburg is a gourmet's paradise. But there are also lots of good-value pubs, too. And there is one thing above all else that makes Hamburg unbeatable: the view, the view and once more the view

> **In a nutshell: the regional cuisine includes fish from the Elbe and the North Sea, fruit from orchards in the Altes Land region and cabbage from Dithmarschen.** Fortunately people in Hamburg like to eat well. Whether champagne soup, calamaretti or Barbary duck: the menus in the better restaurants in Hamburg leave nothing to be desired. As a result, Hamburg has (quite rightly) long had the reputation of being the best (even if not the cheapest) city in Germany for eating out. A willingness to try out

new dishes and the influx of people from different corners of the world have both had an impact on Hanseatic tastes. And what really counts – surprise, surprise – is a view of the Elbe or Alster. For the privilege of dining along the river between the Fish Market and Övelgönne, for example, you will usually have to dig deeper into your pocket. Many trendy bistros opened by former pupils of gourmet chefs can often be found tucked away in side streets. Such chefs like to ex-

Above: the Rive restaurant

FOOD & DRINK

periment with whatever the market has to offer, combined with their experience and imagination. More and more emphasis is being placed on regional produce and meat from ecologically approved farms. Wander off and drop in wherever it takes your fancy. Early reservations, however, are advised for the gourmet restaurants as they are usually fully booked, especially at weekends. One tip for all those who enjoy good food: almost all top restaurants have excellent and moderately priced lunch menus. They generally close again before the evening or have a limited menu for in-between whiles. Cheaper restaurants mostly open their doors at 11 am and the kitchen stays open all the time. The same goes for the cafés and snack bars.

CAFÉS & ICE CREAM PARLOURS

ALEX IM ALSTER PAVILION ⫯ **[123 D3]**
The pavilion dates from 1953 and is the seventh to be built on this site.

CAFÉS & ICE CREAM PARLOURS

Café Wien afloat on the Inner Alster

During the Nazi period Hamburg's jazz youth gathered here and rebelled against the regime. The guests today make quite a noise too, but without the jazz. *Open every day | Jungfernstieg 54 | Tel. 350 18 70 | S-/U-Bahn Jungfernstieg*

Insider Tip **BIOKONDITOREI EICHEL** [136 A1]
Vegan cakes – do they taste of anything? They're absolutely delicious! Try the pear and cream cake (all cakes are made from produce from approved 'green' suppliers). There is always a space free during the week in this simply styled café. *Closed Mon | Osterstr. 15 | Tel. 43 19 31 51 | Bus 4, Schulweg*

BODO'S BOOTSSTEG ✹ [137 D2]
Simply the best place on the Alster. A popular place for office workers to relax during their lunchbreak. The

deckchairs and Hanseatic lifestyle Insider Tip come free with the coffee. *Open every day | Only Sat/Sun in winter | Bootssteg Rabenstrasse | Tel. 4103525 | Bus 109, Böttgerstrasse*

CAFÉ GEYER [136 A5]
A café/bistro with a terrace styled along pure clean lines, between the Reeperbahn and the harbour. A good place in the evening, but the Hein-Köllisch-Platz is especially lovely in the sun. Good breakfasts and homemade cakes. *Open every day | Hein-Köllisch-Platz 4 | Tel. 23 93 61 22 | S 1, 3, Reeperbahn*

CAFÉ KOPPEL [137 E4]
Classical music and cane sugar. The café started out catering for the alternative scene and is ideal for an unhurried breakfast or a snack lunch of carrot and orange soup. Garden open in summer. *Open every day | Koppel 66 (entrance on Lange Reihe) | Tel. 24 92 35 | Metrobus 6, Gurlittstrasse*

CAFÉ LINDTNER [128 C5]
A wooden revolving door leads into the hallowed halls of this café. Well-dressed ladies from Othmarschen are lured here by the Maharani gâteaux and the homemade chocolates. Brunch at weekends. *Open every day | Eppendorfer Landstr. 88 | Tel. 48 06 000 | U 1 and 3, Kellinghusenstrasse*

CAFÉ WIEN ⭐ ✹ ▶▶ [123 E3]
A ship in the city centre and yet miles from the hustle and bustle outside: get into the holiday spirit over a cappuccino with whipped cream and listen to the waves lapping the banks of the Inner Alster. *Open every day |*

Ballindamm, on the ship | Tel. 336342 | S-/U-Bahn Jungfernstieg

CASTING-CAFÉ CATWALK [136 A2]

Extras needed! Every Thursday between 3–5pm casting sessions for television dramas and commercials are held in the café. Drink a cup of coffee and launch your acting career. *Open every day | Weidenallee 10 b (Hinterhof) | Tel. 28051510 | Bus 115, Sternschanze*

EISBANDE [136 A3]

Luxuriously rich ice cream and 50 recipes in its repertoire, including soya milk ice cream. Tip: take a look through the darkened mirror in the shop and watch the ice cream being made. *April–Oct Open every day from 1pm | Tel. 350716530 | S-/U-Bahn Sternschanze*

EISLIEBE ▶▶ [135 D4–5]

In spring everyone in Ottensen descends on the ice cream parlour after its cinnamon and plum speciality or its creamy nougat. *Mid March–Oct Open every day from 12 noon | Bei der Reitbahn 2 | Tel. 39808482 | Bus and S-Bahn station Altona*

KNUTH [135 E4]

Popular breakfast café, an easy-going crowd and some (locally) well-known faces. Becomes a pavement café in good weather. Mind-boggling selection of magazines. *Open every day | Breakfast until 3pm | Grosse Rainstr. 21 | Tel. 46008708 | Bus and S-Bahn station Altona*

WITTHÜS TEESTUBEN [132 C4]

Idyllic Blankenese in the middle of the deer park. At teatime (with a choice of more than 20 blends of tea) try the 'Jellyfish on Sand' (cake with cherries soaked in rum). Gourmet dining in the evening. *Open every day | Closed Mon evenings | Elbchaussee 499a | Tel. 860173 | S1, Blankenese | Metrobus 1 and 22, Mühlenberg*

MARCO POLO HIGHLIGHTS

★ **Café Wien**
Indulge in a piece of cake on an Alster steamer (p. 58)

★ **Le Canard Noveau**
Ali Gungürmös conjures up spectacularly good dishes on the Elbe (p. 62)

★ **Nil**
The 'in' scene with good cooking, young and lively (p. 66)

★ **Schauermann**
Count the container ships while sitting on purple Thonet chairs (p. 67)

★ **Louis C. Jacob**
The best chef in town and a charming host (p. 60)

★ **Tafelhaus**
Exquisite cuisine, cool decor, easy-going staff (p. 63)

★ **Cölln's Restaurant**
An old legend in the city centre has been reawakened to a new life (p. 62)

★ **Fischereihafen-Restaurant**
The uncontested classic among fish restaurants (p. 63)

SNACKS

▪ SNACKS ▪

ASIA IMBISS WOK ▶▶ [136 A3]

It sizzles and spits when Thai curry is being cooked. This top snack bar will be feeding future generations around Sternschanze in years to come, too. *Open every day | Bartelsstr. 28 | Tel. 4303301 | S-/U-Bahn Sternschanze*

ESSZIMMER ▶▶ [136 A2]

Sooo tasty and sooo popular! One of the best lunches in town, and half of Eimsbüttel and the rest of Hamburg knows that. *Only open at lunchtime, closed Sun | Eppendorfer Weg 73 | Tel. 8900 6900 | Metrobus 20, 25, Fruchtallee*

➤ GOURMET RESTAURANTS
High standard, perfect settings

HAERLIN [123 D3]

This is how the true Hanseatic family loves to dine: in an elegant, first class restaurant. The cuisine has a star and has always received lots of praise. The service is – how could it be otherwise – perfect. Set menus from 70 euros. *Only open evenings, closed Sun/Mon | Neuer Jungfernstieg 9 | Tel. 34943310 | S-/U-Bahn Jungfernstieg*

LOUIS C. JACOB ★ ⚜ [133 E5]

The best chef in town is and will remain Thomas Martin. In the splendid surroundings of the hotel restaurant, this is where the elegant Hanseatic style can be seen. Wonderful terrace in the summer with a view of the Elbe. But leave room for the filling *petits fours* with your after-dinner coffee. Set menus from 86 euros. *Open every day | Elbchaussee 401 | Tel. 82255523 | Schnellbus 36, Sieberlingstr.*

POLETTO [128 C4]

Only very few women in Germany have cooked themselves a Michelin star rating – and one of them is the eternally young looking Cornelia Poletto. This distinguished restaurant in Eppendorf, kept entirely in white, is a family-run operation. Her husband, Remigio, is in head of service and stocks up the wine cellar. Set menus from 49 euros. *Closed Sun/ Mon, Sat only open evenings | Eppendorfer Landstr. 145 | Tel. 4802159 | Metrobus 20, 22, 25 Eppendorfer Markt*

SEVEN SEAS SÜLLBERG ⚜ [132 B3]

On the Süllberg in Blankenese it is not only the view that is exceptional but what Karlheinz Hauser produces in the kitchen is unbeatable, too. Have a look in the ballroom and visit the beer garden in summer high above the Elbe: there is hardly a more beautiful spot in Hamburg. Menus from 66 euros. *Closed Mon/Tues (bistro open daily) | Süllbergterrasse 12 | Tel. 8662520 | Schnellbus 48, Waseberg*

SGROI [137 E4]

The name Anna Sgroi has been synonymous with exquisite Italian cooking for ages in Hamburg, and she has been raised to the nobility with a Michelin star. This immensely likeable cook has fulfilled her dream of having her own place in St. Georg. Set menus from 58 euros. *Closed Sun/Mon, Sat only open evenings | Lange Reihe 40 | Tel. 28003930 | Metrobus 6, Gurlittstrasse*

Hanseatic elegance, culinary perfection: Louis C. Jacob on the Elbchaussee

FLEETSCHLÖSSCHEN [137 D6]

To date, this is still the best address for eating out in 'Hafencity'. An exceptional lunch is conjured up by Christian Oehler in the historic walls of the old ship-pilot's house. The maritime museum is being built opposite. *Open every day | Brooktorkai | Tel. 30393210 | Metrobus 3, 6, Bei St. Annen*

JIM BLOCK [137 E4]

If you're tempted every now and then by hamburgers and chips, then this is the place for you. Jim Block is the best address for burgers in the city. And of course, there's always a side salad. *Open daily | Kirchenallee 37 | Tel. 18067955 | S-/U-Bahn Hauptbahnhof*

KERVANSARAY [135 D4]

There are countless Turkish snack bars in Ottensen, but this little shop next to the mosque is one of the best and most friendly. The food is all homemade. *Open every day | Bahrenfelder Strasse 88 | Tel. 397067 | Bus and S-Bahn station Altona*

TEUFELS KÜCHE ▶▶ [135 D4]

Almost a 'gourmet' snack bar and from the very outset an 'in' place to be. Specialities include homemade lamb sausages, pasta and vegan dishes. *Open every day | Ottenser Hauptstrasse 47 | Tel. 39804977 | Bus and S-Bahn station Altona*

■ RESTAURANTS € € € ■

BROOK ▶▶ ☆ [123 D6]

Minimalistic interior and an amazing view over the historic warehouse district. Lars Schablinski, an apprentice of Eckart Witzigmann's and Josef Viehhauser's, now serves his creative fish dishes in his own restaurant. *Closed Sun | Bei den Mühren 91 | Tel. 37503128 | U1, Messberg*

RESTAURANTS €€€

LE CANARD NOUVEAU ⭐ 〰️ [134 C5]
Recently given a Michelin star, Ali Güngörmüs has long been one of the city's elite chefs. The wonderful building above the Elbe in which the restaurant is to be found, was built by Hamburg's 'senior' star architect Meinhard von Gerkan. *Closed Mon,* here too. *Closed Sun | Brodschrangen 1–5 | Tel. 36 41 53 | U3, Rathaus*

COX ▶▶ [137 E4]
Stylish surroundings (rose gold and mirrors on the walls) and 'new German cuisine' for the advertising and television crowd and the well-heeled

Exceptional standard with fantastic views of the Elbe – the Tafelhaus restaurant

Sat/Sun only open evenings | Elbchaussee 139 | Tel. 88 12 95 31 | Bus 115, Schnellbus 36, Hohenzollernring

CÖLLN'S RESTAURANT ⭐ [123 D5]
Holger Urmersbach is a true Hamburg figure through and through and has now brought the historical Cölln's in the city centre back to life: with its little rooms, table bells, original tiled walls and the 'Bismarck Room' – after all the Iron Chancellor used to dine

set from St. Georg. *Open daily, Sat/Sun only evenings | Lange Reihe 68 | Tel. 24 94 22 | Metrobus 6, Gurlittstr.*

DAS WEISSE HAUS [135 D6]
This little house in Övelgönne really launched the TV star-chef Tim Mälzer. Sometimes he is even here in person. Booked up weeks in advance. In the evenings there is just one gala surprise menu for all. *Closed Sun | Neumühlen 50 | Tel. 39 09 0 16 | Bus 112, Neumühlen*

FISCHEREIHAFEN-RESTAURANT ⭐ 🍴 [135 E6]

Famous faces come to dine at the Kowalke's so often that the owner, Rüdiger, is now part of the VIP crowd himself. But what is more important is that the fish dishes are exquisite. Ask for a table in the window and come on Hadag ferry no. 62 (Dockland). *Open every day | Grosse Elbstr. 143 | Tel. 381816 | Bus 383, Van-der-Smissen-Strasse*

HENSSLER & HENSSLER ▶▶ [135 E6]

Yet another bright TV chef on the banks of the Elbe. But Steffen Henssler is better looking than Tim Mälzer, isn't he? And instead of grilled sausages he serves up sushi and other more exotic dishes. However, the acoustics in the old warehouse takes some getting used to. *Closed Sun | Grosse Elbstr. 160 | Tel. 38699000 | Bus 383, Sandberg*

LUTTER & WEGNER ▶▶ 🍴 [135 F6]

Great view! But inside it's huge. It remains to be seen if the locals of Hamburg take to the fine Austrian cuisine that has been imported from the well established restaurant in Berlin … On the ground floor is a wine shop and a café. *Open every day | Grosse Elbstr. 49 | Tel. 809009000 | Bus 383, Fischauktionshalle*

MESS [122 A2]

This little cellar restaurant in the 'Karo' district has proven that Mediterranean dishes can happily be combined with *schnitzel*. Good-value midday menu. *Open daily, Sat/Sun only open evenings | Turnerstr. 9 | Tel. 434123 | U3, Feldstrasse*

RIVE ▶▶ 🍴 [135 E6]

Rive was the first restaurant on this stretch of the Elbe to become popular with the 'in' crowd. And the regulars are always amazed at the good-looking waiters and waitresses. Where do they all come from, one wonders! *Open every day | Van-der-Smissen-Strasse 1 | Tel. 3805919 | Bus 383, Fährterminal | Fähre 62, Dockland*

SALIBA [135 D3]

Hanna Saliba has taught the people of Hamburg just how tasty Syrian hors d'œuvres – called *mazza* – can be. Great atmosphere in old factory workshop. *Open every day | Leverkusenstrasse 54 | Tel. 858071 | S3, 21, Diebsteich*

SHALIMAR [122 C3]

In 1982 Mike Washington opened one of the first Indian restaurants in the Grindel district. A few years ago he moved into the city centre. Don't be put off by the uninspiring surroundings. Inside it's prettily decorated and the food is superb. *Open daily, Sat/Sun only open evenings | ABC-Strasse 46–47 (ABC-Forum) | Tel. 442484 | U2, Gänsemarkt*

TAFELHAUS ⭐ ▶▶ 🍴 [135 D6]

Excellent cuisine with excellent views of the Elbe, with the added bonus of the feel of a big city with the corresponding clientele. Discreet and chic. Christian Rach's cooking is mouth-watering, imaginative and quite simply superb. *Closed Sun, Sat only open evenings | Neumühlen 17 | Tel. 892760 | Bus 112, Lawaetzhaus*

RESTAURANTS €€

ATLAS [135 D3]

Old factory buildings seem to attract good restaurants. The good cooking is supplemented by the friendly staff. The bar offers the ideal place for that last drink of the day. *Open every day | Schützenstr. 9 a (in the Phoenixhof) | Tel. 8517810 | Metrobus 2, Bus 288, Schützenstr. (South)*

BISTRO VIENNA [136 A2]

Can't be indiscreet here – the restaurant is tiny and everyone can hear every word. Regulars know that and come here to indulge in cod or boar ragout. And something else too: everyone waits patiently for a place – no reservations are taken. *Only open evenings, closed Mon | Fettstr. 2 | Tel. 4399182 | U2, Christuskirche*

> SPECIALITIES

Savour typical Hamburg cooking!

Aalsuppe – 'eel' here is the Low German meaning for a typical soup made from left-overs, in which sweet ingredients (prunes) are mixed with savoury (bacon). If there really are bits of eel in it, then it's usually a concession to the tourists.

Alsterwasser – is what is called 'Radler' (shandy) in other parts of Germany: beer with lemonade.

Birnen, Bohnen und Speck – tastes really good even if non-locals their noses up at it. Pears, beans and bacon together with potatoes.

Franzbrötchen – tasty pastries with cinamon, the perfect treat for an upset Hamburg child.

Herbstprinz – an old type of apple from Finkenwerder where the different varieties are still propagated. To be found at the weekly markets. Just ask for regional produce.

Labskaus – looks revolting: salted meat, beetroot, pickled herring, onions and potatoes passed through the mincing machine. Served with a fried egg on top. Come on, be bold! It tastes better than it looks (photo)!

Scholle Finkenwerder Art – generally speaking, these are large fillets of plaice, coated with breadcrumbs and served with fried bacon and fried potatoes. Still one of the Sunday favourites among the locals.

Stinte – a tiny species of salmon that, for a few years now, can be found locally again in the Elbe and has advanced to be a yuppy speciality. Fried in flour, you eat the whole thing, head, tail and all. When: only available a few weeks early in the year.

A good place to take a break while walking around the Outer Alster: Bobby Reich

BOBBY REICH ✻ [129 D6]

Middle class or yuppy: for generations those out for a stroll or 'to see and be seen' have been dropping in to eat here. The superb view across the Alster has to go some way to make up for the overpriced drinks and standard fare served here. *Open every day | Fernsicht 2 | Tel. 48 78 24 | Bus 109, Harvestehuder Weg*

CAFÉ PARIS ▶▶ [123 D4]

'Tout Hambourg' had been waiting to be greeted with a "Bonsoir, Madame" or a "Bonjour, Monsieur" and to take an 'apéro' at a sound level that would do any café in Paris proud. *Open daily | Rathausstr. 4 | Tel. 32 52 77 77 | U3, Rathausmarkt*

CUNEO ▶▶ [136 A5]

Italian dishes have been served up here since 1905, just like at mamma's. That seems to appeal just as much to the media crowd as prominent faces and tourists alike. *Only open evenings, closed Sun | Davidstrasse 11 | Tel. 31 25 80 | S1, 3 Reeperbahn*

EISENSTEIN ▶▶ [135 D4]

When it first opened in the 1980s masked hooligans smashed the windows: too many yuppies in leftish Ottensen. The chicly designed house in the Zeisehallen has now long since been accepted. The charcoal oven pizzas are known as the best in town. *Open every day | Friedensallee 9 | Tel. 39 04 606 | Bus and S-Bahn station Altona*

FISCHCLUB BLANKENESE ✻ [132 B4] *Insider Tip*

The pavilion called 'Op'n Bulln' is right on the jetty in Blankenese. Shortly after opening in 2005, the landlord had to close again: a tanker rammed the pontoon. But don't worry, that only happens once in a blue moon. *Open every day | Strandweg 30a | Tel. 86 99 62 | Bus 49, Blankeneser Fähranleger*

FRIESENKELLER [123 D4]

Unpretentious, North German cooking in pleasant surroundings on Alsterfleet. Despite its location this is not a tourist rip-off. Try the seasonal dishes such as the cabbage. *Open every day | Jungfernstieg 7/Alsterarkaden | Tel. 35 76 06 20 | S-/U-Bahn Jungfernstieg*

LA MIRABELLE [136 B–C3]

The French chef is always in a good mood and the cheese trolley promises heavenly delights. Small, fine and popular. In the Grindel district.

Only open evenings, closed Sun | Bundesstr. 15 | Tel. 4107585 | Metrobus 4, 5, Staatsbibliothek

NIL ★ ▶▶ [136 A4]

What would Hamburg's gourmets do with their Nil? This has long been an address for good food in the cult surroundings of an old shoe shop. And the crew never fails to come up with new ideas. *Closed Tues | Neuer Pferdemarkt 5 | Tel. 4397823 | U3, Feldstr.*

OLD COMMERCIAL ROOM [122 B5]

The 'Michel' tolls from across the way, and photos of stars hang on the walls of this venerable restaurant. The menu is in several languages for the numerous tourists who find their way here – after all, who knows what 'Labskaus' is? Tip for a souvenir: tinned spam. *Open every day | Englische Planke 10 | Tel. 366319 | U3, Baumwall*

OPITZ [137 F3]

Nobody leaves here feeling hungry. The delicious roast potatoes are free on the side. Just as good: the 'Farmer's breakfast' with gherkins and ham. To walk it all off, follow the path around the Outer Alster. *Open every day | Mundsburger Damm 17 | Tel. 2290222 | Metrobus 6, Mundsburger Brücke*

LE PAQUEBOT ▶▶ [123 E4]

The restaurant in the Thalia Theatre is just wonderful. Crowded with interesting looking culture vultures who dine either before the performance or, if ordered in advance, in the interval. Great food and the friendliest service in the city centre. *Open*

Insider Tip

every day, Sun only open evenings depending on performances | Gerhart-Hauptmann-Platz 70 | Tel. 326519 | S-/U-Bahn Jungfernstieg

RESTAURANT ENGEL ▶▶ ⚓ [133 F5]

What a view from the Teufelsbrück moorings of ships sailing by! Christian Rach, the imaginative chef of the restaurant 'tafelhaus', keeps a beady eye on the quality of the food. Scrumptious brunches. *Open every day | Tel. 824187 | Teufelsbrück jetty, Elbchaussee | Schnellbus 36, Teufelsbrück*

Insider Tip

>LOW BUDGET

> *Paparazzi* is really the canteen for editors working for the 'Bild', 'Abendblatt' and 'Hör-Zu'. But you can also go to the first floor in the Axel-Springer Passage. All dishes for less than 6 euros. *Mon–Fri 11.30am–3pm | Caffamacherreihe 1 [122 C3] | Tel. 34 72 51 33 | U 2, Gänsemarkt*

> Special price for the jobless in *Zum kleinen Zinken* and good and cheap food for everyone (midday meal from 4.60 euros). Evenings, the 'Zinkenpfanne' cost less than 10 euros. *Open daily | Rothestr. 50 [135 D5] | Tel. 39 90 61 37 | Bus and S-Bahn station Altona*

> Curry stew, cabbage soup or beef bouillon, served with fresh bread and a cappuccino for less than 2 euros. Nobody goes hungry in the *Souperia* – or pays a fortune. *Closed Sun | Bartelsstr. 21 [136 A3] | Tel. 43099555 | S-/U-Bahn Sternschanze*

RIVERKASEMATTEN ▶▶ [136 A5]
The ancient casemate fortifications can still be seen and – thanks to the restaurateur – have been restored and not ripped out (as was originally planned). The decor takes some getting used to – lots of leather and gold-plated lavatories. East-Asian cuisine – and the terrace is perfect for people-watching. *Open every day | St.-Pauli-Fischmarkt 28 | Tel. 30060190 | S-/U-Bahn Landungsbrücken*

SAI GON [128 C4]
A good, well-established Vietnamese restaurant in the heart of Eppendorf. Discreet and friendly service. *Open every day | Martinistr. 14 | Tel. 46091009 | Metrobus 20, 22, 25, Eppendorfer Marktplatz*

SCHAUERMANN ★ ▶▶ [136 A5]
At the point where three different 'reviers' overlap, the regulars all mix in together here on and above the banks of the Elbe. That this is even possible is typical of Hamburg. The food is modern and light; the purple Thonet chairs were originally in the old television tower! *Only open evenings, closed Sun | St.-Pauli-Hafenstr. 136 | Tel. 31794660 | Bus 112, St.Pauli/Hafenstrasse*

SCHLACHTERBÖRSE [136 B3]
The central meat market is opposite and huge helpings of meat are served surrounded by photos of well-known faces on the walls. *Only open evenings, closed Sun | Kampstrasse 42 | Tel. 436543 | U3, Feldstrasse*

Nil has a trendy atmosphere and creative cooking

RESTAURANTS €

SHIAWASE   [123 D4]

The sushis served up by the Ikebana champion Yoko Higashi are not just a delight to the eye but also taste divine. Nice views of the Alster; downstairs the teas are good. *Open daily, closed Sun in winter | Jungfernstieg 7 | Tel 36099999 | S-/U-Bahn Jungfernstieg*

WEINHEXE   [123 E5]

The best place for antipasti after a visit to the Chilehaus. Lots of journalists do just that. *Closed Sat/Sun | Burchardstr. 13C | Tel. 337561 | U1, Messberg*

■ RESTAURANTS € ■

BARCELONA TAPAS   [135 E5]

Delicious devils on horseback and fried peppers (a portion of *tapas* ranges from 3–8 euros). A bit of Spanish flair can be felt in the bare high rooms. Good selection of Spanish wines. With terrace. *Closed Sun |*

Max-Brauer-Allee 12 | Tel. 38083635 | Bus 112, 115, Altonaer Rathaus

LA BOTTEGA LENTINI   [128 B5–6]

Always a popular meeting place for the chic crowd in Eppendorf who also love the bistro cooking with its Sicilian flair, the tasty wines and the great atmosphere, furnished with simple wooden benches. *Open every day, Sun only open evenings | Eppendorfer Weg 267 | Tel. 46960263 | U3, Eppendorfer Baum*

CREMON   [122 C6]

More of a wine cellar than a restaurant, but the tasty snacks act as a good blotter for the next quarter litre. In summer, guests can sit outside on the pontoon on Nikolaifleet. *Mon–Fri 11.30am–9pm, often longer in summer | Cremon 33 | Tel. 362190 | U3, Baumwall*

DANIEL WISCHER   [123 E4]

Hamburg kids are brought up with

Coffee break in the sun in the Oberhafenkantine

FOOD & DRINK

Daniel Wischer. Parents know that there will be no squabbles here: everyone seems to like the deep-fried fish. Also to take away. *Opening times same as for the shop | Spitalerstrasse 12 | Tel. 32525815 | U3, Mönckebergstrasse*

FISCHERHAUS ☘ [136 A5]
Downstairs there are wooden tables and fried fish; upstairs tablecloths and delicious plaice and a wonderful view over the Elbe. *Open every day | St.-Pauli-Fischmarkt 14 | Tel. 314053 | Bus 112, Hafentreppe*

GOLDBEKER [129 E5]
Typical fried potato bar in Winterhude, wooden tables, pavement terrace, beer and large TV screen. Not only for football fans. *Open every day | Schinkelstr. 20 | Tel. 2708064 | Metrobus 6, 25, Goldbekhaus*

JIMMY ELSASS ▶▶ [136 A2]
The best *tarte flambée* in the north of Germany is perfect for sharing – and instead of cutlery guests are given a roller cutter. Tucked away in a side street. *Open daily, only open evenings | Schäferstr. 26 | Tel. 44195965 | U2, 3, Schlump*

OBERHAFENKANTINE [123 F6]
This is where the dock workers and customs officials used to eat. Now it's in the hands of Christa Mälzer – TV star cook Tim's mum – who fries up hamburgers and schnitzel. It's a little more up-market that in the past, but she has stuck to her filter coffee rather than *latte macchiato*. *Closed Sun | Stockmeyerstr. 39 | no Tel. | U1, Messberg*

RUDOLPH MAL-EBEN [132 B3]
Bernd Rudolph is a wine dealer and one of the dinosaurs of Blankenese. To readings of Ringelnatz's comic verse he serves fried potatoes in the garden. *Only open evenings, Closed Sat/Sun | Blankeneser Landstr. 29 | Tel. 86663018 | S1, Blankenese*

SCHWEIZWEIT [135 D–E4]
This little bit of Switzerland can be found in a basement and – apart from delicious cheeses from the different cantons – guests can indulge in a genuine fondue and all sorts of Swiss specialities. *Closed Mon, Sun only open until 6pm | Grosse Rainstr. 20 | Tel. 3990700 | Bus/S-Bahn station Altona*

TH2 [129 E6]
Lots of bright colours and lots of white: this fancy bistro fits in well in chic Winterhude. The breakfasts (with 'wellness' teas) are superb. *Open daily | Mühlenkamp 59 | Tel. 2788 0088 | Metrobus 6, Goldbekplatz*

TI BREIZH [122 C6]
Pure Brittany with *crêpes* and *cider*. In summer outside on the pontoon on Nikolaifleet. Nextdoor there is a small shop with Breton specialities such as pullovers. *Sun only open lunchtime, closed Mon | Deichstrasse 39 | Tel. 37517815 | U3, Rödingsmarkt*

ZUM STECKELHÖRN [123 D6]
Long established, unpretentious restaurant, and for many office workers in the warehouse district they couldn't imagine life without this institution. *Only open at lunchtime, closed Sat/Sun | Tel. 366560 | Steckelhörn 12 | U1, Messberg*

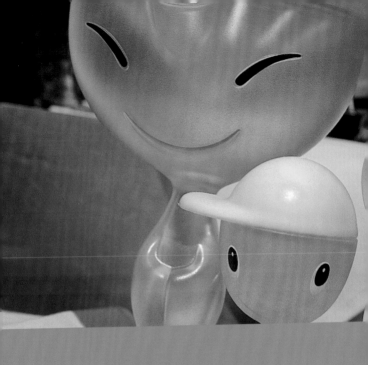

> A SAILOR'S SHIRT OR A DESIGNER DRESS?

Just dive head first into the shopper's dreamworld!

> **Around Jungfernstieg and the Gänse-markt, in the Hanse District, the Hamburger Hof and the ABC streets are all the brand names to be found on international haute couture catwalks. This is also where you will find jewellers', delicatessen shops, tailors and watchmakers.** The Neuer Wall is the top address for Hanseatic traders – but be careful, the security guards will even stop you taking photographs! Nearer the main station are the department stores and less expensive shops. The Europa Passage, with its dome, glass lifts, cafés and bistros, forms a direct link between the exquisite and the affordable. Despite the glamour of the city centre, many Hamburg citizens have stayed faithful to the shops in their district. And that is not surprising either: streets such as Eppendorfer Weg/Eppendorfer Baum, the main thoroughfare in Ottensen, or the Lange Reihe in St. Georg have everything you could possibly want. The Karolinen District has become a real eye-opener over the past

Above: Goods on display in the design temple Stilwerk

SHOPPING

few years. Once passed off as a drab and dreary area, potential stars in the shopping scene now rub shoulders all down the Marktstrasse.

Shops can now stay open around the clock, except Sundays – but there are always some exceptions. In the city centre, department stores are open until 8pm, smaller shops close earlier. Things are different on the Reeperbahn, with many shops staying open well into the night and on Sundays.

AUCTIONS

AUKTIONSHAUS SCHOPMANN [123 E4]

Germany's largest auction house deals with antiques, jewellery and works of art – for purchase or auction. You can also bring your jewellery to be valued. *Speersort 1 | U3, Mönckebergstrasse*

DELICATESSEN

ALSTERHAUS DELIKATESSEN [123 D4]

Fine food aficionados should take the trouble of seeking out the 4th floor of this luxuriously renovated shop of considerable tradition: the cheeses (all called fromages here) are simply too delicious and the wine department too extensive to be missed (850 different wines). Meet at the champagne bar for a chin wag. *Jungfernstieg 16 | S-/U-Bahn Jungfernstieg*

BONSCHELADEN [135 D4]

Insider Tip

Homemade strawberry, liquorice or ginger bonbons along with exquisite cream caramels, all made under the customers beady eye. *Closed Mon | Friedensallee 12 | Bus and S-Bahn station Altona*

CHOCO MONDE [123 D3]

Chocolate with pepperoni or Inca spices are part of the standard range on offer. Outrageously good: the drinking chocolate for that break while shopping. *Colonnaden 54 | S-/U-Bahn Jungfernstieg*

COLONNADEN TEE KONTOR [123 D3]

A realm of peace and quiet among the hustle and bustle: 350 delicious teas and bit and bobs for that perfect little gift. *Colonnaden 39 | S-/U-Bahn Jungfernstieg*

FRISCHEPARADIES
GOEDEKEN ⭐ [135 F5–6]

Fresh fish right on the Elbe, together with wine, pasta, meat and vegetables – everything to make a cook's heart beat faster. Midday snacks. *Grosse Elbstrasse 210 | Bus 383, Sandberg*

KAFFEERÖSTEREI BECKING [135 D–E3]

What a wonderful smell! You'll hardly be able to leave the shop without at least one little bag of coffee. The beans are roasted in the basement, and there

A delicacy: fresh oysters

is freshly brewed coffee for you to sample. It might be a bit off the beaten track but it is worth it, even if only for the atmosphere of this lovely old factory. *Leverkusenstrasse 54 | S3, 21, Diebsteich*

KARSTEN HAGENAH [135 D2]

Eels, oysters and crabs can be found here, complemented by salads and marinated specialities. Fish wholesalers since 1892. The fried fish in the bistro is delicious. *Mon–Fri 7am–4pm, Sat to 11.30am | Schnackenburgsallee 8 | Bus 180, Ruhrstrasse*

K. W. STÜDEMANN [136 A3]

One of the most nostalgic shops in the Schanzen district. Despite the jet-set customers of today, the locals still keep coming to this *chocolatier* for the very best marzipan, tea and coffee, as they have done for decades. *Schulterblatt 59 | Bus 115, Schulterblatt*

FURNISHINGS & CO

CINARIA [128 B6]

...oking is a lifestyle! This specialist ...mple in Eppendorf has more than ...00 articles for the kitchen. Home-...de Italian specialities in the *Cucibar. ...aßenbahnring 12 | U3, Hoheluft-...icke*

...NGEMATTENLADEN [135 B5]

...e name says it all: the hammock ...op. Net hammocks, family-sized ...nmocks, hanging chairs and – what ...kes a nice present – hammocks for ...ies. Not expensive and with com-...ent sales assistants. *Bei der Reit-...n 2 | Bus/S-Bahn station Altona*

...LWERK ⭐ [135 F5–6]

...is restored maltings on the Fisch-...rkt is home to seven floors of differ-...designer labels. Just the right ad-...ss for that rainy day to hunt out a ...fee pot from Alessi or a lamp from ...mburg's own light designer, Tobias ...au. Free crèche Sat/Sun and on open ...vs. *Grosse Elbstrasse 68 | Bus 383, ...dberg*

...SCHEREI ▶▶ [129 F5]

...ndy shopping in a former laundry: ...niture, small accessories and the clothes shop Klementine all under one roof. Tip: hang around a bit longer on Fri as there are always parties held here (until 11pm). *Jarrestr. 58 | U3, Saarlandstrasse*

HANSEATIC SPECIALITIES

BINIKOWSKI [128 C4]

Careful: collecting can be addictive. This little shop (unfortunately not on the harbourside but in Eppendorf) stocks ships in bottles of all sizes, as well as flags, lighthouse goods and captains' whistles. Onlineshop: *www. buddel.de | Lokstedter Weg 68 | Metro-bus 22, Tarpenbekstrasse*

ERNST BRENDLER [123 D5]

Specialist for marine and tropical equipment. This dignified old shop has been here for the past 126 years, and the atmosphere of the colonial days is still hanging in the air. *Grosse Johannisstr. 15 | U3, Rathausmarkt*

HANSEATIC CLASSIC [122 A6]

Blue 'Finkenwerder' fishermen's shirts and the 'Prince Heinrich' caps made popular by the former German chancellor Helmut Schmidt are always in demand. Also stocks everything needed to cope with the local weather.

MARCO POLO HIGHLIGHTS

Globetrotter
...ere buying the right trekking ...uipment turns into an adventure ...76)

Isemarkt
... longest weekly market in ...many. Out of the rain under the ...ed railway tracks (p. 74)

⭐ Stilwerk
Almost too good to buy. Designer shops in an old factory on the banks of the Elbe (p. 73)

⭐ Frischeparadies Goedeken
Fresh fish, cheese, exquisite wines – and all that centrally located on the Elbmeile (p. 72)

MARKETS

The rain hats for children in every imaginable colour are particularly lovely. *Johannisbollwerk 6 | S-/U-Bahn Landungsbrücken*

HARRY'S HAFEN BAZAR [136 A5]

Harry was a sailor who collected anything and everything from stuffed animals to African cult objects. Today it is part shop, part museum, and is run by his daughter. Great place for souvenirs. *Tues–Sun 10am–6pm | Entrance fee 2.50 euros | Erichstrasse 56 | S1, 3, Reeperbahn*

■ MARKETS ■

FLEA MARKETS

There are several flea markets in the city, but their opening times and locations vary. For up-to-date information look in the local papers or *Tel. 314071 or 5315051.*

WEEKLY MARKETS

Arguably the most attractive but undeniably the longest weekly market in Germany is the ★ Isemarkt *(Tues,* *Fri 9am–2pm):* The fruit, vegetable and cheese stall-holders spread out their wares under the stretch of tube running above ground between Hoheluftbrücke and Eppendorfer Baum (U3). A must for those with a sweet tooth is Bonbon Pingel with biscuits and liquorice for everyone to try. The market is often used as a film set. The market on the *Goldbekufer* in Winterhude is also worth visiting *(Tues, Thurs, Sat, 9am–1pm | U3, Borgweg).* Every district has its own weekly market. Times can be found in the local press *www.hamburg.de*.

And for those who can't get enough: every Weds there is an atmospheric evening market on the Spielbudenplatz *(4–11pm Reeperbahn | U3, St. Pauli).*

■ ELEGANT FASHION ■

LADAGE & OELKE [123 D4]

True Hanseatic stock most like to dress like the English: in dufflecoats, blazers, muted colours – elegant but understated. That's exactly what you'll find.

Undercover weekly market: the raised tracks provide a roof for the Isemarkt

SHOPPING

It's always been here and hopefully always will be. *Neuer Wall 11 | S-/ U-Bahn Jungfernstieg*

POLICKE   [137 F4]
There's no such thing here as 'it doesn't suit you!' Huge selection and good value for money. Rows of suits jostle for space over several floors. *Böckmannstrasse 1a | S-/U-Bahn Hauptbahnhof*

STOFFKONTOR
IM KAUFMANNSHAUS   [122 C4]
Classical evening wear, finely che-quered bed linen based on their own designs and exceptionally competent staff. *Grosse Bleichen 31 | S-/U-Bahn Jungfernstieg*

▮ TRENDY FASHION ▮
BROTHERHOOD/SISTERHOOD [136 B3–4]
Fashion for self-confident guys and girls, partly in that much-asked-for retro look. If you don't find what you want here, try the Marktstrasse. *Laeiszstrasse 15 (Ecke Marktstr.) | U3, Feldstrasse*

HERR VON EDEN   [137 E4]
Very chic clothes, very scrumptious sales staff! Everything trendy for him (and quite a lot for her, too) is stocked in this former second-hand shop, much in the style of the 1920s. *Lange Reihe 103 | Metrobus 6, Gurlittstr.*

RUNDUM   [135 D4]
This is where expectant mums feel happy. Tunics, clothes for the office and for festive occasions for all stages of a pregnancy. Hamburg is after all en-joying a baby-boom. *Ottenser Haupt-str. 61 | Bus/S-Bahn station Altona*

THOMAS I-PUNKT   [123 E4]
20 years ago this shop first became a hot tip for the fashion conscious. It still is: lots of extravagant items, lots of sensible things, and on top of that, there is always the elegant Japanese look to choose from. Enjoy a free *latte macchiato* in the conservatory on the 3rd floor. *Mönckebergstr. 21 | U3, Mönckebergstrasse*

WERKHAUS   [135 F5–6]
Scandinavian designer labels such as Tiger of Sweden or Lindeberg in this shop directly on the Elbe run by a young Dane. *Sun viewing only noon–5pm | Grosse Elbstr. 146 | Bus 383, Sandberg*

▮ MUSIC ▮
MICHELLE ▶▶   [123 E4]
In Hamburg's 'one and only' record shop, bands regularly give concerts in the window. Flyers give details about the best gigs in town. *Ger-trudenkirchhof 10 | U3, Möncke-bergstrasse*

STEINWAY   [135 D1]
The name Steinway has been linked to Hamburg since 1880. The largest piano store in northern Germany and the workshops are both in Bahrenfeld. Concerts are held in Steinway's own concert hall. Info under *www.steinway-hamburg.de*. *Rondenbarg 10 | S3, 21, Diebsteich | Bus 180, Rondenbarg*

▮ SHOES & BAGS ▮
FREITAG   [123 F4–5]
This trendy Swiss cult label has bags made of old lorry tarpaulins. The only shop in Germany. *Klosterwall 9 | S-/U-Bahn Hauptbahnhof*

SHOES & BAGS

INGA THOMAS
MODELLSCHUHE ▶▶ [122 A2]
Shoes without even the tiniest bit of leather. The young designer makes her super chic shoes using hi-tech materials and takes customers's measurements in the shop. The finished shoes are sent out by post. Not cheap, but durable. *Marktstr. 113 | U 3, Feldstr.*

SCHUH MESSMER [136 A5]
Pretty Woman eat your heart out: the heels on some shoes are a good 7½ in.! Men come here for their snakeskin ankle boots and over-knee boots are available up to size 46. Cult! *Also open Sun 2–8pm | Reeperbahn 77 | S 1, 3, Reeperbahn*

■ SPECIALIST SHOPS ■
BETHGE [128 C6]
Best quality handmade paper, leatherbound booklets, and the most exquisite wrapping paper in the whole of Germany. *Eppendorfer Baum 1 | U 1, Klosterstern*

FAHNEN FLECK [122 C4]
This shop is as much a part of Hamburg as is the Alsterhaus. Carnival costumes, fireworks and, of course, the flags of every country in the world. *Neuer Wall 57 | S-/U-Bahn Jungfernstieg*

GLOBETROTTER ★ [130 B5]
The more exotic the destination and mode of travel, the more attentive the service: this magnet for all outdoor freaks located in a bright red cube at Bahnhof Barmbek is worth the journey alone. And what is even more exciting – there is a wet room and a walk-in refrigerator for testing specialist equipment. *Wiesendamm 1 | S-/U-Bahn Barmbek*

The well-known trademark blue dominates the interior of the Nivea-Haus

ISTER PARFÜMERIE [128 C5]
ıusual scents for particularly spoilt
ses! A genuinely beautiful shop
ıich has remained in family owner-
ıp since 1888. *Eppendorfer Baum
| U1, Klosterstern*

DELLBAHNKISTE [137 E4]
ɔm highspeed trains to hand-built
ities – nothing is missing in this
lorado for model railway fans.
*ɾchenallee 25 (in the basement) |
/U-Bahn Hauptbahnhof*

VEA-HAUS [123 D3]
vea comes from Hamburg – so what
ıld be more appropriate than a
ge version of the blue tin as a sou-
nir? Or treat yourself to a massage:
ıilable from 16 euros; just drop
no reservation necessary. *Jung-
ıstieg 51 | Tel. reservations under
224740 or directly in the shop | S-/
Bahn Jungfernstieg*

PPNASE & CO [136 C2]
put a smile on anyone's face: balls
juggling, clown outfits and make-
; a comic shop with publications
m around the world can be found
ıt door. *Grindelallee 92 | Metro-
s 4, 5, Grindelhof*

HIRM & CO [123 E4]
institution in Hamburg and, on
ıy days, open longer. The perfect
vice by the Vertein family also in-
des the on-site repair of damaged
ıbrellas. *Rosenstrasse 6 | S-/U-Bahn
uptbahnhof*

EGMANN [123 D3]
one time this was Germany's only
ecialist shop for buttons; this has

since been supplemented by ladies'
clothing, scarves and other accessories.
Jungfernstieg 46 | U2, Gänsemarkt

STEIFF-GALERIE [123 F4]
Soft toys as far as the eye can see:
these much-loved animals with their
distinctive ear tags are piled up high
on the shelves. An absolute paradise
for the young and the young at heart.
*Mönckebergstr. 7 (in the Levantehaus)
| S-/U-Bahn Hauptbahnhof*

THE NEW CYCLIST [128 A–B5]
Michael Schäfer's customers come
from all over Germany. For aficionados of the pure, unadulterated aes-
thetics of bicycles. *Gärtnerstrasse
18E (in rear courtyard) | Metrobus 5,
Gärtnerstrasse*

> ALL CATS ARE GREY IN THE DARK – WHAT RUBBISH!

Hamburg's 'nice but naughty' area no. 1 is the Reeperbahn – but there is an active night-life scene in other districts in the city, too

> **Despite all predictions to the contrary – the Reeperbahn is, and will remain, the centre of Hamburg's nightlife. It is particularly crowded at the weekend.** That is when tens of thousands of punks, yuppies, bourgeois trendies and young hipsters have fun in the clubs, bars, pubs, restaurants and theatres. Those who don't like the crowd can easily avoid it – other 'in' areas are only a short walk or a couple of bus stops away. Musicians have found their meeting places around the Neuer Pferdemarkt and trends are really created – or at least seem to be – in the retro clubs. People in advertising and designers romp around the Schanzen district opposite the anarchists' stronghold Rote Flora. Things are a bit more civilized in Ottensen and St. Georg lives from its proximity to the city and the mobile gay scene. The beach clubs along the Elbe are the hot spots in summer. The city's opening hours are very liberal. Outside service is permitted until 11 pm –

Above: Grosse Freiheit, a side street off the Reeperbahn

ENTERTAINMENT

midnight at weekends. There is really no closing time – when some bars shut their doors at 5 am others are just opening

Hamburg has a lively theatre and music scene in addition to its nightlife. The Staatsoper (State Opera), Thalia Theater, and Schauspielhaus are among the top theatres in the country and there are also 60 private theatres which cover the entire gamut of styles. Premieres and musical are often sold out, especially at the weekend. And, although the people of Hamburg may make a critical audience, they also have their darlings – to be guaranteed a ticket for John Neumeier's ballet performances some fans spend the night before tickets go on sale outside the box office. So, if there is something you particularly want to see, book in advance. The dates are in the dailies, internet and special papers and tickets can be booked via the *Hamburg Tourism* hotline *(see p. 115)*.

■ BARS & TRENDY PLACES ■

If no other times are noted, the fashionable meeting places are open from 10 or 11am. They usually serve breakfast and, on Sundays, often brunch. The bars and clubs generally do not open until evening. When do they close? Most often, when the last guest leaves.

With the flair of the harbour: Au Quai Bar

AU QUAI BAR   [135 D5]

The outdoor terrace of this bar on the Elbe is phenomenal: 130 places, water spray and a view over the Elbe and the docks. The glamorous public knows that, too. *Closed Mon | Grosse Elbstrasse 145b | Tel. 38037730 | Bus 112, Elbberg*

AUREL   [135 D4]

Bar life in Ottensen. If this one is full, there are alternatives around Alma-Wartenberg-Platz. A good place to start a pub crawl. *Open every day | Bahrenfelder Str. 157 | Tel. 3902727 | Bus and S-Bahn station Altona*

BAR HAMBURG ▶▶   [123 F3]

Many celebrities: fashion designers, famous guests from the Hotel Atlantic and bankers meet in the lounges and at the bar. A tiny discreet sign at the entrance is the only indication of where to go. *Rautenbergstr. 6 | Tel. 28054880 | S-/U-Bahn Hauptbahnhof*

BAR ROSSI ▶▶   [136 A3]

'In' bar in a former spa house. If you like cool service, this is the place for you. *Max-Brauer-Allee 279 | Tel. 43254639 | Bus 115, Schulterblatt*

CHRISTIANSEN'S   [136 A6]

If the classical bar atmosphere doesn't soothe your nerves, maybe the profuse selection of whisky and rum (180 and 200 varieties respectively) will. *Pinnasberg 60 | Tel. 3172863 | S1, 3, Reeperbahn*

DIE BANK ★ ▶▶   [122 C3]

Brasserie and bar in a former bank – stunning interior and a hot-spot for the chic. *Hohe Bleichen 17 | Tel. 2380 0330 | www.diebank-brasserie.de | U2, Gänsemarkt*

DIE WELT IST SCHÖN   [136 A4]

The cool rooms of this hip bar on Pferdemarkt are dominated by coloured light and a bright atmosphere. Tip: in summer, drink your cocktails on the rooftop terrace. Good DJs. *Closed Mon | Neuer Pferdemarkt 4 | Tel. 40187888 | U3, Feldstrasse*

ENTERTAINMENT

▮ BEACH CLUBS ▮

★▶▶ When the weather plays along, the beach clubs on the banks of the Elbe are full of life. There, you will find everything from a swimming pool to fitness trainers. It is hard to decide just which club is the most chic; the number is growing all the time, also at the locations in the city centre. Hafenstrasse, Van-der-Smissen-Str., Max-Brauer-Allee. *April–Sept.*

▮ CLUBS & DISCOS ▮

ANGIE'S NIGHTCLUB ▶▶   [136 A5]

The long-standing success in the district. There is live music every evening – either with Angie's house band or invited guests. Soothing, danceable soul, funk or pop. *Thurs–Sat from 11.30pm | 8 euros | Spielbudenplatz 27 | Tel. 31778811 | www.angies-nightclub.de | S1, 3, Reeperbahn*

Insider Tip

CHINA LOUNGE ▶▶   [136 A5]

Female guests who want to bewitch the professional footballers or other celebrities go heavy on the makeup. Still the chicest club in the area. *Tues (hip-hop) and Thurs from 10pm, Fri/ Sat from 11pm | from 8 euros | Nobistor 14 | Tel. 31976622 | www. china-lounge.de | S1, 3, Reeperbahn*

FRAU HEDI/
FRAU HEDIS LANDGANG   [136 A4]

A somewhat different harbour tour. In summer the barge 'Frau Hedi' cruises around the harbour – you can chill out or dance on board. *(May–Sept, hourly from 7pm | Landungsbrücke 10). Frau Hedis Landgang (shore leave) is on Pferdemarkt; off-beat music parties are held in the tunnel-like room. Tues–Sun from 8pm | Neuer Pferdemarkt 3 | Tel. 42102823 | www.frauhedi.de | U3, Feldstrasse*

Insider Tip

GOLDEN PUDEL CLUB ▶▶   [136 A5]

The music artist Rocko Schamoni's club is the address for musicians and nightowls who want to see the sun rise over the harbour. Coffee is served upstairs during the day – if the staff is in the mood – and there is also a space for cabaret. *Open every day from 11pm | Café, irregularly from noon | Fischmarkt 27 | Tel. 3195336 | www.pudel. com | S-/ U-Bahn Landungsbrücken*

MARCO POLO HIGHLIGHTS

★ **Staatsoper/Hamburg Ballet**
Two cultural favourites of the Hanseatic city (p. 86)

★ **Die Bank**
Rush hour after shopping on a Saturday (p. 80)

★ **beach clubs**
Quite amazing: the Costa del Sol in Hamburg (p. 81)

★ **Uebel & Gefährlich**
The 'in' scene is alive and well: dancing in a former air-raid shelter (p. 84)

★ **Schmidt Theater**
Glamour, show and song of legendary status (p. 86)

★ **Thalia Theater**
The best theatre in town (p. 87)

PUBS & WINE BARS

MANDARIN KASINO/BAR ▶▶   [136 A5]
The right address for concerts, you will really work up a sweat. Dance floor, jazz, electro and funk. You can drink a cool Astra at the relaxed bar if it gets too hot for you. *Parties Fri/Sat from 10pm, concerts from 8pm | 7–10 euros | Reeperbahn 1 | Tel. 435 23 28 | www. mandarin-kasino.de | U3, St. Pauli*

TANGO BALL   [136 C2]
The locals love tango. The ball in the Museum of Ethnology is a fixed institution for those with a passion for dancing. *Thurs 9.30pm–1am | 3.50 euros | Rothenbaumchaussee 64 | Bus 34, Museum für Völkerkunde*

WAAGENBAU   [136 A3]
Off-beat area, off-beat club. This club in the Bermuda triangle underneath the Sternbrücke is particularly popular with young people. Hip-hop, electro, reggae. *Usually Mon–Thurs from 10pm, Fri/Sat from 11pm | Max-Brauer-Allee 204 | Tel. 24 42 05 09 | www.waagenbau. com | Bus 115, Sternbrücke*

◼PUBS & WINE BARS◼◼◼◼
BORCHERTS   [128 C4]
The other districts in the city are envious of Borcherts. A beautiful beer garden under old trees. Friday, with DJ; Sunday, the legendary brunch for 12 euros. *Geschwister-Scholl-Strasse 1 | Tel. 46 26 77 | Metrobus 20, 22, 25 Eppendorfer Marktplatz*

FINNEGAN'S WAKE   [123 D5]
Full-blooded Irish pub in the city and the meeting place of exiles from the

❯ SPECTATOR SPORTS
Pure ice and green lawns

When the Hamburg Freezers turn out for an ice-hockey match in the Color-Line-Arena [126 B–C5] all hell breaks loose. Sing along when Freddy Quinn barks "Come back soon, mate" through the loudspeaker when one of the players is sent off to the penalty bench. Tip: buy cheap tickets and then go up to the Skylight restaurant during the game and enjoy the match with a drink and a good view right over the fan enclosure. *Tickets from 19 euros | Season: Sept–March | Tel. 30 05 15 10 | www. hamburg-freezers.de*
A football match with FC St. Pauli is always a cult event. True fans display a skull or a brown T-shirt with 'Wir sind zweitklassig' ('We're second rate')

on it, and drink canned beer from the main sponsor Astra. The stadium at Millerntor [136 A–B4] has been a building site for ages, but that hasn't effected the atmosphere at all. *Tickets from 13 euros | Ticket hotline 01805/ 56 00 152 | www.fcstpauli.de*
And then of course there is the HSV with its chic stadium in Stellingen [126 B–C5]. But it's not any more sedate in the fan enclosure here either; the sponsor is Holstenbier. And most important thing is that this team is the only one to have been in the German league table without interruption since it started. *Tickets from 15 euros | Ticket hotline 01805/47 84 78 | www.hsv.de*

ENTERTAINMENT

shamrock isle. Guinness, British pop and football on TV mean that the atmosphere is always great – and, there is karaoke on Monday! *Mon–Thurs from 4pm, Fri–Sat from 11.30 am, Sun from noon | Börsenbrücke 4 | Tel. 374 34 33 | U 1, Messberg*

FRANK UND FREI ▶▶ [136 A3]
Design-free zone in the Schanzen district for two decades. With its wooden tables, billiards and beer it is perfectly

thirty-somethings can amuse themselves. *Open every day | Hindenburgstrasse 2 | Tel. 275054 | www.land hauswalter.de | U 3, Borgweg*

CINEMAS

ABATON [136 C2]
Hamburg's most attractive repertory cinema. Many European films and high-class American productions. After the film, the *Abaton Bistro* (with its terrace) is the ideal place to discuss

Classic bar of old: Frank und Frei in the Schanzen district

suited for a chat with your friends. In summer: there is a terrace and especially strong beer! *Open every day | Schanzenstr. 93 | Tel. 43 48 03 | S-/U-Bahn Sternschanze*

LANDHAUS WALTER [129 F4]
This is not just the only *real* beer garden in Hamburg (in the City Park) but there are also live concerts and the 'Downtown Blues Club' where the

what you have just seen. *Allende-Platz 3 | Tel. 41 32 03 20 | www.abaton. de | Metrobus 4, 5, Grindelhof*

STREITS [123 D3]
Big screen, comfortable seats: the way cinemas used to be. The perfect place to watch Hollywood productions à la *Titanic*. Charming lounge. *Jungfernstieg 38 | Tel. 34 60 51 | S-/U-Bahn Jungfernstieg*

LIVE MUSIC

ZEISE KINOS [135 D4]
The best films, but no blockbusters, are shown in the old ship propeller factory. Often full at the weekend. *Friedensallee 9 | Tel. 3908770 | Bus and S-Bahn station Altona*

■ LIVE MUSIC ■
BIRDLAND [128 A6]
This Eimsbüttel jazz club is where you can find the real thing. The jam sessions will really set your ears on fire. *Jam sessions Thurs–Sun from 9pm, June–Aug Thurs only | Gärtnerstrasse 122 | Tel. 405277 | www.jazz club-birdland.de | Metrobus 20, 25 Goebenstrasse*

>LOW BUDGET

COLOR LINE ARENA [126 B–C5]
A hall for anything that draws a crowd (16,000 places). This is where Eric Clapton and Shakira perform. Otherwise, sporting events: handball, ice hockey, boxing. *Sylvesterallee 10 | Tel. 881630 | www.colorline-arena. com | S3, 21, Stellingen, then shuttle bus (when there are events)*

FABRIK [135 D4]
This is a guarantee for good live music; some bands perform here regularly. The acoustics are not the best but the atmosphere makes up for that. Often parties on Saturdays – 1st Saturday, 'Dance through the Night'; 3rd Saturday, 'Flirt party'. *Barner Str. 36 | Tel. 391070 | www. fabrik.de | Bus and S-Bahn station Altona*

FREILICHTBÜHNE IM STADTPARK [130 A3]
Concerts are not even cancelled on account of Hamburg's summer showers. Many German bands, as well as superstars such as Sting, perform open air in the green City Park. *Ticket tel. 4147880 | www.karsten-jahnke.de | S1, Alte Wöhr*

KNUST [136 B4]
With its new home in the old slaughterhouse, this club, which was once an infamous dive for intimate dancing, is developing into a concert location. *Neuer Kamp 30 | Tel. 87976230 | www.knusthamburg.de | U3, Feldstr.*

UEBEL & GEFÄHRLICH ★ [136 B4]
Sub-culture and mainstream – the music club in the world-war bunker is starting to make a name for itself. Often live music or parties which are

really the place to be. *Tues–Sat from 9pm, or as announced | Feldstr. 66 (in the media bunker) | www.uebelundge faehrlich.com | U3, Feldstrasse*

■ MUSICALS ■

All the musicals listed here are produced by Stage Entertainment and run from Tuesday–Sunday. Central booking office: *Tel. 01805/4444*; tickets online: *www.stage-entertainment.de*. Tickets 25–115 euros; special offers during the week.

DER KÖNIG DER LÖWEN [136 B6]

Disney's lion king has long become a classic. The African fairy tale dazzles with its fantastic masks and costumes. A ferry transports you from the jetty to the other bank of the Elbe. *Theater im Hafen | Norderelbstr. 6 | S-/U-Bahn Landungsbrücken*

DIRTY DANCING [135 F3]

Nowhere can you see more beautiful hip-swinging than here. The dance show enthrals its audience with its *Theater Neue Flora | Stresemannstr. 163a | S11, 21, 31, Holstenstrasse*

ICH WAR NOCH NIEMALS IN NEW YORK (I'VE NEVER BEEN TO NEW YORK) [136 A5]

The newest musical in Hamburg is being performed at a historical site – the Operetta House on the Reeperbahn. The legendary Cats ran there for more than ten years – now it's *Aber bitte mit Sahne. Spielbudenplatz 1 | U3, St. Pauli*

■ SHOWS & CABARETS ■

DAS SCHIFF [123 D5]

Top-rank satirists entertain you on this cultural steamer. In summer, Europe's only seaworthy theatre ship casts off and makes guest performances along the Elbe. *Tickets from 25 euros | Holzbrücke 2/Nikolaifleet | Tel. 696505-80, Kartentel. -60 | www. theaterschiff.de | U3, Rödingsmarkt*

Sport and concerts: Color Line Arena

FLIEGENDE BAUTEN [122 A3]

Strollers along the city walls become curious when they hear applause coming from the theatre tent. Circus performances also still take place. Reserve a table with dinner. Prices vary, from around 25 euros. *Glacischaussee 4 | Tel. 471106 33 | www.fliegende-bauten.de | U3, St. Pauli*

NACHTASYL [123 E4] Insider Tip

The bar and cabaret stage in the Thalia Theatre. The furnishings are simply pushed aside when readings, cabaret or concerts take place. If there are no cultural events, the bar – with its retro atmosphere without any droning music – is perfect for relaxing after shopping. *Open daily from 7pm | Alstertor 1 | Tel. 32 81 44 44 | www.thalia-theater.de | S-/U-Bahn Jungfernstieg*

POLITTBÜRO [137 E–F4]
Left wing cabaret in St. Georg: the frontwoman Lisa Politt has made the former cinema a fixed institution in Hamburg's cabaret scene. *Tickets from 15 euros | Steindamm 45 | Tel. 28 05 54 67 | www.polittbuero.de | U 1, Lohmühlenstrasse*

SCHMIDT THEATER ★ ▶▶ [136 A5]
Corny Littmann's crew made the Reeperbahn socially acceptable once again. Since then, Schmidt's and the *Tivoli* next door have achieved cult status. The midnight show is first-rate.

Spielbudenplatz 24 | Tel. 31 77 88 99 | www.tivo li.de | S 1, 3, Reeperbahn

■OPERA & CLASSICAL MUSIC■
HAMBURGISCHE STAATSOPER/ HAMBURG BALLETT ★ [122 C3]
The Australian Simone Young is the opera director and the American John Neumeier is in charge of the ballet. Both have become firmly established in Hamburg and are the stars of the local cultural scene. *Grosse Theaterstrasse 25 | Tel. 35 68 68 | www.staats oper-hamburg.de | www.hamburg ballett.de | U 1, Stephansplatz*

LAEISZHALLE [122 B3]
The Laeiszhalle will remain the city's concert house until the Neue Elbphilharmonie opens its doors. Internationally renowned soloists and orchestras perform here and it is also the home of the Hamburg Symphony Orchestra and the North German Radio Symphony Orchestra. A tip: visit the square in the

Always a good address for the cool and way-out: the Schmidt Theater on Spielbudenplatz

evening when the neo-baroque building is illuminated – very romantic!
*Johannes-Brahms-Platz | Tel. 346920
| www.laeiszhalle.de | Metrobus 3,
Bus 112, Johannes-Brahms-Platz*

■ CASINO ■

CASINO ESPLANADE [122 C3]
The magnificent white building on
the Esplanade is the perfect setting
for trying your luck. There are gam-
ing machines in the hall for taking a
quick chance *(open every day from
noon)*; in the Casino itself, the stakes
are higher *(open every day from
3pm).* With restaurant. *Entrance fee
2 euros | Stephansplatz 10 | Tel.
4501760 | www.spielbank-hamburg.de
| U1, Stephansplatz*

■ THEATRES ■

DEUTSCHES SCHAUSPIELHAUS [123 F3]
The largest traditional German theatre
has always had difficulties finding its
audience. It will not be any easier for
Friedrich Schirmer in his third sea-
son as director in 2008 either. However, his mixture seems to be working.
In particular, his troupe has earned
much praise for their performances of
plays for children and young people
in the Junge Schauspielhaus (Young
Theatre). *Kirchenallee 39–41 | Tel.
248713 | www.schauspielhaus.de |
S-/U-Bahn Hauptbahnhof*

der Tip

HAMBURGER KAMMERSPIELE [136 C2]
A private theatre, steeped in tradition,
in the Grindel area. Sometimes light
fare, sometimes avant-garde. *Hartung-
strasse 9 | Tel. 0800/4133440 | www.
hamburger-kammerspiele.de | U1,
Hallerstrasse*

IMPERIAL THEATER [136 B5]
Hamburg's crime thriller theatre.
From *The Mousetrap* to *The Avenger*.
*Reeperbahn 5 | Tel. 313114 | www.
imperial-theater.de | U3, St. Pauli*

KAMPNAGELFABRIK [129 F5–6]
This dance and experimental theatre
on a former factory site has become
mellowed with age. *Jarrestr. 20–24 |
Tel. 27094949 | www. kampnagel.de
| U3, Saarlandstrasse*

OHNSORG-THEATER [122 C4]
This is where you can try to get a
grasp of the Low German dialect –
a lot of down-to-earth fun. *Grosse
Bleichen 23–25 | Tel. 35080321 |
www.ohnsorg.de | S-/U-Bahn Jung-
fernstieg*

ST.-PAULI-THEATER [136 A5]
Local theatre with a long tradition
and a lively programme. *Spielbuden-
platz 29/30 | Tel. 47110666 | www.
st-pauli-theater.de | U3, St. Pauli*

THALIA THEATER ★ [123 E4]
An amazing, decades-long, success
story. The director Ulrich Khuon will
soon be heading for Berlin. This
theatre on Gaussstrasse in Ottensen
has made some successfully daring
experiments on its small stage. *Alster-
tor 1 | Tel. 32814444 | www. thalia-
theater.de | S-/U-Bahn Jungfernstieg*

Insider Tip

WINTERHUDER FÄHRHAUS [129 D4]
The most successful, private, German
comedy theatre. *Hudtwalckerstr. 13 |
Tel. 48068000 | www.komoedie-winter
huder-faehrhaus.de | U1, Hudtwalcker-
strasse*

> SLEEP ON THE WATER'S EDGE

A bunk-bed, a luxury suite or a waterbed in a designer hotel – there are an unbelievable number of ways to spend the night in Hamburg

> Hotel beds in Hamburg are as plentiful as pebbles on a beach. All major chains are represented in the city. Or would you prefer a family-run hotel in one of the beautiful villas, or even a night on a ship? Let your dreams come true!

The official figure for 2007 was that there were 286 places to stay, with new hotels opening all the time. The historical water tower on the Sternschanze near the trade fair has now been converted by Mövenpick into a luxury hotel. The towering *Empire Riverside Hotel* on the docks has changed the city's skyline. The 'Harbour City' district is, however, still unchartered territory on the hotel map but that will change very quickly in the next couple of years. Events such as the Harbour Birthday or a visit by the 'Queen Mary' send prices climbing to exorbitant heights, as do trade fairs. And all centrally located hotels will be fully booked – so plan your trip in good

Above: room in the Hotel Gastwerk

ACCOM MODATION

time. Good value weekend rates can be called up from the Hamburg Tourist Information Office under the heading 'Happy Hamburg Travel' *(www. ham burg-travel.de)*. A number of the private hotels around the Alster have created their own showcase under *www. hamburg-kleinehotels.de*. Many hotels also offer special low-season packages. Up-to-the-minute rates and special offers can be found under the German website *www.ihr-hamburg-hotel.de*.

■ HOTELS € € € ■

ABTEI ★ 📶   [129 D6]

This town villa in Harvestehude is furnished with English and French antiques. An unusual feature is a Victorian billiard table that is available to use – complete with an instructor, if required. The hotel is home to the *Prinz-Frederik-Room* restaurant. Frequently fully booked. *11 rooms | Abteistr. 14 | Tel. 44 29 05 | Fax 44 98 20 | www. abtei-hotel.de | U 1, Klosterstern*

HOTELS €€€

DORINT SOFITEL ❄ 📶   [122 C5]

You may be surprised by the long corridors – but the hotel used to be a post office. The minimalist design adds an

Cool hotel bar in the Royal Méridien

understated and modern touch. The rooms with a view of the water are delightful. *241 rooms | Alter Wall 40 | Tel. 369 50 20 00 | Fax 369 50 10 00 | www.sofitel.de | U 3, Rödingsmarkt*

GRAND ELYSÉE 📶   [123 D1]

Eugen Block, the 'king' of Hamburg's steak house restaurants, has created a monument to himself in the form of the *Grand Elysée*. Perhaps a little on the pompous side, but there's certainly no shortage of space here: either in the rooms or while dancing off the calories in Hamburg's biggest ballroom. *511 rooms | Rothenbaumchaussee 10 | Tel. 41 41 20 | Fax 41 41 27 33 | www. elysee.de | S 21, 31, Dammtor*

LOUIS C. JACOB ❄   [133 E5]

Arguably the most beautiful, privately-run hotel in the city, with an idyllic view of the river from the Elbchaussee. Meticulously furnished right down to the last oil painting over the mantelpiece. Everyone who is anyone in Blankenese will have either had their wedding reception or at least a birthday celebration here. And dinner on the terrace under the lime trees – immortalized by the artist Max Liebermann – is simply divine. *85 rooms | Elbchaussee 401–403 | Tel 82 25 50 | Fax 82 25 54 44 | www.hotel-jacob.de | Bus 36, Sieberlingstrasse*

MÖVENPICK HOTEL HAMBURG   [136 B3]

Spectacularly designed: spend the night within the thick walls of the second largest water tower in Europe and enjoy the view from the (unfortunately unopenable) windows over the trade fair grounds. Situated in 'bohemian' Schanzenpark, this million euro project was bitterly fought over for a number of years. *228 rooms | Sternschanze 6 | Tel. 33 44 11 0 | Fax 33 44 11 33 33 | www.wasserturm-schanzenpark.de | S-/U-Bahn Sternschanze*

ACCOMMODATION

PARK HYATT [123 F4]

This hotel is famous for its comfortable beds, well-loved by numerous famous names who frequent this converted counting house. Unadulterated American luxury is also offered in the *Apples* restaurant and 🔊 *Park-Lounge*. *252 rooms, 30 apartments | Bugenhagenstr. 8–10 | Tel. 33 32 12 34 | Fax 33 32 12 35 | www.hamburg.park. hyatt.com | S-/U-Bahn Hauptbahnhof*

LE ROYAL MÉRIDIEN 🌿 🔊 [137 E3]

A gleaming glass façade outside, light colours and a warm light inside. The conference rooms are under the roof with their own restaurant. A glass lift whisks guests up to the restaurant *Le Ciel* where there is an extensive view of Hamburg's skyline. *284 rooms | An der Alster 52–56 | Tel. 2100 00 | Fax 21 00 11 11 | www.le meridien.com | Metrobus 6, Gurlittstrasse*

STEIGENBERGER HAMBURG 🔊 [122 C5]

Luxury hotel on one of the islands in the river – that's Hanseatic style! Lovely views of the Elbe from the day spa on the 8th floor. *233 rooms | Heiligengeistbrücke 4 | Tel. 368060 | Fax 36806777 | www.hamburg.steigenberger.de | S 1, 3, Stadthausbrücke*

■ HOTELS €€

HOTEL ALSTER-HOF 🔊 [123 D2] *Inside Tip*

Good news for dogs: they're welcome here at no extra charge – but best to bring a blanket. The hotel is near pleasant walks along the banks of the Alster. *117 rooms | Esplanade 12 | Tel. 35 00 70 | Fax 35 00 74 14 | www.alster-hof.de | U 1, Stephansplatz*

ALTE WACHE [137 E4]

Elegant hotel next to the main railway station and ideal for those who like to be central. Internet PC in the lobby. *100 rooms | Adenauerallee 21 | Tel. 28 40 6 60 | Fax 28 01 7 54 | www.hotel-alte-wache.de | S-/U-Bahn Hauptbahnhof*

BASELER HOF 🔊 [123 D2]

With its relaxed Hanseatic flair this hotel can look back on a 100-year-old tradition. Member of the Guild of Christian Hoteliers (VCH). The staff is exceptionally courteous and, in ad-

MARCO POLO HIGHLIGHTS

⭐ **Gastwerk Hotel**
The perfect mixture: modern designer hotel slap bang in the middle of an old industrial area (p. 93)

⭐ **Youth Hostel on Stintfang**
Nowhere else can you get such views for so little money (p. 94)

⭐ **Fairmont Hotel Vier Jahreszeiten**
Simply one of the best hotels in the world (p. 92)

⭐ **Strandhotel Blankenese**
A beach on the Elbe and the Blankenese 'Steps District' right outside (p. 94)

⭐ **Wedina**
Hamburg's literature hotel with a garden terrace right in the heart of St. Georg (p. 95)

⭐ **Abtei**
English country-house flair on the Alster – magnificent (p. 89)

dition to the usual saunas etc., there is a quiet room for contemplation. *151 rooms | Esplanade 11 | Tel. 35 90 60 | Fax 35 90 69 18 | www. baselerhof.de | U1, Stephansplatz*

CLIPPER ELB-LODGE 🔊 [135 F5]
Perfectly equipped apartments for one night or a long-term stay are available in this building in the old timber dock. The people of Hamburg will envy you such a location. Full service available if required. *57 suites | Carsten-Rehder-Str. 71 | Tel. 80 90 10 | Fax 80 90 19 99 | www.clipper-hotels. de | Bus 383, Sandberg*

HOTEL AM DAMMTOR 🔊 [136 C3]
Once home to students, this old townhouse now provides beautifully furnished rooms. Friendly service – and the campus is just a stone's throw away. *33 rooms | Schlüterstrasse 2 | Tel. 45 00 5 70 | Fax 41 06 3 00 | www. hotel-am-dammtor.de | Metrobus 4, 5, Staatsbibliothek*

EAST ▶▶ 🔊 [136 A–B5]
A designer hotel in a converted steel foundry in St. Pauli. The king-sized beds –waterbeds also available – are in the middle of the rooms, with the bathroom area curtained off. Both the

❯LUXURY HOTELS
Exquisite by day and night

ATLANTIC KEMPINSKI [123 F2]
For almost 100 years, the Atlantic has dominated the east side of the Outer Alster. A portrait of Germany's last emperor, who was a guest here, hangs in the lobby. Today, commoners enjoy afternoon high-tea in the inner courtyard or an evening in the elegant hotel bar. The *Tsao Yang* restaurant on the ground floor serves Chinese delicacies of the highest quality. *252 rooms | doubles 290–470, suites 800–4,900 euros | An der Alster 72–79 | Tel. 28880 | Fax 24 71 29 | www.kempinski.atlantic.de | S-/U-Bahn Hauptbahnhof*

FAIRMONT HOTEL VIER JAHRESZEITEN ⭐ [123 D3]
This traditional hotel on the Inner Alster has changed ownership every few years. But this hasn't flustered the hotel director, Ingo Peters, who continues to manage this luxury hotel –

which is one of the best in the world – with an unflappable serenity. Many Hamburg couples celebrate their golden weddings here and can recall with pride their confirmation lunch in the same four walls. *157 rooms | double from 300, suites 475–4,000 euros | Neuer Jungfernstieg 9–14 | Tel. 349 40 | Fax 34 94 26 00 | www.fairmont-hvj.de | S-/U-Bahn Jungfernstieg*

SIDE 🔊 [122 C3]
Even a trip to the loo is a lesson for design aficionados. The US theatre director Robert Wilson designed the lighting; in the hotel wood and clear-cut lines are the dominating features; the ▶▶ *Side-Bar* with its red leather chairs provides a flamboyant contrast. *178 rooms | doubles 160–315, suites 235–710 euros | Drehbahn 49 | Tel. 30 99 90 | Fax 30 99 93 99 | www.side-hamburg.de | U1, Stephansplatz*

ACCOMMODATION

restaurant and the bar are hot spots for the people of Hamburg. *125 rooms, 2 apartments | Simon-von-Utrecht-Str. 31 | Tel. 30 99 30 | Fax 30 99 32 00 | www.east-hamburg.de | U3, St. Pauli*

DAS FEUERSCHIFF [122 B6]

In a bright red former lightship you can bed down for the night like an old salt – in a bunk that may be small but is nonetheless comfortable. At night, listen to the Elbe swishing against the planks. Monday is the 'Blue Monday Jam Session' *(8.30pm)*. Ear plugs are put out on the pillows. *6 rooms | City-Sporthafen | Vorsetzen | Tel. 36 25 53 | Fax 36 25 55 | www.das-feuerschiff.de | U3, Baumwall*

GASTWERK HOTEL ★ 🔊 [135 D3]

Hamburg's most stylish hotel is to be found in a former industrial complex and boasts lots of brick and lots of light. Slightly off the beaten track, but for that, both the atmosphere and the price are right. *141 rooms | Beim alten Gaswerk 3 | Tel. 89 06 20 | Fax 89 06 22 0 | www. gastwerk-hotel.de | Metrobus 2, 3, Bornkampsweg*

HOTEL HAFEN HAMBURG 🔊 [136 B5]

Towering above the jetties, this hotel is virtually a landmark building. Rooms are divided into categories ranging from 'Sailors' rooms to the 'Admiral's Suite'. The view from the ☀ *Tower-Bar (open every day from 6pm | 12th floor)* doesn't just take the tourists' breath away but is something that the locals like to boast about, too. *353 rooms | Seewartenstr. 9 | Tel. 31 11 30 | Fax 31 11 37 55 | www. hotel-hamburg.de | S-/U-Bahn Landungsbrücken*

HOTEL HEIMHUDE [136 C2]

A hotel with a regular clientele. A personal service is provided in a grand, Hanseatic setting. *24 rooms | Heimhuderstrasse 16 | Tel. 41 33 00 | Fax 41 33 04 0 | www.hotel-heimhude.de | S21, 31, Dammtor*

Tower-Bar in the Hotel Hafen Hamburg

JUNGES HOTEL [137 E5]

Popular by families: baby extras are free of charge. Inside it is modern and comfortable. Close to the main station. 🔊 Restaurant. *133 rooms | Kurt-Schumacher-Allee 14 | Tel. 41 92 30 | Fax 41 92 35 55 | www.jungeshotel.de | S-/U-Bahn Hauptbahnhof*

LANDHAUS FLOTTBEK 🔊 [133 F3]

Country-house feeling in the lovely western part of Hamburg. Tastefully modernised thatched house with a delightful garden and gourmet restaurant. On some days, however, it can be a little loud when the planes approach Fuhlsbüttel from the west. *25 rooms | Baron-Voght-Str. 179 | Tel. 8227410 | Fax 82274151 | www.landhaus-flottbek. de | Schnellbus 37, Flottbeker Kirche*

NIPPON HOTEL HAMBURG 🔊 [137 F2]

Japanese lifestyle: where clear and harmonious lines are in the forefront. Guests walk on tatamis – Japanese grass mats – and sleep on futons. The in-house Japanese restaurant has more to offer than just sushi. *42 rooms | Hofweg 75 | Tel. 2271140 | Fax 22711490 | www.nipponhotel.de | Metrobus 6, Zimmerstrasse*

RADISSON SAS HOTEL HAMBURG 🔊 [122 C1]

Don't ask for a room with a balcony as there aren't any in this dizzily high building. To compensate, you can enjoy a marvellous view, attentive staff, the distinguished atmosphere of a business hotel and the 🔆 *Top of Town* nightclub *(Mon–Sat from 9.30pm | 5 euros entrance fee on Fri/Sa). 560 rooms | Marseiller Str. 2 | Tel. 35020 | Fax 35023530 | www.hamburg.radissonsas.com | S21, 31, Dammtor*

STRANDHOTEL BLANKENESE ⭐ [132 B4]

This is where you will really have the feeling of being on holiday, staying in a white-washed turn-of-the-century villa, with a walk on the beach thrown in. For those who like combining sightseeing with a little relaxation, this is the place for you. Rooms with a view of the Elbe are the most popular – and the most expensive. *16 rooms | Strandweg 13 | Tel. 861344 | Fax 864936 | www.strand-hotel.de | Schnellbus 48, Landungsbrücke*

25 H/TWENTY FIVE HOURS 🔊 [135 D3]

Recently opened design hotel: a bit hip and kind to the under 25s who get 25% off room rates. A large TV screen in the lounge is an open invitation to watch DVDs. *104 rooms | Paul-Dessau-Strasse 2 | Tel. 855070 | Fax 85507100 | www.25hours-hotel.de | Metrobus 2, 3, Bornkampsweg*

>LOW BUDGET

> The view from the ⭐🔆🔊 *CDJ Youth Hostel on Stintfang* on the harbour is unbeatable. Book well in advance! *357 beds | up to 26 yrs. | 15.90 to 24.90 euros | 3 euros more for older guests | Alfred-Wegener-Weg 5 [122 A5] | Tel. 313488 | www.djh.de | S-/U-Bahn Landungsbrücken*

> New and sparklingly clean is 🔊 *Backpackers St. Pauli* opposite the Studio cinema, tucked into a quiet corner. *10 rooms | dorm beds from 19, doubles from 55 euros | Check-in until 1am | Bernstorffstrasse 98 [136 A4] | Tel. 23517043 | www.backpackers-stpauli.de | Metrobus 3, Bernstorffstr.*

> In *Stella Maris*, a former lodging house for sailors in the Portuguese district in the harbour, rooms are available from 30 euros, although the WC is on the landing. Free use of internet PC on the ground floor. *49 rooms | Reimarusstr. 12 [122 A6] | Tel. 3192023 | Fax 3174313 | www.stellamaris-hamburg.de | S-/U-Bahn, Landungsbrücken*

ACCOMMODATION

WEDINA ⭐   [137 E4]

No room in your luggage for books? Then stay in this blue town house in Hamburg's literature hotel. Every room is dedicated to a different author whose works fill the shelves. The hotel owns four colourfully painted houses

| *Fax 28 41 91 41* | *www.yoho-hamburg. de* | *U2, Christuskirche*

HOTEL YORK 📶   [137 E1]

Lovely old building in Uhlenhorst, popular among opera singers and actors who are attracted by the peace and

Wood and warm colours: a room in the Hotel Wedina

in St. Georg – a tip for artists. *59 rooms* | *Gurlittstr. 23* | *Tel. 28 08 9 00* | *Fax 28 03 8 94* | *www.wedina.de* | *Metrobus 6, Gurlittstrasse*

YOHO 📶   [136 A2]

Small designer hotel in a town villa. The Wilhelminian style has been cleverly combined with the modern. This Eimsbüttel hotel offers price reductions to the under 26s. The Syrian hotel restaurant *Mazza* serves superb food. *30 rooms* | *Moorkamp 5* | *Tel. 28 41 91 0*

quiet. *10 rooms, 3 apartments* | *Hofweg 19* | *Tel. 22 71 4 20* | *Fax 22 73 1 19* | *www.hotel-york.de* | *Metrobus 6, Averhoffstrasse*

▮ HOTELS € ▬▬▬▬▬

HOTEL BAURS PARK 📶   [132 C3]

Slap in the middle of Blankenese village life, 5 mins. from the market square. If travelling with children, ask for a family room. Following the complete renovation of the building, these are especially love. *24 rooms* |

HOTELS €

Elbchaussee 573 | Tel. 866 66 20 | Fax 86 66 62 20 | www.baurspark.de | S 1, 11, Blankenese

CRISTOBAL HOTEL 🔊   [129 E6]
Far from the madding crowd: this small, intimate hotel is situated near the Alster in lovely Winterhude. Expensive when trade fairs are being held. 18 rooms | Dorotheenstr. 52 | Tel. 357 03 00 | Fax 35 70 30 70 | www.hotel-cristobal.de | Metrobus 6, 25, Gertigstrasse

HOTEL HANSEATIN   [122 B3]
Pretty, listed town house opposite the Laeiszhalle for women only. Individually styled rooms. For those travelling on their own, the women's café endlich is the perfect place to unwind over a cup of coffee and a paper. 13 rooms | Dragonerstall 11 | Tel. 34 13 45 | Fax 34 58 25 | www.hotel-hanseatin.de | Metrobus 3, Johannes-Brahms-Platz

Insider Tip

HOTEL KÖNIGSHOF ▶▶ 🔊   [137 E4]
Bright and breezy and exceptionally friendly. Located in a quiet side street (with garden) this hotel is not just popular by gays. 21 rooms | Pulverteich 18 | Tel. 28 40 740 | Fax 28 40 74 74 | www.koenigshof-hamburg.de | S-/U-Bahn Hauptbahnhof

KOGGE ▶▶ 🔊   [136 A5]
It may look a bit shabby on the outside, but this rock-'n-roll hotel is wonderful. Lots of musicians stay here and the rooms were designed with the help of a number of artists. The reception (which is also the bar) is open until 4 am. 12 rooms | Bernhard-Nocht-Str. 59 | Tel. 31 28 72 | Fax 33 44 21 85 | www.kogge-hamburg.com | S 1, 3, Reeperbahn

HOTEL MICHAELIS HOF 🔊   [122 B5]
This hotel in the Catholic Academy offers good value for money. Whether it's because of the cosy rooms or the other Christian guests, visitors automatically feel at home here. No breakfast, some rooms with use of kitchen, underground garage free of charge. 22 rooms | Herrengraben 4 | Tel. 35 90 69 12 | Fax 35 90 69 11 | www.michaelishof-hamburg.de | S 1, 3, Stadthausbrücke

Inside Tip

MOTEL HAMBURG 🔊   [128 B6]
Most importantly: there's somewhere to park your car. And that in Eimsbüttel, slap in the city centre, is worth a lot. 35 rooms | Hoheluftchaussee 117–119 | Tel. 42 04 41 | Fax 42 29 905 | www.hamburg-hotels.de/motel | Metrobus 5, 20, 25 Gärtnerstrasse

SCHANZENSTERN   [136 A3]
Hamburg's newest low-budget hotel has become so popular that there is now a second hotel that has opened in Altona. Apart from single and double rooms, there are also 5-bed rooms (19 euros). Breakfast is available in the hotel's own 🔊 'green' restaurant/-café. 20 rooms | Bartelsstr. 12 | Tel. 43 98 441 | Fax 43 93 413 | www.schanzenstern.de | S-/U-Bahn Sternschanze

SEEMANNSMISSION 🔊   [135 F5]
Rooms for sailors and landlubbers alike: simple, clean and safe. When there are floods, this is the most exciting place to be. Some reduction in capacity during renovations during spring 2008. 40 rooms | Grosse Elbstr. 132 | Tel. 30 62 20 | Fax 30 62 218 | www.seemannsmission.org | Bus 383, Sandberg | S 1, Königstrasse

Ins T

Brightly-coloured mix of styles: the rock-'n'-roll hotel Kogge

HOTEL ST. ANNEN 🔊   [136 A4]

Charming hotel in a quiet part of St. Pauli; garden terrace, garages and PCs for use by guests. *36 rooms | Annenstr. 5 | Tel. 3177130 | Fax 31771313 | www.hotelstannen.de | U3, St. Pauli*

STADTHAUSHOTEL   [135 F4]

The façade may be uninviting but inside the atmosphere is all the more positive. A hostel managed by people of varying disability for guests with similar handicaps – and of course for others. *13 rooms | Holstenstr. 118 | Tel. 3899200 | Fax 38992020 | www.stadthaushotel.com | Metrobus 20, 25, Bus 115, Max-Brauer-Allee (Mitte)*

■ CAMPING ■

The *Schnelsen-Nord* campsite is centrally located, next to Ikea, standard rating. *April–Oct | 2 pers./tent 19.40 euro, dormobile 25.50 euros | Wunderbrunnen 2 [140 C2] | Tel. 5594225 | Fax 5507334 | www.campingplatz-hamburg.de | A 7, exit Schnelsen |*
U2, Niendorf Markt, from there Bus 191, Dornröschenweg.

The campsite at *Falkensteiner Ufer* is beautifully located, but is off the beaten track. *April–Oct | no electricity hookups | 2 pers./tent from 15 euros | Falkensteiner Ufer 101 [132 A4] | Tel. 812949 | www.elbecamp.de.*

From 8.50 euros for caravans at the fish market in *St.-Pauli-Hafenstr. 89 [136 A6] | Tel. 230120*

■ PRIVATE ROOMS ■

BED AND BREAKFAST

Rooms and apartments available in various districts throughout the city, from 50 euros. *Office: Markusstr. 9 | Tel. 4915666 | Fax 4914212 | www. bed-and-breakfast.de | S1, 3, Stadthausbrücke*

HADLEY'S BED AND BREAKFAST   [136 B2]

Two flats in a former hospital, cosy and centrally located. *4 rooms | double room 85 euros | Beim Schlump 85 | Tel. 417871 | www.bed-and-breakfast-hamburg.de | Metrobus 4, Bus 115, Bundesstrasse*

THE PERFECT CITY FOR FAMILIES

Hamburg is ideal for a short outing with the children

There are big ships in the harbour and little paddleboats on the Alster, sand for building castles along the Elbe and many museums with a children's programme. On top of that, there are a number of musicals for all the family such as 'The King and the Lion', Germany's oldest children's theatre and even a hotel for children. What could families want more?

HAGENBECKS TIERPARK ⭐ [127 E4]

A spanking new tropical aquarium with crocodiles, snakes and thousands of fish; a sensational orang-utan house and elephants which can be hand fed. And all this is in one of the most beautifully landscaped zoos in the world with out-door enclosures and a very long tradi-tion: in 2007 Hagenbeck celebrated its 100th birthday. *March–June, Sept/Oct open daily 9 am–6 pm, July/Aug 9 am–7 pm, Nov–Feb 9 am–4.30 pm | Entrance fee 10 euros (children under 16), 15 euros | Lokstedter Grenzstr. 2 | Tel. 53 00 3 30 | www.hagenbeck.de | U2, Hagenbecks Tierpark*

KINDERHOTEL
BENGEL UND ENGEL [127 F6]

Everything's there, just as for adults: reception desk, welcome cocktail, towels and, in addition, attentive carers. 8 places for children between 6 months and 12 years. Child care from 6 pm to 10 am the next day, 55 euros incl. meals. *Stellinger Weg 49 | Tel. 43 17 94 90 | Fax 4317 94 9 10 | www.bengel-engel.de | U2, Lutterothstrasse*

MUSEUMS

All state-run museums are free of charge for children under 18. And all of them – incl. private museums – have a children's programme. Just ask, for example at the museums' information service *(Tel. 428 13 10 | www.museumsdienst. hamburg.de)*. Fun for children and free for everyone is the *Zollmuseum* custom's museum in the warehouse district *(Tues-Sun 10 am–5 pm | Alter Wandrahm 16 [123 E5–6] | www.museum.zoll.de | U2, Messberg)* and the *Zoologische Samm-lung der Universität* (University Zoological

>TRAVELLING WITH KIDS

Collection) with its stuffed animals which almost look as if they are still alive. A walrus named Antje, familiar to many Germans from TV, can also be seen here. *(Tues–Sun 10 am–5 pm | Martin-Luther-King-Platz 3* [136 B2] *| www.biologie.uni-hamburg. de | Metrobus 4, 5, Grindelhof).*

SHOPPING WITH THE CHILDREN

The *Stilwerk* doesn't just have chic designer shops and a glass lift, but also provides a free child-minding service on Sat *(from 4 yrs upwards | Grosse Elb-strasse 68* [135 F5–6] *| Tel. 30621100 | www.Stilwerk.de).* During Advent there are prettily decorated steam ships moored at the Jungfernstieg jetty [123 D3] where children can listen to fairy tales or bake biscuits while their parents go off hunting for Christmas presents.

CHILDREN'S THEATRE/ ALLEETHEATER   [135 E4]

This is where children are taken seriously – as has been the case for the past 35 years! In the evening there are opera performances for adults. Tickets from 11 euros. Performances usually on Fri, Sat and Sun. *Max-Brauer-Allee 76 | Tel. 382538 | www.theater-fuer-kinder.de | Bus 20, 25, 115, 183, Gerichtsstrasse*

SHIPS' WELCOMING SYSTEM/ 'SHIP-IN-A-BOTTLE' MUSEUM   [140 B3]

Ships sailing into or out of Hamburg are greeted with music through a loud-speaker system or wished 'bon voyage'. Retired captains dip the flag and record the ship's tonnage and land of origin. A great place to visit for the whole family – and not just because there are neither computers nor interactive games. Everything is authentic here: from the coffee jugs to the ships-in-a-bottle in the museum on the lower floor. *Wedel | Schulauer Fährhaus | Open every day from 9 am | Museum: open every day 10 am–6 pm from mid March until mid October; Weds/Sat/Sun only from mid Oct until mid March. | Entrance fee 1.50 euro | www.schulauer-faehrhaus.de | S 1 Wedel, from there Bus 189, Elbstrasse*

> COUNTING HOUSES, THE OUTER ALSTER AND BLANKENESE

Hamburg is great for walkers

The walking tours are marked in green on the map on the back cover and in the Street Atlas

1 DISCOVER THE COUNTING HOUSE DISTRICT

This walk leads us through the economic heart of the city. The first demolition and reconstruction activities began at the end of the 19th century. Craftsmen, bakers and ferrymen left and ship owners, brokers and agents took their place. The stroll takes 1–2 hours; it depends on your mood. U1, Messberg

The starting point is Oberbaum-brücke 1, the entrance to the Deichtor-center (on Willy-Brandt-Strasse). Surprised? The tapering office building is a typical Hamburg 'Kontorhaus' (former counting house); however, it is not an old brick construction but new and made completely of glass and steel. The architect Hadi Teherani got raked over the coals in 2002 for his daring design even though the glass giant is in line with the Hanseatic tradition. The very first office building of this type was the Dovenhof. It used to be

Above: The Warehouse District

WALKING TOURS

opposite the mirrored skyscraper you see today. Its architect, Martin Haller, was famous in his time. He designed the Laeiszhalle *(p. 86)*, the Hapag Building on Ballindamm, the old Alster Pavilion and Hamburger Rathaus *(p. 30)*. His plans for the first counting house in Hamburg, which was completed in 1886, had the greatest impact on the appearance of the city. The building was unbelievably modern for its time. There was a paternoster lift, an internal postal system and heating costs were calculated precisely per square metre. The Dovenhof was partially destroyed during the War and, later, demolished. As with the former building, the Deichtorcenter is also equipped with cutting-edge technology. Its state-of-the-art ventilation system makes it possible to do without any air-conditioning at all. Hadi Teherani can also appreciate that – his office is on the fourth floor.

But, don't you want to visit a genuine old 'Kontorhaus'? Go back towards the city centre and in a few minutes you will find yourself in front of the magnificent brick façade of the Chilehauses on the corner of Klingberg and Pumpen *(p. 26)*. It was necessary to demolish houses to fulfil the plans of the architect Fritz Höger. Go into the inner courtyard from the left and have a look at the staircase *(Portal A, left | only open Mon–Fri)*. The figures of South American animals are an indication of how the building's commissioner Henry B. Sloman made his fortune dealing with saltpetre from Chile – and that is how the building got its name: 'Chilehaus'. Leave the courtyard heading for Burchardstrasse and you will discover another beautiful staircase on the right *(Portal C, Burchardstr. 13)*. The Sprinkenhof *(Burchardstr. 4–6)* is opposite; here you should also go into the inner

courtyard. The building is even bigger than the Chilehaus and, in 1932, was considered the largest office building in the world. Construction took 16 years and, in addition to Fritz Höger, the brothers Hans and Oskar Gerson were also involved as architects. Pay particular attention to the net-shaped pattern on the façade and the gilded terracotta stones. The round staircase is fantastic.

Leave the Sprinkenhof and walk via Altstädter Strasse, Schopenstehl and Grosse Reichenstrasse to Brandstwiete. You will see old counting houses all along the way: the Montanhof *(Kattrepel 2)*, Laeiszhof *(Trostbrücke 1)* and Pressehaus on Cathedral Square *(Speersort 1)*. You will also come across some interesting new buildings such as the Rolandsbrücke 4 office complex which was built by Carsten Roth in 2005. The Neue Dovenhof *(Brandstwiete 1)* would really be nothing special without the

A globe crowns the façade of the Hotel Atlantic on the Alster

glass lifts in the courtyard. Take the one to the right of the entrance – but be discreet; this is an office building, not a tourist attraction. The view from the top is absolutely fantastic. On the left, you can see the 'Kontorhaus' district with its brick buildings, white wooden windows and green bronze railings on the roofs and, to the right, the 'Harbour City' and warehouse district. They are only a stone's throw away. And it won't take you three guesses to work out what is being built there – modern 'counting house-styled' offices, of course. The word *Kontor* originated from the French word *comptoir* meaning 'counting room'. This brings us back to the 'pepper sacks'. A respectable Hamburg merchant doesn't go to the office but to the 'counting house'!

2 ONCE ROUND THE OUTER ALSTER

The magnificent tour around the Outer Alster (Aussenalster) will show you many sides of Hamburg: sport and culture, the citizens' pride and patronage. Count on walking for a good 2–3 hours.

The path around the Outer Alster is 7.5 km long. It is perfect for jogging and that is what countless locals do every day. But, you want to see something. The snow-white Hotel Atlantic *(An der Alster 72–79, p. 92)*, which was built in 1909, is a lovely place to start your tour. That was the time when cruises started to boom and the well-heeled voyagers waited for their ships in the Atlantic. You might even see the rock legend and house ghost Udo Lindenberg in the lobby – he has

lived here for more than ten years. Go down to the banks of the Alster and turn right. Have you ever thought about getting a sailing license? You can do that at the *Pieper Sailing School (Atlanticsteg | Tel. 247578 | www.segel schule-pieper.de).* Note: there are special regulations on the Alster: those approaching from the right have priority and, naturally, so do the Alster steamers. The Literaturhaus is located at Am Schwanenwik 38; you can spend an entire day in the building with its stuccoed garden hall, bookshop and many readings. *(Open every day | Schwanenwik 38 | Tel. 22702011 | www.literaturhaus-ham burg.de).*

You now continue along the Schönen Aussicht: nomen est omen – this means 'beautiful view' in German. Don't panic when you see a lot of policemen in front of house number 26. They are there for security reasons. This Alster villa was built by Martin Haller in 1868 and is now the official Guesthouse of the Senate. The Queen was the first visitor to stay here after the war; Diana and Charles came here later, too. A bit further on, you will see a completely different type of building: the Imam-Ali-Moschee. It was built in 1961 and, today, is an important centre for Hamburg's Shiite Moslems. The world returns to its Hanseatic state opposite this. This is the seat of the NRV, Hamburg's most traditional sailing club and you can only become a member if you have two sponsors. You cannot get lost even though the road now takes you away from the Alster; after a short stretch along Sierichstrasse you turn left onto Bellevue with its row of magnificent town houses.

You should take a break at the Krugkoppelbrücke at the top of the Alster. Why not drop in at the Bobby Reich Restaurant *(p. 65)*? If the way back is too far for you, you can take one of the Alster steamers and cruise back to the Jungfernstieg in comfort.

Otherwise continue along the green west bank. The land along the Alster where you are now walking has only been accessible to the public since 1953. It used to belong to the large villas on Haverstehuder Weg. It is incredibly packed here on sunny weekends. Heinrich Heine's publishers Hoffman und Kampe still have their offices at number 42. You now pass Pöseldorf where Jil Sander began her career on Milchstrasse. Today, there are several fine galleries and a few chic shops and restaurants there.

The city's music academy has now taken up residence in the former Budge Palais at Milchstrasse 12. There is another 'White House' at the end of your stroll: the US Consulate. This was the main administrative office during the Nazi period; the road in front of the building has been completely closed since 2001 (take the path to the left along the water with its romantically positioned benches!). If you still haven't had enough, the *Alsterwanderweg* takes you from here, through the city centre, directly to the Elbe. Take the pedestrian tunnel under the Kennedy and Lombard Bridges, turn into the Alsterarkaden at the Jungfernstieg, then go straight ahead along the Alsterfleet to the Schaartorschleuse. Alster, town houses, inner-city, the canals and now the Elbe: This is as multifaceted as a stroll through Hamburg can be.

3 UP AND DOWN THE STEPS DISTRICT IN BLANKENESE

What was that? Mountain hiking in Hamburg? Of course! Put on your walking boots and head for the 'Positano of the north'. You won't need any provisions either; there are a number of lovely resting places 'en route'. Duration: as long as you want, but at least 2 hours.

Start at Blankenese Station and get warmed up on the mini ascent to the Gossler Haus, on the right-hand side of Blankenese Landstrasse. As was the case with many beautiful old villas in West Hamburg, this magnificent white building was used as a district office for decades before being purchased by the city. You now cross at the traffic lights and find your first refreshments: scones at Lühmanns Café *(Open every day | Blankeneser Landstr. 29 | Tel. 863442).*). Pass the venerable high school on the left, cross the street and a carpark before reaching Hessepark. Go past Hessehaus (also a former district office) on the right and leave the park towards the right.

The real ascent over the Charitas-Bischoff-Stiege begins directly opposite. You are now in the heart of the Treppenviertel ('Steps District'). It is stunningly attractive here! The old houses to the left and right are just a stone's throw away, only separated by steep flights of steps and narrow paths. You can look into the gardens and kitchen windows; you will see the flag on the Süllberg above you to the right and the glittering water of the Elbe flowing below. Understandably, almost everyone wants to live here! But, it is not so easy – many of the former captains' houses have been in the same family for generations.

Now go downhill and cross Blankenese Hauptstrasse. Maybe one of the mini-buses – the so-called 'mountain goats' – will happen to come by. You can hop on and be driven down to the banks of the Elbe. However, the path over Schlagemihls Treppe is nicer. Cross the main road once again, walk

historical Dreehuhs built to house three fishing families at numbers 4–6. You now reach the Süllbergterrasse. A short way to the left and then to the right brings you to *Schuldt's Kaffeegarten* which has been in the same family for 130 years. The cakes are home-made, the cream whipped by hand, and the atmosphere unique *(open every day from midday, in winter*

Insider Tip

A pretty sight: view from the Süllberg in Blankenese of the Elbe

past number 38 and turn left onto Hans-Lange-Strasse (this is only a path). You are almost at the Elbe. Are your feet now longing for warm sand, does you stomach want a tasty plaice at the Fischclub Blankenese *(p. 65)*? Forget it! Show what you're made of! Take a deep breath and go up to the Silberbergterrasse on your right. This is really steep. Turn onto the Elbeterrasse and take a look at the

only Sat/Sun | Tel. 862411). Now, you have almost made it. Leave the café to the left, go downhill about 200 metres and take the next left. Only a few more metres and you will be standing in front of the steep ascent to the ☼ Süllberg (p. 60). A luxury restaurant, a hotel and – above all – a beer garden. An unbelievable view over the Elbe and a glass of cool beer – what bliss!

A DAY IN HAMBURG

Non-stop action and one-off experiences.
On tour with our scene scout

BREAKFAST FOR EVERYONE

7:30

In the morning down at the slaughter house, the world is still in order. Early risers, taxi drivers and night hawks all meet at Erikas Eck for a minced meat roll and a café au lait or why not order a juicy steak? Nobody needs to leave with an empty stomach! What a way to start the day. **WHERE?** *Sternstr. 98 | Tel. 43 35 45 | Sat, Sun only until 9 am, Mon only opens at midnight) | www.erikas-eck.de*

10:00

A BOAT TRIP IS ...

... great fun. A boat trip is cool. Canoes can be hired at Kübis Bootshaus. The white villas along the shore are best viewed from the water. Drift along but keep your eyes peeled: perhaps you'll see one or two famous faces too. But don't forget to wave! **WHERE?** *Possmoorweg 46e | Canoes from 7 euros | April–Oct, open every day 9 am–10 pm | Tel. 279 67 41*

FRESH FISH

12:00

Just follow your nose – the fish is ready! Hamburg's typical fried fish shops can be found a few hundred yards from the fish market heading for Övelgönne. If you want the best and cheapest fried scampi, try the *Meeres-Kost* fish shop. But don't eat too much: you will need to leave some room for some fried fish and a jar of pickled Hamburg herring. **WHERE?** *Grosse Elbstr. 135 | Tel. 380 56 21*

14:00

ACTION-PACKED CLIMBING

Shin up the wall: the highest outdoor climbing wall in the north of Germany, in Flora Park, opens up whole new perspectives. Clip on the climbing harness and hold on tightly to that hand grip, pulling your feet up behind you. Repeat this a number of times until you are 20 metres above the ground. Going down is faster. Just abseil down the wall, gliding safely to the bottom. **WHERE?** *Lippmannstrasse 60a | Entrance fee: donations welcome | Free climbing: Sun | www.kilimanschanzo.de*

24 h

THE PERFECT SNIP

15:30

Fancy a new hairdo? Then the *Schneideraum* is the right place for you. Haircutting has been made into an event here – even on Sundays! DJs make sure the atmosphere in the salon is just right and a make-up session for your evening out on the town is all part and parcle of the experience. Sink into the chair and let maestro do his bit. Tip: don't open your eyes before the hairdryer has been turned off. **WHERE?** *Grosse Elbstrasse 146 | Tel. 38 03 85 70 | www.schneideraum-hamburg.de*

17:30

IN WITH THE 'IN' CROWD

Hamburg's most 'in' place is waiting for you – the Schanzen district opposite Flora Park. But be quick: the street cafés fill up very fast. If you don't get a seat, don't worry – it's just as cool to order at the bar and to drink standing outside. And don't be surprised if you get drawn into your neighbours' conversation – that's quite normal here! **WHERE?** *Schulterblatt*

LET'S DANCE

20:30

And back to the harbour for a sundowner. Let the romantic in you come to light. From the terrace of the Beachclub you can watch the sun turn the Elbe a deep red. And as if that were not enough, Tuesday is tango day, and couples dance into the setting Sun Itchy feet? Then grab your dance partner and stride out across the floor. **WHERE?** *St.-Pauli-Hafenstr. 89 | Mai–Oct | www.strandpauli.de*

22:30

OUT ON THE TOWN

Location hopping in the night-club district: US-style table dancing can be seen in *Dollhouse*, the best hotdogs can be found in *Danmark-Snack* and, a few steps away, the travel agents even stays open until 11pm – so if you fancy booking your next holiday between drinks, this is the address for you! Still fit? Try the early morning sports club in the *Kurhotel*, Grosse Freiheit 35, which opens at 6am on Sundays. Everything and anything is possible in the night-club district! **WHERE?** *Grosse Freiheit, Reeperbahn*

> FROM THE DYKE TO THE WOODS

A container, museums, fruit and wolves:
What an assortment of different outings!

The outings are marked in green on the map on the back cover and in the Street Atlas

1 CYCLE TOUR TO ALTENWERDER CHURCH

The past, present and future of the harbour are the theme of this unusual bike tour. This is not for lovers of un-spoilt nature – the trip also takes you through industrial areas. You will need around 5 hours, including the round trip by boat. Take a picnic with you!

Above: Fruit trees in blossom in Altes Land

It starts with a short trip on a boat. Take the Hadag Ferry 61 from the 'Landungsbrücken'. You only need a normal HVV ticket, bikes are free *(only Mon–Fri | every 2 hours | departure times: Tel. 31 17 07 10 | www. hadag.de)*. You travel to the **Walters-hof** pier where you can still feel the atmosphere of the old harbour with its lighters, coal stacks and tugboats.

OUTINGS

The big, white-domed building on the left is the **Festmacherzentrale (Mooring Centre)**; the mooring ships make certain that the enormous vessels are made fast to their anchor places and the work is among the most dangerous jobs in the harbour. On the right, you will see the gigantic Eurogate portainer cranes.

Pedal left to the end of Rugenberger Damm. This is not very pretty,

but it is exciting: you are right under the Köhlbrand Bridge! Turn into Finkenwerder Strasse at the Waltershof customs office (border of the free port). After a few minutes, turn right to Hornsand. Follow the signs to Neugraben/Finkenwerder. Turn left at the Paul Günther company sign and a surprisingly idyllic bike path under the autobahn takes you to

Dradenstrasse. Turn left onto Waltershofer Strasse towards Altenwerder at the BAB Waltershof bus stop on the major junction and then, after around 200 metres, once again to the left onto Altenwerder Hauptdeich. Can you see the red church steeple in the small wood off to the right? That's where you're heading for. Follow the signs to the church on the Altenwerder Kirchdeich. The former Altenwerder village church of *St. Gertrud* lies completely isolated – surrounded only by a small wood and cemetery – at the end of the path. Bear in mind that this was once the lively centre of a village with 2,000 inhabitants! In 1973, the Senate decided to do away with the village in order to expand the harbour. All the protests made were without success and the only concession was that St. Gertrud would be preserved. Weddings and funerals still take place and the church is always full on Christmas Eve.

Can you hear the twittering in the trees? It comes from the electronically controlled container carriages in Europe's state-of-the-art **Altenwerder Container Terminal**. There is always new construction underway here. When the bike path from St. Gertrud to the Terminal is completed, there will be lookout points and places to take a break. You can either ride back now or extend your tour. The (still) idyllic hamlet of **Moorburg**. is a few kilometres away but it will also have to make way for the harbour at some time in the future. You can now pedal back to the city centre by way of Wilhelmsburg and the Elbe Bridges. For this, you need a good map and a couple of extra hours: It's worth the effort: this tour will make a real Hamburg expert out of you!

Omnipresent in Sachsenwald: Bismarck

2 VISIT THE 'IRON CHANCELLOR' IN SACHSENWALD

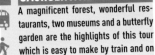

A magnificent forest, wonderful restaurants, two museums and a butterfly garden are the highlights of this tour which is easy to make by train and on foot. **You should allow at least half a day for it. The district line 21 will bring you directly from the main railway station to Aumühle in 33 minutes. The station lies in the centre of the Sachsenwald (Saxon Forest).**

In 1871, Emperor William I gave his 'Iron Chancellor' Bismarck this largest single area of forest in Schleswig-Holstein as a sign of his gratitude for his faithful service. The enormous forest area is still in the family's possession and they live in Schloss Friedrichsruh (Friedrichsruh Castle). A leisurely 30–40 minute stroll from Aumühle through the forest takes you to the castle. Leave the train station to the right, cross the road and go into the forest – the path is signposted. Here, you will already be tempted by the first charming country inns with their wonderful terraces and inviting menus.

Walk past the stables. Above these, on the right, is the wonderful Eisenbahnmuseum (Railway museum) *(only Sun 11am–5pm | entrance free)*. Big, old steam locomotives have been lovingly restored. Make a donation, they have earned it! The first thing you will see when you reach the park walls of Friedrichsruh Castle is a sign to the Schmetterlingsgarten (Butterfly Garden) in the grounds of the princely forest administration. The idea of creating Germany's first butterfly garden reputedly came from Princess Elisabeth of Bismarck on one of her many journeys to the tropics *(20 March until the end of Oct, open every day 9am–6pm | Entrance fee 5 euros | Tel. 04104/6037 | www.garten-der-schmetterlinge.de)*. Going further along the castle walls and down the road to the left you will come across the Bismarck Museum where, among many other ex-

hibits, you can admire the impressive boots made for the more than 1.90-metre-tall old chancellor. Bismarck's Mausoleum is just a few minutes' walk away *(April–Oct, open every day 10am–6pm, Nov–March, Weds, Sat, Sun 10am–4pm | Entrance fee 4 euros)*. The Bismarck Foundation, located in the former railway station, almost appears to be competition. The exhibition 'Bismarck and his Time' which is on display here is much less focused on a personality cult than the one in the museum *(In the old railway station | March to Oct Tues–Sun 10am–6pm, Nov–Feb 10am–5pm | Tel. 04104/97710)*.

Now you have really earned a break. How about venison fillet in the Forsthaus Friedrichsruh Restaurant? The boxer Max Schmeling used to train where you're enjoying your meal today *(Open every day | Tel. 04104/692366 | €€)*. The local railway makes several trips back to Hamburg every day. Or, you could wander back through the park to Aumühle and take the regional line

3 APPLES, PEARS, CHERRIES: THE 'ALTES LAND'

Spring is the best time to visit Hamburg's orchards. That is when you can see the cherry trees blossoming see off against the magnificent old farmhouses. This car trip will take around 4 hours.

There are millions of them: apple and cherry trees, pears and plums – the Altes Land is the largest, single, fruit-growing area in Central Europe. In this case 'Alt' has nothing to do with the German word for 'old'. The first settlers here came from Holland and 'Olland' was the original Low German name for this district. This gradually developed from 'olles Land' into 'Altes Land'. The small villages have charming names like Francop, Jork, Ladekop and Cranz and their houses, built on dykes, really do remind one of Dutch coastal villages.

The easiest way to reach the region is via the A7 motorway, taking the Waltershof exit and then through Finkenwerder towards Cranz. On your way you will drive past the gigantic Airbus complex. As on the tour to Altenwerder, the wounds which industrialization has cut into the beautiful old cultural landscape become painfully apparent. The little town of Steinkirchen is especially lovely with its cluster of half-timbered houses in the centre. There is a magnificent Arp Schnitger organ in the village church. The famous North-German organ builder died in 1719 and was buried in the nearby village of Neuenfelde where his grave was discovered in 1971. He was just one of the many organ builders active in the Altes Land.

You now reach the larger town of Jork. This is where Gotthold Ephraim Lessing married Eva König on 8 Oct, 1776 – after a five-year engagement! The great event almost didn't take place: on a stroll over the marshy fens, the great German writer and philosopher fell into some 'slimy water'. Enraged, he wanted to leave the place of this disgrace for ever, but his later wife convinced him to stay. She had a tragic fate and died in childbirth one year later. It is still possible to sink into the mud in the meadows. However, the flowering

trees and, especially, the grand estates with their magnificent entrance gates make wonderful photo motives. The Altes Land Museum (April to Oct, Tues–Sun 11 am–5 pm; Nov–March, Weds, Sat, Sun 1–4 pm | Entrance free | Westerjork 49).

The Obsthof Matthies (Matthies Orchard), not far from Jork, is a great place to take a break. You can have brunch on Sundays or enjoy the apple cake any afternoon in the fully glazed restaurant. There are tours of the farm and many local specialities (Open every day | Am Elbdeich 31 | Tel. 04162/91580 | www.obsthof.de). One of the most popular country inns near Hamburg is the Estehof with many inviting dishes on the menu including the 'Estebrügger Quarkbüddel' – delicious wild duck with a generous helping of red cabbage and dumplings. (Thurs–Mon 11 am–7 pm | July/ Aug, call in advance – sometimes closed for holidays | Estebrügger Str. 87 | Tel. 04162/275 | €€). Additional information on the Altes Land: www. 3meilenvorhamburg.de

4 WOLVES AND PIGS IN THE HARBURG HILLS

This excursion is a tip for families with children – but not only for them. In the Schwarze Berge (Black Hills) Game Park you will encounter bison and foxes, and you can bake bread in the traditional manner and take part in many other activities at the Kiekeberg Open Air Museum. The easiest way to reach the Harburg Hills is by car (A7 motorway, Marmstorf exit) but you can also get to the two locations relatively quickly by train or bus (S3 and S31 to Neuwiedenthal, then Bus 340, Wildpark or Museum Kiekeberg stop | total travel time approx. 45 min.). The **Wildpark (Game Park) Schwarze Berge** is a paradise for all animal lovers, young and old. There are wolves, lynxes and bats and – most importantly – funny pot-bellied pigs that dash around grunting if you have bought the right food. The playground with its gigantic swings and slides is a real magnet – even for stay-at-homes. You can bring your own sausages and grill them on the barbecues in the park. *8am–6pm, in winter 9am–5pm | Entrance fee 7 euros, children 5 euros | Tel. 81977470 | Am Wildpark 1 | Rosengarten | www. wildpark-schwarze berge.de*

The **Freilichtmuseum (Open Air Museum) Am Kiekeberg** is only a stone's throw away. Thirty beautiful farmhouses have been restored or reconstructed here. The whole village with its animals and human inhabitants, who are sometimes clothed in historical costume, is bursting with life and is an open invitation for you to join in. Find out about the special days – for baking bread, making candles and so on – before you go. The kids will also like being able to ride on the tractor and there are great gifts in the museum shop. *Tues–Fri 9am–5pm, Sat/Sun 10am–6pm | Am Kiekeberg 1 | Rosengarten-Ehestorf | Tel. 7901760 | www.kiekeberg-museum.de*

The surrounding area in the **Harburg Hills** is perfect for hiking. They are even high enough for some restaurants to call themselves 'mountain huts' – that is a bit of an exaggeration!

Schwarze Berge Game Park: my friends, the pot-bellied pigs

> FROM BANKS & CREDIT CARDS TO TIME ZONE

Holiday from start to finish: useful addresses and information for your trip to Hamburg

■ BANKS & CREDIT CARDS ■

Cash dispensers *(Geldautomat)* can be found everywhere. General banking hours are from 9am to 6pm.

■ CITY SIGHTSEEING TOURS ■

Sightseeing tours vary from straight forward trips around the city to three-hour illuminated tours in the evening. For those new to the city, the red double-decker buses and the *Hummelbahn* are to be recommended. Tours begin at the main station, exit Kirchenallee, and from the jetties ('Landungsbrücken'), in summer from 9.30am–5pm, departing every 30 minutes, in winter every hour until 4pm. *(15 euro)*. The day pass allows passengers to embark and disembark at any stop. *(Tel. 7928979)*. *Hamburg-Rundfahrt: Tel. 6413731 | www.hansa-rundfahrt.de*

Insider Tip Explore the port, its ships and docks in *Jasperreisen's* three-hour 'Trip round the Giants'. *Sat/Sun (May–Sept incl. Fri) | Departs Vorsetzen/Überseebrücke | 26 euros | Reservations and ID/passport essential | Tel. 22710610 | www.jasper-hamburg.de*

Insider Tip You can zoom around the city standing up on a single-axle, motorized Segway. Looks pretty amazing and is certain to turn a few heads. *From 48 euros | approx. 2½ hrs. | Tel. 47113300 | www.segway-citytour.de*

Bicycle Rickshaws: Young cyclists will peddle you around the city. *April–Oct | from 2.50 euros | Tel. 0162/1089020 | www.trimotion.de*

■ CITY TOURS ■

Stattreisen Hamburg e. V. offers a number of different tours of the city including some unusual subjects. *Tel. 4303481 | www.stattreisen-hamburg.de*

StadtkulTour: Tours tracing the steps of Heinrich Heine or torchlight tours around the warehouse district. *Tel. 366269 | www.hamburger-nachtwaechter.de*

Jogging-Tour: Yet another way of getting to know Hamburg. Gösta Dreise, who works as a cycle courier and is a passionate triathelete, is your sporty tour guide. You specify the pace and length of your tour depending on what you want and how fit you are. *By appointment only | Groups and individuals | Duration approx. 1–1 ½ hrs. | Tel. 0163/1738780 | www.touristjogging.de*

■ CONSULATES ■

British Embassy Berlin – Wilhelmstr. 70–72 | 10117 Berlin | Tel. 030/204570 | www.british-embassy.de
US Consulate – Alsterufer 27–28 | Tel. 411710 | S-Bahn Dammtor | hamburg.usconsulate.gov
Canadian Consulate – Ballindamm 35 | Tel. 460027-0 | S-/U-Bahn Jungfernstieg | www.international.gc.ca

■ CUSTOMS ■

Travellers from other EU countries are no longer subject to custom checks. EU citizens may bring the following

BACK TO BASICS

items into Germany: max. 90l of wine, 10l of spirits, 800 cigarettes. Duty-free for non-EU citizens are: 50g perfume, 2l of wine, 1l of spirits and 200 cigarettes.

ELECTRICITY

Current is 220 volts AC, 50 cycles. Plugs are two-round-pin continental types; UK and North American visitors will require an adaptor. North American visitors should check wether 110/120-volt AC appliances require a voltage transformer.

EMERGENCIES

Fire/police/ambulance: *Tel. 112*
Emergency medical service: *Tel. 22 80 22 (24-hr. service)*
Emergency doctor's surgery: *Stresemannstr. 54, Mon/ Tues, Thurs/Fri 7pm–midnight, Weds 1pm–midnight, Sat/Sun 7am–midnight*
Emergency dental service: *Tel. 0180/50 50 5 18*
Duty chemist: *Tel. 01805/93 88 88*

GETTING TO HAMBURG

BY AIR

Hamburg is served by most international airlines. Timetable information: *Tel. 507 50 | www. airport.de.* The city centre can be easily reached by public transport: buses run every ten minutes, for example, to the underground and district line station in Ohlsdorf. The *Airport Express (from 5 euros, every 15 min.)* goes to the main station. The trip to the city centre by taxi takes about 20 mins, and costs 18–22 euros.

WHAT DOES IT COST?

> CAPPUCCINO	2.50 EUROS	inside a café
> ICE CREAM	1.80 EUROS	for two scoops
> WINE	FROM 3.50 EUROS	per glass inside a bar
> PIZZA	FROM 7 EUROS	in a restaurant
> BOAT TRIP	APPRX. 10 EUROS	for a trip round the harbour
> BUS TRIP	1.65 EUROS	for a single journey

BY CAR

Via the A7 motorway along the north-south axis (Flensburg-Hanover/Kassel); via the A1 from the east and west (Lübeck/Bremen); via the A24 from Berlin and the A23 from Heide/Husum. There are often traffic jams on the A7 around the Elbe Tunnel during rush-hour. For information on the automatic parking guidance system see *www.parkinfo.com.*

BY TRAIN

Four intercity stations – Hauptbahnhof (with connections to all underground and district lines), Dammtor (CCH), Altona and Harburg – link Hamburg with all major cities in Germany.

■ INFORMATION ■

HAMBURG TOURIST CENTRE
Postfach 102249 | 20015 Hamburg | Hotline 040/3005 13 00 | Mon–Sat 9 am–7 pm | Fax 3005 13 33 | www.hamburg-tourismus.de

Welcoming in a ship in Wedel

TOURIST INFORMATION
– Main Station | Exit Kirchenallee | Mon–Sat 8 am–9 pm, Sun 10 am–6 pm – St.-Pauli-Landungsbrücken | between jetties 4 and 5 | April–Oct Mon, Weds, Sun 8 am–6 pm, Tues, Thurs–Sat 8 am–7 pm, Nov–March: daily 10 am–6 pm – Airport | Terminals 1 and 2, arrivals area | Open every day 6 am–11 pm

■ INTERNET ■
Useful and informative addresses: *www.hamburg-tourismus.de; www.hamburg.de; www.hamburg-magazin.de*

'What's on': see local daily newspapers and city magazines (in German): *www.mopo.de; www.abendblatt.de; www.szene-hamburg.de*

The online street plan *www.hamburg-tourismus.de/Stadtplan* is useful. It marks every museum or hotel and also has aerial views. *www.hafen-hamburg.de* lists the arrival times of all passenger liners.

Using *www.hvv.de* you can create your own personal timetable.

■ INTERNET CAFÉS ■
Hamburg has the greatest number of WLAN remote internet hot spots of any city in Germany. In the city centre laptops work almost anywhere and many cafés and restaurants often display signs offering 'free WLAN' on the door. Hot spots in Germany can be viewed under *www.businesshotspot.de*.

MATCH GAMES   [136 C2]
Internet café with computer games. *Mon–Sat 11 am–midnight, Sun 2 pm–midnight | Rothenbaumchaussee 61 | Tel. 41 49 76 26 | www. matchgames.de | U 1, Hallerstrasse*

SATURN ELEKTROMARKT   [123 F4]
In-store internet café. *Mon–Weds, Sat 9.30 am–8 pm, Thurs/Fri 9.30 am–9 pm | Mönckebergstr. 1 | S-/U-Bahn Hauptbahnhof*

■ LOST PROPERTY ■
Bäckerbreitergang 73 [108 B3] *| Tel. 35 18 51 | U 2, Gänsemarkt*

■ PASSPORT & VISA ■
Visas are not reqired for EU citizens; citizens of the US or Canada require a visa only if staying for longer than

three months. A valid identity card or passport is sufficient to allow entry to Germany.

PUBLIC TRANSPORT

The Hamburg Public Transport Association (HVV) provides an extensive network. Single tickets, day passes and group tickets (also valid for Elbe ferry services operated by the HVV) are available from ticket machines for all destinations. At weekends, the metrobuses, district and underground lines run around the clock. With the *Hamburg-Card* discounts are given on entrance fees to museums, on theatre tickets, in certain restaurants and on sightseeing tours of the city, harbour and Alster: day passes 8 euros (1 adult/ 3 children), group tickets (up to 5 people) 11.80 euros, three-day ticket 18 euros (groups: 29.80 euros). For those who want to explore the surrounding area as well, the *Metropol-Card* is to be recommended. It is valid for one year and includes free travel on the local public transport system

for one day, plus reductions on the entrance fee to 140 cultural and leisure attractions (adults 18.50, children 8.50 euros, families 38.50 euros). Available from all HVV service points, the Tourist Information Office, and online under *www.metropolcard.de*. For information on the times the HVV service runs, ring *Tel. 19449*, or *www.hvv.de*

SIGHTSEEING FLIGHTS

Lufthansa Ju 52 Team: sightseeing flights and short trips on the 'Tante Ju': *April to Oct | Book well in advance | from 159 euros | Tel. 50701717 | www.dlbs.de*

In a hot-air balloon over Hamburg. Hot-air balloon trips. *April–Oct, in winter on application | Approx. 1½ hrs. | from 185 Euro | Tel. 484677 | www.ballons-ueber-hamburg.de*

SPORT

FITNESS & WELLNESS

All major hotels have wellness and sauna areas available for use by non-

> SAIL AWAY!
Which boat and what tour?

An overwhelming choice can be found at the 'Landungsbrücken' jetties. The smaller barges chug around the narrow canals in the Warehouse district, the bigger boats can make it across to the container ship terminals. Just ask: all services run from the 'Landungsbrücken' or towards Baumwall near the Überseebrücke. Most tours cost the same (duration 1 hr.). Just as nice as a trip round the harbour is a tour of the Alster. The elegant white boats

start from the Jungfernstieg. You can even get married on board. All sorts of different tours are available, e.g. a round trip of the Alster *(daily, every 30 mins. | approx. 50 min. | 10 euros).* The 'Fleetfahrt' (waterway trip) takes you into the Warehouse district *(3 daily | approx. 2 hrs. | 15 euros);* the 'Dämmertörn' (dusk sailing) is romantic *(daily 8pm | approx. 2 hrs. | 15 euros).* When: March/April–Sept/ Oct | Tel. 357 42 40

residents. It's worth asking. The Meridian Spa is popular: *Mon, Weds, Fri 7am–11pm, Tues, Thurs 9am–11pm, Sat/Sun 9am–10pm | From 16 euros | Quickbornstr. 26 | Tel. 65891350 | www.meridianspa.de*

GOLF

Hamburg's most exclusive club is in Rissen. Open to members of other clubs on weekdays. *(Hamburger Golf-Club e.V. Falkenstein | In de Bargen 59 | Tel. 812177).* For further clubs, see *www. golfverband-hamburg.de*

CANOEING & ROWING

There are many places in Hamburg where you can splash around: many hire boat companies rent out canoes, paddleboats and rowing boats. A general rule of thumb: the further away you go from the Alster, the cheaper it is. On the Alster the steam ships have right of way, otherwise it's right before left. From 9 euros/hr.
– Bobby Reich | Fernsicht 2 (near the restaurant) | Tel. 487824

– Bootsverleih Dornheim | trips in gondolas from 140 euros | Winterhude | Kaemmererufer 25 | Tel. 2794184 | www.bootsvermietung-dornheim.de
– Bootsvermietung Goldfisch | with sushi picnic on board | Isekai 1 | Tel. 41357575 | www.goldfisch.de

Inside
Tip

CYCLING

There are many cycle paths which make trips with the children that much easier. Bicycles can be taken on the HVV free of charge – at any time of the day during school holidays, otherwise not before 9am or between 4–6 pm, Mon to Fri.

Really good tips for cycling tours can be found in the *ADFC-Infoladen* in St. Georg *(Tues–Fri 10am–5pm | Koppel 34 | Tel. 393933 | www. hamburg.adfc.de).* Cycle hire (ID/passport essential) from the Deutschen Bahn at the Main Station next to the travel centre (Reisezentrum) *(from 10 euros/ day | Tel. 391850475 | Open every day 7am–10pm);* bike station at Dammtor/Rothenbaum *(from 3 euros/*

WEATHER IN HAMBURG

	Jan	Feb	March	April	May	June	July	Aug	Sept	Oct	Nov	Dec
	36/2	37/3	46/8	56/13	64/18	72/22	73/23	73/23	67/19	56/13	45/7	39/4
Daytime temperatures in °F / °C												
	27/-3	27/-3	32/0	37/3	45/7	52/11	56/13	56/13	50/10	43/6	36/2	30/-1
Night-time temperatures in °F / °C												
	2	2	4	6	8	8	7	6	6	2	2	1
Sunshine hours/day												
	12	10	8	10	10	10	12	11	10	10	11	11
Precipitation days/month												

BACK TO BASICS

day | *Schlüterstr. 11* | *Tel. 41468277)* where the free leaflet 'Exploring Hamburg by bike' can be picked up.

ICE-SKATING & IN-LINE SKATING

The lovely open-air rink is centrally located in the 'Wallanlage'. From April onwards, in-line skaters can skate here free of charge. Ice-skating: mid Nov–mid March, four skating times. *Adults 3.10 euros, children 2.50 euros* | *am Holstenwall* | *Tel. 3193546* | *www.eisbahn-wallanlagen.de* | *U3, St. Pauli* | *Bus 112, Handwerkskammer*

SWIMMING

Insider Tip

The renovated *Holthusenbad* in Winterhude provides swimming at its best with a wave pool, heated outdoor pool, sauna facilities and spa area. Fri from 7pm onwards, by candlelight. *Goernestr. 21* | *U1, 3, Kellinghusenstrasse*

Near the city centre, opposite the hospital in St. Georg, is the *Alsterschwimmhalle* with its 50-metre pool. *Ifflandstr. 21* | *U1, 2, Lübecker Str.*

In summer, the *Naturbad Stadtparksee* is pure bliss. *Südring 5b* | *U3, Saarlandstrasse*

Information on all swimming pools: *Tel. 188890* | *www.baederland.de*

TAXI

Autoruf Taxizentrale: *Tel. 441011* | das taxi: *Tel. 611122* | Hansa Funktaxi: *Tel. 211211* | Taxi Hamburg: *Tel. 666666*

TELEFON

The international dialling code for Germany is 0049, the area code for Hamburg is (0)40. Dial 0044 for Great Britain and 001 for US and Canada connections.

THEATRE & CONCERT TICKETS

– *Kurt Collien* | *Eppendorfer Baum 25* | *Tel. 483390*

– *Konzertkasse Gerdes* | *Rothenbaumchaussee 77* | *Tel. 45035060*

Störtebeker memorial in the Warehouse district

– *Kartenhaus* | *Schanzenstr. 5* | *Tel. 01805/969000*

– *Konzertkasse Hauptbahnhof* | *In Tourist Information Office* | *Mon–Fri 8am–9pm, Sat/Sun 10am–6pm* | *Tel. 32873854*

– *Hamburg-Hotline für Veranstaltungstickets* | *Tel. 30051300*

TIME ZONE

Germany is six hours ahead of US Eastern Standard Time and one hour ahead of Greenwich Mean Time

> ## ON THE ROAD IN HAMBURG

Please refer to the back cover
for an overview of this Street Atlas

STREET
ATLAS

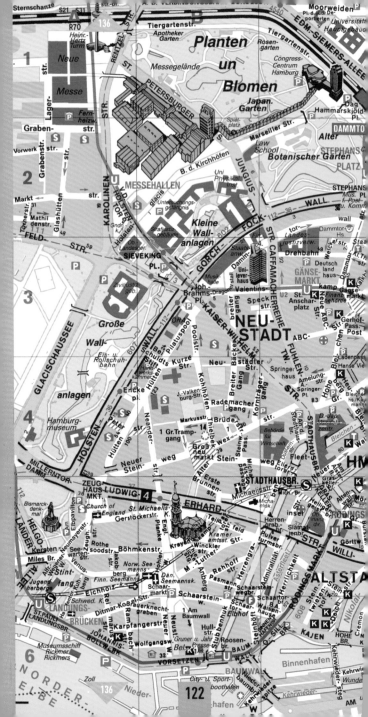

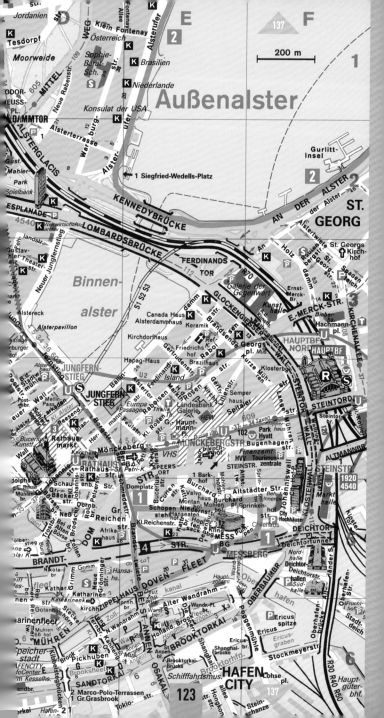

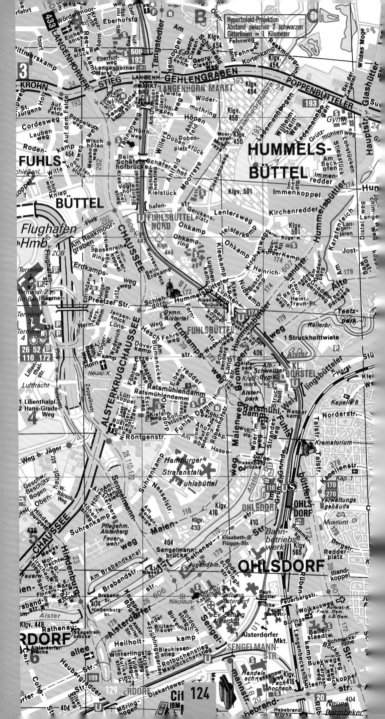

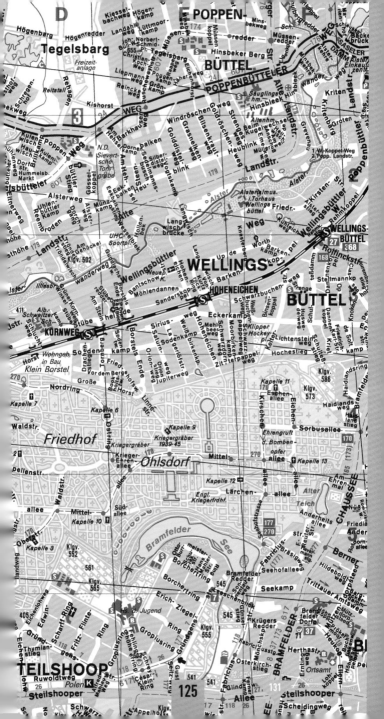

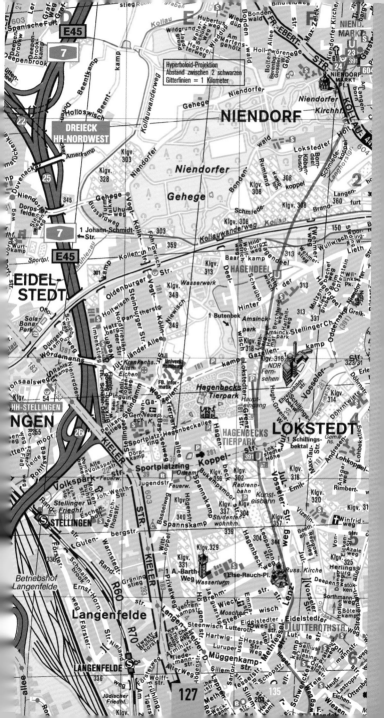

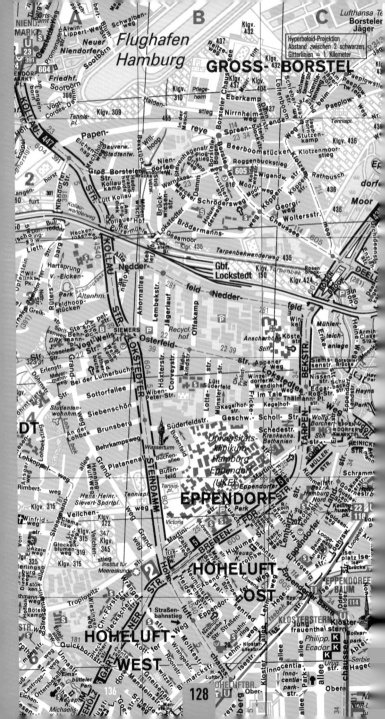

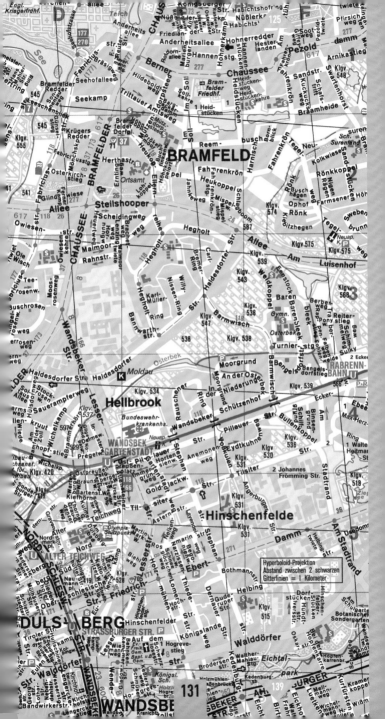

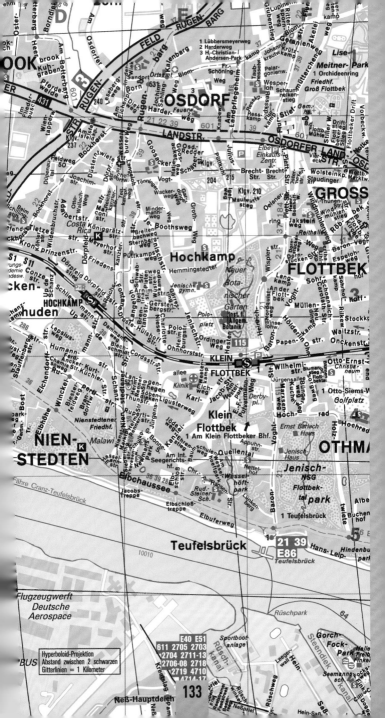

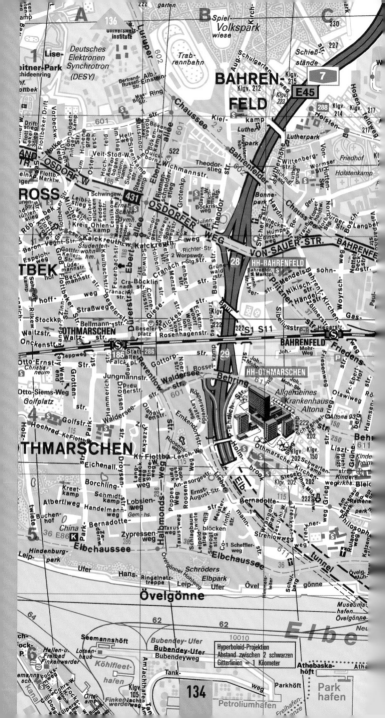

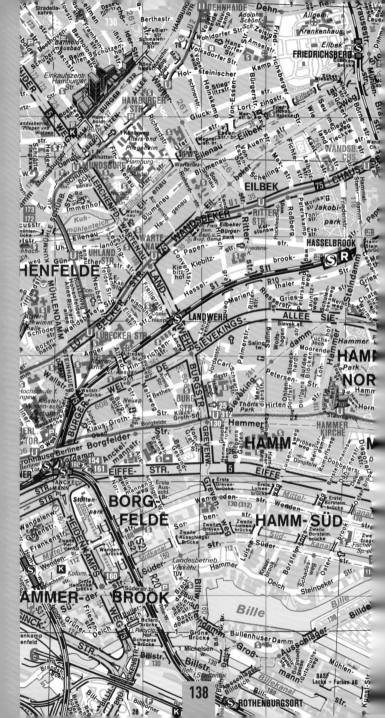

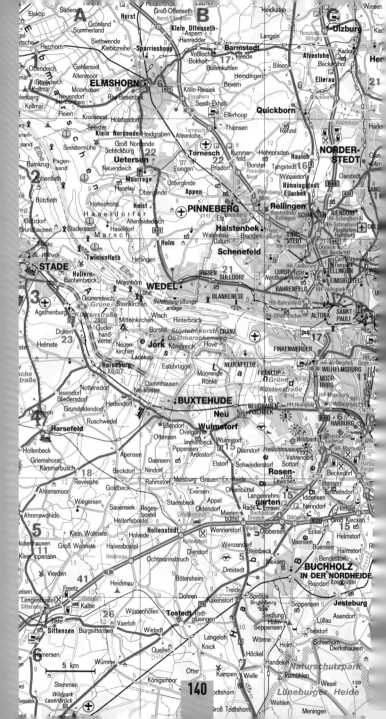

This index lists a selection of the streets and squares show in the Street Atlas

STREET ATLAS INDEX

KEY TO STREET ATLAS

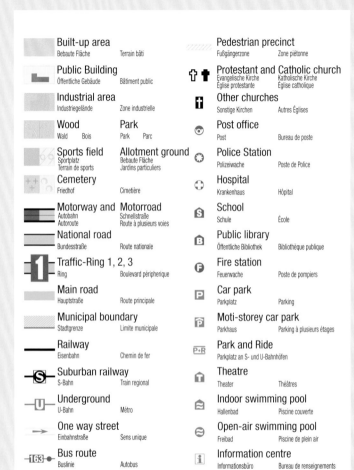

Built-up area	Bebaute Fläche	Terrain bâti
Public Building	Öffentliche Gebäude	Bâtiment public
Industrial area	Industriegelände	Zone industrielle
Wood Wald Bois	**Park** Park Parc	
Sports field Sportplatz Terrain de sports	**Allotment ground** Bebaute Fläche Jardins particuliers	
Cemetery Friedhof	Cimetière	
Motorway and Autobahn Autoroute	**Motorroad** Schnellstraße Route à plusieurs voies	
National road Bundesstraße	Route nationale	
Traffic-Ring 1, 2, 3 Ring	Boulevard périphérique	
Main road Hauptstraße	Route principale	
Municipal boundary Stadtgrenze	Limite municipale	
Railway Eisenbahn	Chemin de fer	
Suburban railway S-Bahn	Train regional	
Underground U-Bahn	Métro	
One way street Einbahnstraße	Sens unique	
Bus route Buslinie	Autobus	
Walking tours Stadtspaziergänge	Promenades en ville	

Pedestrian precinct	Fußgängerzone	Zone piétone
Protestant and Catholic church Evangelische Kirche Église protestante	Katholische Kirche Église catholique	
Other churches Sonstige Kirchen	Autres Églises	
Post office Post	Bureau de poste	
Police Station Polizeiwache	Poste de Police	
Hospital Krankenhaus	Hôpital	
School Schule	École	
Public library Öffentliche Bibliothek	Bibliothèque publique	
Fire station Feuerwache	Poste de pompiers	
Car park Parkplatz	Parking	
Moti-storey car park Parkhaus	Parking à plusieurs étages	
Park and Ride Parkplatz an S- und U-Bahnhöfen		
Theatre Theater	Théâtres	
Indoor swimming pool Hallenbad	Piscine couverte	
Open-air swimming pool Freibad	Piscine de plein air	
Information centre Informationsbüro	Bureau de renseignements	

The map projection (hyperboloid)
causes a change in scale between the city centre and the suburbs. Using this method the city centre can be shown in a readable format (as if using a magnifying glass). The black grid lines help when working out distances; the grid lines are exactly one kilometre apart.

INDEX

This index lists all sights, museums and destinations plus the names of important people featured in this guide. Numbers in bold indicate a main entry, italics a photograph

PICTURE CREDITS

Rathaus 11, 24, **30f**
Rathausmarkt 33
Reeperbahn **37**, 78, 107
Rickmer Rickmers 37f
Sachsenwald 110f
Schauspielhaus 11, 79, **87**
Schanzenviertel 78, 107
Schumacher, Fritz 19, 29, 34, 54f
Speicherstadt (Warehouse District) 9, 11, 19, 22, **38ff**, *100/101*
Speicherstadtmuseum 42f
Spicy's 43

Sprinkenhof 102
St. Georg 12, 23, 70, 79
St. Pauli 32ff
St.-Pauli-Theater 87
Staatsoper 79, **86**
Stadtpark **55**, 84
Steinkirchen 112
Stilwerk *16/17*, **73**, 99
Stolpersteine 51
Süllberg 10, 60, 105
Teherani, Hadi 19, 27, 47, 100, 102
Teufelsbrück 33, 47, **48f**
Thalia-Theater *8*, 66, 79, **87**

Theater für Kinder 99
U-Boot 43
Veddel 9, 11, 22, 54
View Point Hafencity 44
Waltershof 108f, 112
Wedel 45, 99
Wildpark Schwarze Berge 112f
Willkommhöft (Wedel) 99
Winterhuder Fährhaus 87
Zeisehallen 49
Zentralbibliothek 28
Zollmuseum 98
Zoologische Sammlung 98

> GET IN TOUCH!

Dear reader,

We make every effort to ensure you get the most up-to-date information available for your trip. Although our authors have done their research very carefully, errors or omissions do sometimes occur. We regret that the publisher cannot be held responsible for the consequences of such mistakes.

We do, however, look forward to receiving your comments.

Please write to the editorial team at
MARCO POLO Redaktion,
MAIRDUMONT, Postfach 31 51,
73751 Ostfildern, Germany
info@marcopolo.de

PICTURE CREDITS

Cover photograph: Alsterarkaden (Laif: Vogel)
Beiersdorf (76); W. Dieterich (72); Erika's Eck (106 top left); Fotolia: Otmar Smit (106 centre right); R. Freyer (5); Gastwerk Hotel Hamburg & 25hours Hotel (15 bottom); HB Verlag, Mike Schröder (20/21, 98/99, 113, 147); D. Heintze (151); Huber: Gräfenhain (11, 22/23, 36, 64, 78/79, 100/101, 108/109, 110); © iStockphoto.com: Elena Korenbaum (107 centre left), Lori Sparkia (107 bottom right); I. Knigge (2 left); Laif: Gaasterland (28, 46, 116), Modrow (80), Selbach (flap, left, 3 left, 3 centre, 88/89, 90, 93, 95, 97, 102), Vogel (1); Look: Engel & Gielen (43), Pompe (49, 83); Mauritius: Imagebroker.net (51), Rosenfeld (3 right), Waldkirch (19); D. Renckhoff (flap, centre, 2 right, 4 left, 4 right, 8/9, 16/17, 20, 31, 35, 38, 40, 44, 53, 54, 56/57, 61, 62, 65, 67, 68, 70/71, 74, 85, 86, 99, 119, 120/121); Ilka Sassen (13 bottom); Schapowalow: Atlandide (flap, right); Tilman Schuppius (12 top, 12 centre, 12 bottom, 14 top, 14 bottom, 15 top, 106 centre left, 106 bottom right, 107 top left, 107 centre right); White Star: Pasdzior (27, 32, 47, 58, 98, 105), Reichelt (21); Jens Wilhelmi (13 top); M. Zegers (6/7, 18)

3rd revised edition 2008 © MAIRDUMONT GmbH & Co. KG, Ostfildern
(14.) German edition 2008
Publisher: Stephanie Mair-Huydts; Chief editors: Michaela Lienemann, Marion Zorn; Author: Dorothea Heintze; Editor: Jochen Schürmann; Programme supervision: Leonie Dlugosch, Nadia Al Kureischi; Picture editors: Barbara Schmid, Gabriele Forst; Translated from the German by Robert McInnes and Christopher Wynne; copy-editor of the English edition: Christopher Wynne
Cartography for the Street Atlas: © Falk Verlag, Ostfildern
Scene/24h: Wunder Media, Munich
Design and Layout: Zum goldenen Hirschen, Hamburg; Title page/pp. 1–3: Factor Product, Munich

NOTES